DATE DUE

JУ 1 1 '00	Nov 6		
OC 1 9 '00			
NO 8 '00			
NO 2 9 '00			
JУ 2 3 '02			
AU 9 '02			
DE 1 9 '02			
JУ 2 '02			
FE 1 1 '03			
AP 2 5 '03			
DE 1 8 '03			
FE 1 2 '04			
DE 2 1 '07			

DEMCO 38-296

The Making of Microsoft

How Bill Gates and His Team
Created the World's Most
Successful Software Company

DANIEL ICHBIAH
and SUSAN L. KNEPPER

Prima Publishing
P.O. Box 1260DI
Rocklin, CA 95677
(916) 624-5718

For Chris

Copyright 1991 by Daniel Ichbiah

Copyediting by Anne Montague
Interior Design by Renee Deprey
Jacket Design by Kirschner-Caroff Design

Prima Publishing
Rocklin, California

Library of Congress Cataloging-in-Publication Data

Ichbiah, Daniel
    The making of Microsoft: how Bill Gates and his team created
the world's most successful software company / by Daniel
Ichbiah and   Susan L. Knepper.
    p.   cm.
    Previously published in France under title: New magicians,
1989.
    Includes index.
    ISBN 1-55958-071-2
    1. Microsoft—History. 2. Computer software industry—
United States—History. 3. Gates, Bill, 1956-   I. Knepper,
Susan L. II. Ichbiah, Daniel. New magicians. III Title.
HD9696.C64M535 1991   91-6639
338.7'610053'0973—dc20   CIP

91 92 93 94 RRD 10 9 8 7 6 5 4 3 2 1

Printed in the United States of America

How to Order
Quantity discounts are available from the publisher, Prima Publishing,
P.O. Box 1260DI, Rocklin, CA 95677; telephone (916) 624-5718. On your
letterhead include information concerning the intended use of the books
and the number of books you wish to purchase.

U.S. Bookstores and Libraries: Please submit all orders to St. Martin's
Press, 175 Fifth Avenue, New York, NY 10010; telephone (212) 674-5151.

Contents

Contents   **v**

Contents

Acknowledgments

I would like to thank the following people for their support in the process of writing this book. They were remarkably patient, willing to help, and intellectually honest.

Paul Allen
Jabe Blumenthal
Betsy Davis
Bill Gates[1]
Doug Klunder
Neil Konzen
Michel Lacombe
Barry Linnett

Miriam Lubow
Bob O'Rear
Jeff Raikes
Charles Simonyi
Michel Suignard
Bernard Vergnes
Steve Wood

I would also like to thank Jean-Philippe Courtois, Elisabeth Floch, and Dominique Kulig of Microsoft France, and Pam Miller of Pam Miller Communications for arranging my meetings with programmers.

Finally, I would like to collectively thank the staff of the Microsoft Corporation library for giving me free access to documents and videos about the history of the company.

—Daniel Ichbiah

---

[1] I have interviewed Bill Gates several times in my career as a journalist.

Preface to the English Edition

The question I have often been asked in the course of this project is, "Why are you translating a *French* book about an *American* company?" People assume, as I did, that there must already be several books in English about a major software company like Microsoft. While the general and trade press have published countless articles about Microsoft's past, its products, and its personnel, Daniel Ichbiah's *Microsoft: Les nouveaux magiciens* is the first attempt at putting the whole story together in one volume.

The next question invariably is, "Why did a French author write about Microsoft?" After covering the company for years as a computer journalist, Daniel Ichbiah decided to write a book about Microsoft simply because he was fascinated by the company and its founder. As it turned out, the French were also intrigued by the story of the self-made American billionaire. Ichbiah used material from his past interviews with Bill Gates as well as from the extensive documentation placed at his disposal by Microsoft France and the Microsoft corporate library in Redmond, Washington. He talked with many of the early Microsoft employees and interviewed Gates again specifically for the book. Finally, he rounded out this information with previously published articles.

So, why translate the French book? In deciding whether to accept this assignment, I had to answer that question myself. Clearly, Americans will also enjoy reading the complete story of Microsoft's amazing success. But couldn't someone else just write a similar book in English? The advantage of translating Ichbiah's work was that I could draw on all that research without having to start from scratch. I did need to do a great deal of additional research in order to obtain the original quotations, clarify details, and verify sources, but that is an inherent part of any translation project. And even there, Daniel made my job much easier by providing me with some of his files and the cassettes of his interviews.

Although I have been using the term *translation,* the present volume is a translation only in the broadest sense. *Adaptation* is perhaps more accurate. Translating is never a mechanical task of taking each word in the French and replacing it with a corresponding English word—anyone with a pocket bilingual dictionary could do that, but the result would be a relatively meaningless string of words. Still, for the purposes of the English edition, I was instructed to take much more "poetic license" than I would normally have taken on a translation project, primarily because an American audience approaches this particular subject very differently than does Ichbiah's original French audience. As a result, some sections have been significantly condensed, rewritten, or eliminated altogether; several chapters have been restructured; and new paragraphs and a new chapter have been added to bring the book up to date.

None of this could have happened, however, without the following people. First and foremost, Carolyn McFarlane deserves thanks for her excellent editing of this English version. Her thoroughness and hard work have been inspiring. And, had she not introduced herself to a couple of fellow Americans hanging out at the Eiffel Tower one sunny afternoon—a meeting that turned out to be nothing short of providential—I would never have had this exciting opportunity.

Daniel Ichbiah's willingness to help proved invaluable, and his excitement about the Microsoft story was contagious.

Bill Gladstone and Matt Wagner of Waterside Productions took care of the business side of things and kept the enthusiasm fresh, as did Ben Dominitz of Prima Publishing.

Microsoft co-founder Paul Allen, and two of the company's earliest employees, Bob O'Rear and Miriam Lubow, were very gracious in answering my additional questions to help ensure accuracy.

Much of my job would have been infinitely more difficult without the capable assistance of many reference librarians in Santa Cruz and throughout the San Francisco Bay Area. I am especially grateful to Rosanne Macek of the Apple Computer library for allowing me free rein in that excellent facility.

Finally, my husband Chris not only helped edit the more technical portions, but also provided constant support and encouragement, occasional exhortation, and unconditional love every step of the way.

—Susan Knepper
Santa Cruz, California

Introduction

In 1968, officials at Lakeside School in Seattle made a seemingly minor decision whose impact ended up changing the face of modern society. Even though computer technology was in the Stone Age of its development, Lakeside School had the vision to secure the use of a computer for its students, something many schools have still failed to achieve although computer literacy has since become as important as learning the ABCs.

One of the Lakeside students most eager to seize the opportunity of working on the computer was an eighth grader named Bill Gates. Today, just over two decades later, billionaire Bill Gates runs a software empire called Microsoft, located in a creative campuslike setting in Redmond, Washington. And in the meantime, our civilization has been transformed. This book unfolds the drama of that process scene by scene. It is a compelling story for the computer buff and the technological neophyte alike.

Much of the story centers around software. Software is what gives life to the hardware, almost creating the illusion that the machine can think. It is the lifeblood of our information age.

In many respects, a creator of software is as much an artist as is a painter or a novelist. Depending on the skills and creativity of its developer, a software program can "teach" a computer to accomplish a wide range of socially useful tasks. If a program is fast, easy to use, and visually appealing, it can also provide intellectual stimulation and aesthetic satisfaction for the user.

Programmers put in countless hours of hard work and creative problem-solving to write thousands of lines of code. Although the code itself makes sense only to those trained in the field, together the lines of code become a program, which is displayed for the user on the computer screen. A program may be an electronic spreadsheet that allows users to simulate financial scenarios before making a decision; a word processing program that offers a new standard of quality for reports and business correspondence; or a database that helps keep information and statistics organized and up to date. Thus the software—a creative work—transforms the computer—a piece of hardware with a collection of circuits and a central processing unit—into a useful, interactive, and sometimes even entertaining tool.

Many software programs have now sold millions of copies: Microsoft Windows, Microsoft Multiplan, Microsoft Word, Lotus 1-2-3, dBASE, WordPerfect, and WordStar are just a few. When a product meets with such success, its impact on society is every bit as great as that of a work of art or literature.

This new form of communication became a central feature of the commercial sector in the 1980s and will be an integral part of our home lives by the year 2000. In order for this to happen, however, software applications must become increasingly accessible to the average person. Bill Gates embraced such a vision in 1975 when he founded his company. Today, Microsoft is leading the way in a process of change which is gradually making our societies more efficient, automated, and interconnected.

Gates is not, of course, the only traveler on this bold, visionary journey. The microcomputer industry is teeming with talented creators whose products change the work habits of everyone from financial analysts to musicians. Companies such as Apple, Compaq, and Lotus, which have catapulted to positions of leadership in the market in a few short years, have had a very visible influence on the development of microcomputing. Others, like the researchers at the Xerox Palo Alto Research Center who defined the user interface implemented today on Macintosh computers and in Microsoft Windows, have worked more behind the scenes but have also made a lasting impression on our society.

The engine of growth and progress in microcomputing is fueled by the fierce competition that began with the release of the IBM PC in 1981 and intensified with the introduction of the Apple Macintosh in 1984. Today, Microsoft dominates the software market, but faces serious competition from firms such as Lotus, WordPerfect, and Borland. As long as this competition continues, Microsoft will not be tempted to rest on its laurels but will remain a driving force in the industry.

And to think that it all began with a young boy's fascination with software. . . .

PART 1

CHILD PRODIGY
TURNS
PROGRAMMER

I read a sentence by a French author one time which
said, "Le plus difficile n'est pas de monter, mais en
montant, de rester soi-même." *[The hardest thing is not*
getting to the top, but remaining yourself in the process.]
That completely applies to Bill.

–Miriam Lubow, Microsoft's sixth employee

1

William Henry Gates, III

In the midst of the scenic splendor of the Pacific Northwest lies Seattle, an ultramodern city nestled between the Olympic and Cascade mountain ranges. Seattle is home to Boeing and many other aviation companies. The 606-foot-tall Space Needle offers a spectacular view of the surrounding forests, mountains, and water.

The Gates family is well respected in this dynamic community. William Henry Gates, Jr., is a prominent attorney whose intellectual prowess and integrity command the respect of his peers. His wife, Mary, a former schoolteacher, is an active participant on the boards of many charitable organizations such as the United Way.

William Henry Gates III was born October 28, 1955, his parents' second child and only son. Bill led an uneventful childhood in well-to-do surroundings. He attended Sunday school at the Congregational church and sang in the choir. He joined the Boy Scouts as well, although he never exhibited great enthusiasm for these activities.

"He comes from a wonderful family, and they have had a wonderful influence on him, his education, his upbringing, and his philosophy on life," says Miriam Lubow, one of Bill's first secretaries, who worked with him for 15 years.

At the dinner table, the Gates family enjoyed animated discussions about each member's activities and experiences. "It was a rich environment in which to learn," Bill Gates recalls.

While his childhood appeared outwardly typical, Bill was in fact an unusual child who spent long periods of time in his room deep in reflective thought. He liked science and showed a particularly strong aptitude for math.

He read many of Edgar Rice Burroughs's Tarzan and Martian stories, and he devoured biographies of famous men, such as Franklin D. Roosevelt, Napoleon, and great inventors. Music didn't particularly interest him. An attempt at learning to play the trombone was quietly abandoned. He claimed no interest in philosophy, describing himself instead as a "scientist."

Academically, this frail-looking blond was a gifted student who always ranked at the top of his class. He scored a perfect 800 on the math section of the Scholastic Aptitude Test.

High school English teacher Anne Stephens was astounded by Bill's remarkable memory. He once memorized a three-page soliloquy for a school play in one reading. William Dougall, his science teacher, recalls that when a teacher was not going fast enough, "Bill always seemed on the verge of saying, 'But that's obvious.' "

Most of the people who observed Bill in his early years agree on one point: He could be a huge success in any career. Bill chose to apply his genius to computers, which were first produced commercially just ten years before he was born.

While a student at Lakeside School, a private middle and high school known for its academic excellence, Bill boasted to a teacher that he would be a millionaire someday. He underestimated himself.

2

The Birth of a
Passion

The late 1960s marked the computer's entry into the business world—even though one computer would occupy an entire room.

International Business Machines dominated the market, exceeding $3 billion in sales and commanding worldwide stature as virtually the sole proprietor of a revolutionary new form of information technology. Control Data Corporation sought government action to stop IBM, petitioning the U.S. Justice Department for an antitrust suit against it. Yet IBM marched on—until one computer company devised a strategy it hoped would catch the giant napping.

Inspired by chief executive Ken Olsen, Digital Equipment Corporation (DEC) created the first minicomputer, smaller and less expensive than IBM systems, yet more than adequate in capacity for most businesses. DEC's new product expanded the computer market into thousands of additional companies, and was so successful that IBM was forced to respond with a competitive product several years later.

In 1968, the administration of Seattle's Lakeside School made what turned out to be a fateful decision. Ahead of its time, the private school sought a way to expose students to the new technology and new language of computers. The price of a computer was then far beyond the means of the school budget, so Lakeside decided to enter into a time-sharing relationship, in which "machine time" would be rented from a corporate computer owner. With a Teletype machine, users could communicate with the computer over the phone lines.

To carry out this plan, the school principal asked the Mothers' Club to raise money to purchase a Teletype and help pay for machine time. The group emptied the club's kitty, investing $3,000 so that each Lakeside class could learn to use nearby General Electric's DEC PDP-10 mini-computer.

In the fall of 1968, Bill Gates entered the eighth grade at Lakeside School, and his best friend, 15-year-old Paul Allen, entered the tenth grade. When the computer courses began in January 1969, both Bill and Paul immediately discovered a passion for programming. Very few teachers knew anything about computers, so the two boys taught themselves by carefully studying all the manuals they could find. Fascinated by the possibilities opened to them via the terminal, they learned rapidly. To their teachers, the boys seemed to display an instinctive grasp of computers and their future possibilities.

Although Paul and Bill were in different grades, they grew closer through their common interest in programming the PDP-10. Often, one boy would sneak into the school building at night only to find the other boy already at the terminal. Some days they cut gym class to gain extra time on the computer.

Each boy developed special interests. Bill set out to formulate programs for practical uses, while Paul was charmed by the subtleties of assembly language, a low-level language that allows the programmer to control all parts of the computer. While Paul plunged into the complexities of assembly language, Bill wrote his first program, a ticktacktoe game. In their enthusiasm, the two computer whizzes decided to make the PDP-10 simulate thousands of plays in order to discover which strategies worked best. The annual budget, however, could not support these experiments, and after six months, Lakeside School had to ask parents to help pay the bill from General Electric. Eventually, Bill and Paul's access to the terminal was restricted, as their parents reached their limits in paying for computer time.

The boys' excitement about programming remained unquenchable. Finding access to a computer was difficult, because computers were rare and computer time was expensive. Yet the two students soon found an unexpected source of virtually unlimited computer use.

COMPUTER CENTER CORPORATION

Several recent graduates of the University of Washington had just founded a company called Computer Center Corporation (CCC). They obtained a PDP-10 with the intention of renting machine time to other companies. CCC founders signed an agreement with Digital whereby payments for the purchase of the machine would be deferred for as long as CCC discovered bugs in the PDP-10 software.

Bugs are anomalies in a computer program that cause it to act in an incorrect or incomprehensible manner. For example, a company's accounting or stock information could show up with erroneous data, or the computer could "crash," becoming temporarily unusable. Restarting it often resulted in losing all the information entered that day.

During this period, DEC's PDP-10 software was thoroughly infested with bugs, which caused massive headaches for DEC and its customers, but delighted the young engineers at CCC, for they kept payments deferred and the DEC collections department at bay. CCC promised to buy the machine once it became reliable, and provide frequent bug reports in the meantime.

When Bill and Paul first introduced themselves, CCC engineers were more than a little skeptical of the teenagers' claims of DEC programming prowess. Bill, however, already evidencing strong persuasive powers, convinced CCC of their skill and value, and the company signed an agreement with the "Lakeside Programming Group," as Bill and Paul called themselves.

In exchange for computer time, the two boys were to regularly supply CCC with lists of bugs in the PDP-10 software, including details on the circumstances that caused the computer to crash.

Every night around 6 o'clock, a strange shift change took place. The regular CCC daytime programmers left the office while Bill, Paul, and two companions—Rick Weiland and Kent Evans—arrived on bicycles to begin their work on many different programs in a room full of Teletype machines. "We stayed up until all hours of the night because we just loved working on software so much. It was a fun time," Paul Allen recalls.

During this time, they substantially deepened their knowledge of the subtleties of the minicomputer's hardware and software. They filled dozens of pages in the CCC logbook documenting crashes. Determined to find every last bug, Gates and Allen subjected the PDP-10 to the most rigorous tests. In familiarizing themselves with every minute operation of this computer, however, they ended up venturing into unauthorized domains.

PIRACY AND PUNISHMENT

Normally, a PDP-10 user was required to enter his name and password to gain access to the computer and only the information he or she was authorized to use. More for the challenge than out of malice, Bill found a way to bypass the password protection, thus tricking the computer's security system. This then gave him access to information he was not authorized to have, which at the time thrilled him immensely—until his shenanigans caused the system to crash.

The CCC engineers were furious. They strongly reprimanded Bill and revoked his computing privileges. He then learned that the University of Washington's PDP-10 was connected to Cybernet, a national computer network run by Control Data Corporation (CDC). Despite the mishap with CCC, Bill felt challenged to clandestinely break into this network too. He began studying the structure of the CDC machines and their software. Pretending that he was studying for a test, he went to the University of Washington and managed to obtain detailed information about how the network was set up. No one seemed to worry about harmless questions from a 16-year-old who didn't look his age.

Bill's plan worked perfectly. He successfully accessed Cybernet and installed his own program in the main computer, which then distributed the program to all the other computers on the network.

It was all according to plan—until a few minutes later, all the computers crashed.

Bill was caught again, thanks to the excellent design of the Cybernet system, which made it possible to trace the source of sabotage. This time, he was chastened to such a degree that his passion for computers temporarily diminished. He promised he would never touch a computer again, and during his junior year of high school, Bill Gates kept his word.

In the meantime, Paul Allen, Rick Weiland, and Kent Evans continued working at CCC, ferreting out the bugs in the PDP-10 software. The list was growing out of control: their Problem Report Book was now 300 pages long. Unfortunately, DEC finally decided that the agreement with CCC had lasted long enough. The manufacturer demanded payment for the computer time, but CCC could not pay and declared bankruptcy.

The person sent to remove the chairs from the CCC offices walked in and discovered three teenagers busily working on the computers and not in the least concerned by this intruder. Even without chairs, the Lakeside group continued to work. The rest of the furniture was removed, but that still did not discourage these programming aficionados. It wasn't until the computers themselves were confiscated that the programmers gave up working.

A YEAR-LONG RESPITE

After the remonstrances from the CDC engineers, Bill spent most of 1970 away from computers. Thoughts of a future career were on his mind, and the choice that seems so obvious now—blazing trails in information technology—was still far from determined.

At home, Bill was exposed principally to the legal profession. Most of his father's friends who came to the house were lawyers who were well-spoken and knowledgeable about business and politics. They made cogent comments about important matters in the community, where they enjoyed stature and influence. With his computer career temporarily derailed, Bill began to be pulled into more traditional directions, and he started to make plans for college.

SAVING THE LAKESIDE CLASS SCHEDULE

Yet programming pursued Bill Gates while he was still in high school. Expert DEC programmers were rare, and the reputation of the two teenage computer whizzes spread across the border to Oregon. In December 1970, Bill and Paul were contacted by a firm called Information Sciences and offered PDP-10 time in exchange for their programming expertise.

After evaluating the boys' technical competence, Information Sciences asked them to write a payroll program for the company in COBOL. In return, the company gave Bill and Paul $10,000 worth of computer hours, which they used throughout the school year.

In June 1971, Lakeside School identified Gates, the math whiz who loved computers, as the ideal person to write a program for creating class schedules. Done manually, this job was very complex and inevitably led to overcrowded classes.

Gates, however, turned down the offer. He had not yet decided what role programming would play in his life. A bizarre series of mishaps, however, thrust this task back upon him.

An engineer who had just come to Lakeside to teach math was assigned the class scheduling job. He was killed in an airplane accident. The school administration again asked Bill Gates, along with Kent Evans, if they would consent to doing the programming task. Then Kent died while mountain climbing.

Fortunately, Bill was not superstitious. Once he got over the shock of his friend's death, he called Paul Allen to the rescue. Paul had just graduated from high school in June. He helped Bill develop the class schedule, writing the program in FORTRAN. Paul remembers working night and day with Bill in the otherwise deserted school, grappling with this programming challenge: "It was a really interesting problem because everybody had different classes that they wanted to take, and [we had] to make sure that all the class sizes were the same. [There were] all these constraints."

Gates and Allen received computer time in exchange for programming and made $2,400 in spending money. During the 1971-72 school year, it took them several months to exhaust the substantial computer-time credit they had accrued.

Later, in refining the program, Bill combined business with pleasure and wrote the class scheduling program so that in every possible case, he would be the only boy in a certain course, surrounded by cute girls.

TRAF-O-DATA

In the fall of 1971, Paul Allen entered Washington State University as a computer science major. The work world, however, attracted Allen, who believed he and Gates could put their talents to practical use. He told Bill about an interesting idea he wanted his friend to help him carry out.

In Seattle, rubber strips had been placed across some highway and city-street intersections to analyze traffic flow. A company in south Seattle connected the rubber strips to small gray boxes that produced punched paper cards containing traffic information. Allen believed there had to be a way to analyze these punched cards using computers. From there, it should be possible to furnish the traffic statistics that cities and counties needed to qualify for highway funds.

Bill liked the idea, so the duo tried to buy a computer, but quickly discovered that minicomputers were still prohibitively expensive. Then Paul, a regular reader of many electronics magazines, discovered that Intel had released a new microprocessor called the 8008.

A microprocessor is a small version of the processors essential for the functioning of large computers. The processor (large or small) handles the data that are entered into the computer's memory—for example, it saves the text of a letter and calculates the totals for a budget. Previously, in 1969, the California company Intel had successfully integrated millions of microscopic circuits into a silicon chip, which was a miniature reproduction of the set of circuits and wires that in the past would have filled an entire room. Intel called its microprocessor the 4004. The 4004 was too limited to handle writing software, so Intel expected to use it as a controller in household appliances, not in computers. A successor to the 4004 was released in 1972. Although the 8008 was much more promising, it was difficult to imagine that this chip could handle a computer program that would serve any useful function.

Paul was very excited about the 8008 and first tried to convince Bill that they should create a programming tool for the chip. They chose BASIC, a programming language they had used extensively at Lakeside School. Bill, however, said that it wasn't worth the effort because the chip was too slow. He correctly assessed that the microprocessor was not powerful enough to support BASIC.

Paul then realized they could use this chip to make a minimal computer that could analyze the traffic data generated by the gray boxes used on Seattle streets. In order to carry out their operation, the two friends formed a company and named it Traf-O-Data.

For $360, they bought one of the first 8008 chips produced by Intel. Then they had an electronics technician build a programmable machine for the Traf-O-Data. This ancestor of the microcomputer had no sophistication whatsoever. The wires were rolled up haphazardly inside, and the outside wasn't much to look at either. The machine was not intended to be a marketable product, just a tool for programming the 8008.

The division of labor occurred naturally, with each of the two programmers working on what interested him most. Paul, still a student at Washington State, developed a program in assembly language on the PDP-10 to make it simulate the behavior of the 8008 chip. From Paul's simulator, Bill wrote the program to monitor traffic flow. It took an extremely long time to develop, since the Traf-O-Data team was attempting to do something that had never been done before.

Once the machine was set up and the program was written, the punched cards from the gray boxes in Seattle provided the data for the Traf-O-Data machine. Paul and Bill also wrote to agencies responsible for monitoring traffic in other parts of the United States and Canada, offering traffic flow reports. During the 1972-73 school year, Traf-O-Data earned $20,000 from clients that included the state of Maryland and the province of British Columbia.

The 1972 presidential campaign pitted George McGovern against Richard Nixon. Bill, an Eagle Scout, found a summer job as a congressional page. He bought 5,000 McGovern-Eagleton badges for 3 cents each. When Eagleton was dropped from the Democratic ticket, Bill began selling the badges as collector's items, asking as much as $20.25. In the process he refined his selling techniques and perfected his powers of persuasion.

TRW CALLS

In January 1973, in the middle of Bill's senior year of high school, an unexpected opportunity arose with TRW. The defense contractor was involved in building a computer system to monitor and control all the dams in the Pacific Northwest, including the Columbia basin area. Several PDP-10 computers were supposed to analyze the electricity needs of the area and then control the amount of electricity generated by the dams. TRW was writing the necessary programs to use on the PDP-10s.

For several months, the company had been experiencing terrible problems caused by all types of bugs in the PDP-10 software. The firm was on the verge of paying indemnities to its client because of delays in the project and had just made an international appeal for PDP-10 experts. They were considering all potential candidates. During this crucial period, a TRW technician discovered the CCC Problem Report Book. In it, he found a mind-boggling list of bugs already identified on the PDP-10. He also noticed that the names of two PDP-10 experts, Gates and Allen, appeared on almost every page. TRW checked with Information Sciences in Portland to confirm the expertise of these two programmers. From there, it was easy to find them.

The two boys went to TRW for interviews. Paul Allen, weary of college life, needed no coaxing. He was increasingly interested in a job in the private sector. And, as luck would have it, students at Lakeside School had the option of finishing their senior year in an internship at a private company. So Bill asked for and easily obtained permission to work at TRW. "I don't think that the company had any idea how young we were," he recalls.

Once again, the two programmers used their talents in very different domains. Allen worked on restoring the system after it crashed, while Gates worked on data storage and run-time code.

At TRW, Gates and Allen met John Norton, who amazed them with his ability to memorize a 5,000-page listing of the operating system. Gates credits Norton with helping him hone his programming skills. Norton would review Gates's code with him and make him remove anything he felt was not logical or could be simplified.

Despite the high quality of their work, Paul and Bill received student wages. "We got paid $165 a week," Paul says. "That was our first paying job. We had an apartment in Vancouver and didn't have many expenses, so we thought it was great." TRW saved its contract. Bill and Paul's participation helped tremendously in the project's final success.

Meanwhile, in their free time, Gates and Allen continued to look for prospective clients for Traf-O-Data's traffic statistics. That spring, however, they found themselves facing unexpected competition. The federal government had decided to offer a similar service at no charge. Traf-O-Data shut down.

Bill graduated from high school in June, and was getting ready to go off to college. In the summer of 1973, Honeywell offered him a job with one of its subsidiaries in the state of Washington. Since Honeywell really wanted to recruit a full-time programmer, however, Bill recommended Paul Allen, who got the job.

AT HARVARD

As Bill wondered what to do with his life, sometimes the idea of starting a company right away sounded tempting. At other times, he was unsure which route to take. Abstract mathematics and economics interested him most, but he also liked the idea of becoming a lawyer. He finally decided to go to Harvard. A few months later, Paul Allen arranged to be transferred to Boston.

When Bill entered Harvard in the fall of 1973, he had already decided to study láw. His parents were thrilled with his decision and happy that a legal career had won out over his childhood "hobby." Yet his heart was not in it. He spent countless hours playing poker and, he says, sitting in his room "being a philosophical depressed guy, trying to figure out what [he] was doing with [his] life." At other times he immersed himself in novels such as *Catcher in the Rye* and *A Separate Peace,* which appealed to him because they dealt with the reality of growing up even when you don't want to.

At Harvard, Bill became friends with Steve Ballmer, whose intellectual intensity was matched only by his incisive wit. Steve introduced Bill to his friends by blind-folding him in the university cafeteria and making him deliver a speech on the virtues of computers.

Paul Allen often visited Bill on evenings and weekends, engaging in fervent debates about the prospects of starting a computer company. In 1974, Intel released a new micropro-cessor, the 8080. In contrast to the 4004 and the 8008, this chip opened up the possibility of writing programs that could be released to thousands of users. This time, Intel wanted to market the 8080 on a wide scale.

Paul had a vision. How could they meet the challenge of the microprocessor, this invention that reduced a large-system processor to the size of a matchbox? A revolution was beginning and they could not miss it. "We need to write a BASIC for the 8080," he told Bill. Gates thought long and hard about such an opportunity, but did not see any concrete application for it. What they needed was a computer built around the 8080 . .

Thousands of miles away, in Albuquerque, a certain Ed Roberts and his company named MITS were already taking on this challenge.

PART 2

BASIC BEGINNINGS

*Gates is to software what Edison was to the light bulb—
part innovator, part entrepreneur,
part salesman and full-time genius.*

–*People* magazine, December 26, 1983

3

Altair BASIC

A handful of manufacturers—including IBM, DEC, and Hewlett-Packard—dominated the computer market in 1975. These firms had combined revenues in the billions of dollars, based primarily on large systems and minicomputers. They had not yet grasped the significance of the microprocessor and were making plans to use it. That left a dramatic opening for small-scale entrepreneurs, who soon launched a technology that radically changed the rules of computer design and use.

Computer magazines also played a large part in fostering this technology. Before any personal computer ever reached the market, publications such as *Radio Electronics* and *Popular Electronics* were sparking an interest in the potential of microcomputers. Computers were embraced as a hobby by many subscribers, and amateur clubs were formed throughout the United States. The most notable of these was the Homebrew Computer Club, started in March 1975 in Menlo Park, California. Its early members included Steve Jobs and Steve Wozniak, who later founded Apple Computer. When the first microcomputer appeared, it aroused immediate and enormous demand from thousands of hobbyists whose interest had been fueled by monthly reports in the magazines.

THE MITS ALTAIR: THE FIRST MICROCOMPUTER

In 1974, a small company in Albuquerque, New Mexico, built the first personal computer to have any real impact. Ed Roberts had founded MITS (Micro Instrumentation and Telemetry Systems) in 1968 as a small electronics company and later began to manufacture calculators. In 1973, Texas Instruments entered the calculator market and implemented an aggressive price-reduction policy. This strong competition so seriously affected MITS that just one year later Ed Roberts was on the verge of bankruptcy. Fortunately, his pioneering instincts led him to take interest in the 8080 chip produced by Intel in April 1974. Convinced that this microprocessor could serve as the basis for a microcomputer, Roberts decided to build his own, which he called the Altair. *Popular Electronics,* which had been looking for a scoop for six months, agreed to feature the product on the cover of its January 1975 issue.

That magazine hit the newsstands in mid-December 1974 with an eye catching headline: WORLD'S FIRST MINICOMPUTER KIT TO RIVAL COMMERCIAL MODELS. Inside was an article describing the Altair and a form to order it from MITS. The announcement triggered an avalanche of checks, far surpassing Roberts's expectations.

As presented in *Popular Electronics,* the Altair fit the minimal definition of a microcomputer. Once assembled, it looked like a metal box. It had no keyboard or monitor; data entry and output took place via a panel of switches. Inside the box were two logic boards and a power supply. One board contained the processor, including the Intel 8080 chip, and the other provided 256 bytes of memory. [1]

Altair buyers needed not only the $397 to purchase the kit, but a soldering iron and tremendous patience as well. The machine required very careful, piece-by-piece assembly, a task that took hours to complete. Once assembled, the Altair

---

[1] A byte corresponds to a series of eight binary numbers, or "bits." A byte represents characters such as the letters of the alphabet.

presented another challenge. It couldn't store data permanently. What's more, using the computer was very complex, requiring programming expertise. Programs and data had to be entered into the machine via toggle switches on the front panel. The instructions were programmed in machine language—series of zeros and ones—which required a high degree of technical knowledge as well as great manual dexterity. The smallest error meant starting all over again. Blinking lights on the front panel communicated the result of the Altair's calculations. When the machine was turned off, the program and results were lost because the computer's memory was volatile RAM (random access memory).

These shortcomings notwithstanding, the Altair met with unexpected success, triggering the beginning of the microcomputer revolution. The low price provided all the additional incentive enthusiasts needed. Ed Roberts was able to keep the price down because he had negotiated with Intel to obtain the 8080 chips for $75, one-third their normal price.

Roberts's traditionally negative bank balance miraculously turned positive, and he began anticipating a healthy financial future based on a steady stream of daily orders. Thousands of hobbyists who had always dreamed of owning their own personal computer blindly ordered a practically unusable product. Yet only a few, such as Steve Dompier, actually managed to find a use for the Altair. Having discovered that the Altair caused interference with a nearby radio, Dompier awrote a program to control the frequency and duration of the static and make the computer play the Beatles' "Fool on the Hill" through the radio. At a Homebrew Club meeting in April 1975, he methodically entered each line of his program by moving the switches and made the Altair play the song for the stupefied audience.

SEIZING THE ALTAIR OPPORTUNITY

One icy December morning in 1974, Paul Allen was in Harvard Square when he happened upon the *Popular*

Electronics magazine featuring the Altair computer kit. He ran to find Bill Gates and tell him the incredible news. An inexpensive microcomputer is now available! What he read left him flabbergasted: "The first computer kit to rival professional models!" The magazine contained the first in a series of articles that would become famous: "Build the Altair Computer Yourself."

"Look, it's going to happen! I told you this was going to happen!" Allen cried. "And we're going to miss it!" These words struck a chord in the 19-year-old Gates. He and Allen clearly grasped the significance of the moment, as Gates told interviewer Mark Stevens (*M. Inc.*, December 1990). "What excited us more than the kit itself was the realization that the personal computer miracle was going to happen."

Gates and Allen became determined to implement a computer language for the Altair. Their Traf-O-Data experience with the 8008 chip and their Lakeside School work with BASIC would prove valuable in this undertaking. They chose BASIC as the language to work with because it was simpler to program than any other computer language and infinitely more accessible than the microprocessor's machine language. John G. Kemeney and Thomas E. Kurtz had created BASIC in 1964 with the goal of making programming as easy as possible, so BASIC was an obvious choice for the Altair microcomputer, which was targeted for the general public.

In Albuquerque, Ed Roberts watched in awe as orders for the Altair poured in from all over the country. Once the initial wonder wore off, however, Roberts realized that to attract a broader public, he needed to offer a simple programming language with the computer. Only a few rare-gifted individuals dared to struggle with the machine's switches to try to program it at its most basic level. If a form of BASIC were available, it would open up a whole world of applications on the Altair in areas likely to interest businesses, such as accounting, bookkeeping, and letter writing. However, representatives from Intel had assured Roberts that the 8080 chip was not powerful enough to run a language like BASIC. Roberts agreed but kept his eyes open for anyone who could prove him wrong.

One week after reading the *Popular Electronics* article, Bill Gates and Paul Allen called MITS. They introduced themselves as representatives of a Seattle firm called Traf-O-Data. Without hesitating, Bill claimed that he had already adapted BASIC for the Altair and asked whether Roberts was interested.

Ed Roberts was somewhat wary of such offers, having received several already. "Of course I'm interested," he replied. "Show me what you've got."

A short time later, MITS received a letter on Traf-O-Data letterhead in which Bill and Paul claimed to have a BASIC interpreter that ran on all 8080 computers. The writers said they were interested in selling copies of the software to hobbyists through MITS in the form of cassettes or diskettes. They proposed royalties of 50 cents a copy and asked Roberts to respond if he was interested.

The letter piqued Roberts's curiosity. He rushed to the phone to dial the number on the Traf-O-Data letterhead. He reached a boarding school in Seattle, and found no one at the other end of the line who knew anything about a BASIC interpreter. What should he think of the offer from these apparent pranksters?

Fortunately, he soon received another sign of life from Traf-O-Data. Bill and Paul had been working hard to implement BASIC on the Altair. Their first major problem was that they didn't have an Altair computer. Nonetheless, they decided to repeat a strategy that had worked well for them at Traf-O-Data. They would simulate the Altair microprocessor on the large PDP-10 system in Harvard's Aiken Computer Laboratory. Paul had mastered this art.

Some time earlier, a certain David Osborne had written a manual detailing the functioning of the 8080. Bill and Paul acquired a copy, which, along with the *Popular Electronics* article, became the basic reference tools for the two programmers. They began by studying the specifications of the 8080, and Paul tried to program the DEC to make it act like the Intel chip. He spent two weeks developing a simulator of the Altair's processor on the PDP-10, as well as an assembler for programming the chip. The assembler takes the assembly language's input and produces the machine instructions. During that time, Bill wrote the design specifications for Altair BASIC.

The two friends had still never seen an 8080 when they called Ed Roberts again to tell him they had practically finished implementing the language. This time Roberts asked them whether they could come to Albuquerque to demonstrate their program. Bill swallowed hard and responded that they could, in less than three weeks.

The Altair had a maximum capacity of only 4 kilobytes (4K), or approximately 4,000 characters. (Within ten years, IBM computers and compatibles would offer 160 times more memory than the MITS machine.) Since the language Gates developed would be used to write and run programs, which also required memory, he had to keep his BASIC to less than 4K. Fortunately, he had already accumulated vast expertise in writing efficient, concise, and bug-free code.

For four weeks Bill worked day and night, between classes, in his small dorm room at Harvard and in the computer lab. He and Paul sometimes nodded off in front of the PDP-10 screen. Speed was all the more crucial because, according to Roberts, other firms were also working to develop BASIC for the Altair.

Bill and Paul faced another problem: inputting the data. It was not realistic to introduce thousands of lines of BASIC using the Altair's switches. When they phoned to ask the MITS technicians whether they were going to produce a keyboard for the machine, the technicians were intrigued by the question: they had no plans to do so. The partners borrowed an old Traf-O-Data technique and recorded Bill's 8,000 lines of machine language code onto punched paper tape.

When they found the time to distance themselves from their work, Bill and Paul were struck by the magnitude of their challenge. They had never touched an Altair. The success of their operation depended largely on the reliability of the 8080 simulator Paul had written.

BASIC PASSES THE TEST

In February 1975, on the eve of their appointment with Ed Roberts, the two friends worked very late. Paul caught an early morning flight to New Mexico. Suddenly, a sobering thought occurred to him: They had forgotten to write the code needed to load BASIC into the Altair memory. He began writing as the plane began its descent into Albuquerque.

Paul felt strange in Albuquerque. Residents wore lightweight, casual clothes and cowboy hats in this sun-drenched city. A man of about 40 drove up in a truck and introduced himself as Ed Roberts. "I'll take you to our development laboratory," he told Paul, who was expecting to arrive at a large downtown building with spacious offices. The Altair had been featured on the cover of *Popular Electronics*; he assumed that MITS was a big company. But he soon discovered that it was a small shop located between a laundromat and a massage parlor.

When they entered the "development laboratory," Paul saw an assembled Altair for the first time. It was an advanced model with 6K of memory. Paul wanted to test BASIC immediately, but Roberts insisted that there was no hurry.

Bill had stayed behind in Cambridge, and was anxiously awaiting word of the outcome of the meeting. He had very little hope left. There were too many unknowns. Was Paul's simulator accurate? Was his own BASIC completely free of bugs? That night, Paul telephoned and tried to reassure him that everything would be fine, although he wasn't convinced himself.

The crucial moment arrived the next day in Roberts's office. Paul fed the punched tape into the tape reader he had connected to the computer. Roberts looked skeptical. Minutes ticked away while the data were slowly loaded into the Altair's memory.

Suddenly, the Altair reacted, writing the word READY on the Teletype machine connected to it. This meant that the

Altair was ready to receive a program written in BASIC. "It works!" Ed Roberts exclaimed.

Paul was even more surprised (and relieved!) than Roberts. He still had to prove, however, that the BASIC worked effectively. The first software tested on the machine, from a programming book on BASIC, was a simulation of a spaceship landing on the moon. It was the first time the Altair had been put to practical use. Bill's BASIC worked without a glitch, and Roberts was very impressed. Now negotiations could begin: He was ready to order immediately.

Paul ran to the phone and told Bill about their triumph. Confused about his future, Bill needed just that boost, and he exploded with joy.

Later, whenever they recalled that moment, they marveled that Bill's BASIC had actually worked, considering how it was developed. One single error would have meant failure. If they had misread the book on the 8080 or if Paul's simulator had contained the slightest mistake, nothing would have happened when Paul entered the code from the punched tape.

Having BASIC was significant for the Altair—and the industry. Now practical applications for areas like accounting and statistics could be developed. Understandably, Roberts wanted to market BASIC as soon as possible, but Gates wanted to put some final touches on it before it was released. He continued at Harvard, working on his law studies and refining his BASIC on Harvard's central computer. His professors couldn't imagine why he logged so many hours of computer time.

Allen returned to Honeywell and kept in touch with Roberts, buying time as Gates improved his BASIC. Eventually Roberts offered Allen the job of developing software for the Altair. He joined MITS in May 1975. At age 22, he was promoted to software director. He in turn persuaded Gates to join him in Albuquerque at the beginning of Harvard's summer vacation. Gates continued to improve the Altair BASIC before it was officially released for sale.

Gates's BASIC was very reliable for the standards of that time. If a user made a mistake, an error message would appear. BASIC did not produce incorrect results or, worse yet, cause the Altair to crash. It was so well written that it dominated the microcomputer market for the next six years.

The Altair's paper tape data entry procedure became automated, but Paul realized this solution was still imperfect and that the ideal setup would be to connect a disk drive to the Altair. He shared his idea with Bill, who then planned to start working on the necessary changes.

MICROSOFT IS BORN

In order to carry out the negotiations with MITS, Gates and Allen formed a business partnership called Micro-Soft (for microcomputer software; the hyphen was later dropped) in Albuquerque, New Mexico, in July 1975. Its goal was to develop languages for the Altair and other microcomputers that would soon appear on the market. It was the first company created with the specific purpose of producing software for this type of machine.

Microsoft's first contract was to write the BASIC for the Altair. Paul Allen supervised all negotiations in the name of MITS with Ed Roberts's approval. In this contract, Microsoft granted MITS a license to distribute Microsoft BASIC. In other words, Microsoft essentially sold MITS the right to use and market its software, but the contract specified that no manufacturer, developer, or end-user would ever be 100 percent owner of the software. This became the basis for the legal relationship that currently exists between software developers and anyone marketing or using their product.

Microsoft's contract also stipulated that MITS would promote sales of BASIC licenses among third parties such as other developers. The buyer received limited rights to use the language. Developers were considered as intermediaries, in the sense that they could transfer the license from Microsoft to end-users.

An Albuquerque lawyer drew up the agreement, but Bill's legal knowledge no doubt played an important role in the precision and adroitness of the contract. In fact, that contract became a model for future software licensing agreements, because it allowed Microsoft to retain ownership of its language regardless of who used or sold it in the future.

The first BASIC sold for the Altair was called 4K BASIC and took up one-third that amount of memory. It left enough memory for a 50-line program.

At the beginning of the 1975-76 school year, Bill left Albuquerque for Harvard. A few months later, though still officially a student, he returned to work with MITS. Bill and Paul worked to give the Altair a solid software base. They wrote an assembler—to translate the assembly language into machine instructions for the microprocessor—and made a few refinements to their BASIC.

MITS developed memory expansion cards for adding memory to its computer. Bill spent three months writing some complex programs to test the cards, and found that none of the cards worked correctly. Tension mounted between the Gates-Allen duo and Roberts, who wanted to continue selling his cards despite their obvious defects.

Ed Roberts frequently walked past the vacuum cleaner dealer and sewing machine store separating Paul Allen's software department from the MITS administrative office to visit the two programmers and encourage them to write applications for the Altair. Allen and Gates, however, were not convinced of the computer's reliability and urged Roberts to improve the quality of his memory expansion cards. Despite protests from Roberts, they preferred to use a Data General computer to handle MITS's accounting. The Altair also lacked a data entry mechanism. Data entry from punched tape was a hybrid solution that inhibited marketing application software for professional use.

Paul again asked Bill to write a version of BASIC to manage files on a diskette, but Bill's mind was on other things. Now that he had founded Microsoft, his primary concern was expanding his company. For that, he needed to interest other microcomputer manufacturers in the BASIC.

4

Microsoft's First Year

Microcomputer diskettes for storing programs and data first appeared on the market in 1972. They were simply a smaller version of the disks that had been used in computers since 1956. Disk drives for the new diskettes were bulky but were preferable to other data access devices like magnetic tape drives, punched tape readers, and cassette players because they allowed users to jump immediately to the desired information rather than having to "fast forward" through other data first.

Knowing that MITS needed to offer the capability to use a disk drive with the Altair, Allen became more insistent that Gates write the necessary software routines. In February 1976, Gates, still a student at Harvard, finally bowed to Allen's pressure. He flew to Albuquerque and holed up in the Hilton Hotel with a stack of yellow notepads. Five days later, he emerged with hundreds of pages of notes. He then went to enter the code on a DEC PDP-11 belonging to the Albuquerque public school system. Less than a week later, DiskBASIC for the Altair was ready to run. Paul Allen still remembers that as "a real feat of programming."

The file managing method in DiskBASIC was different from the ones Gates had used previously. A file allocation table handled the distribution of available space and managed all files on a diskette. According to Gates, this setup provided an enormous increase in speed. In fact, he created a concept that was widely used in the computers of the 1980s.

DiskBASIC was ready, but the price of disk drives was still very high. The first inexpensive disk drive (by Shugart) did not appear until December 1976. The Shugart disk drive, however, was not sufficiently reliable. The heads often lost their alignment, which meant that a diskette containing data written on it by one computer could not be read by another machine. Even with these limitations, the availability of a convenient storage medium such as the diskette was another step toward the wide-scale marketing of applications software such as accounting packages, budgeting software, and computer games. DiskBASIC was becoming the programming language of choice for such applications.

PIRACY PROBLEMS

Since the fall of 1975, MITS had had the exclusive right to distribute the license for Microsoft BASIC. After a few months, however, Microsoft found that its revenues had subsided to a mere trickle. The reason lay in a new, insidious phenomenon: pirating. Many hobbyists attending computer club meetings were openly copying BASIC and freely distributing it to any interested party.

After reading the *Popular Electronics* article, many people had ordered an Altair and later MITS products, such as memory cards and Microsoft BASIC. Delivery delays were excessively long, and MITS products were far from satisfactory. The Altair memory cards were a primary source of disappointment because they just didn't work. To unload the cards, Roberts employed a marketing trick: Microsoft's BASIC sold for $500 alone, or for $150 when purchased with a memory card. In the end, the hobbyists received a memory card that didn't work and a notice that BASIC was not yet ready.

In mid-1975, Ed Roberts began a special promotion for the Altair. The "MITS Mobile Caravan" drove all over the country, stopping in major cities to demonstrate the microcomputer. The goal was to encourage hobbyists to begin Altair user groups. The blue GM truck was soon baptized the "MITS-mobile."

In June 1975, the MITS Mobile Caravan stopped at Rickey's Hyatt House in Palo Alto. Members of the Homebrew Computer Club heard the news and decided to come out in force to show their discontent with MITS's unkept promises. They then discovered that the Altair being demonstrated ran BASIC, whereas none of the hobbyists had yet received their copies. The language was loaded in memory using a punched tape reader, and information was printed on a Teletype machine. This was too much for the computer fans, most of whom had waited weeks to obtain nonfunctional hardware or were still waiting for a BASIC that they had long since paid for.

One member of the Homebrew Computer Club snatched the punched tape that had fallen to the ground and gave it to Dan Sokol so he could copy BASIC from it. Sokol took the paper tape to work and duplicated it many times. At the next meeting of the Homebrew Computer Club, Sokol handed out free copies of Microsoft BASIC. Everyone was encouraged to pass it on to other Altair users, including members of other amateur computer clubs.

In December 1975, when Bill Gates found out what had happened, he was furious because, first of all, this pirating of his software meant a loss of income for him. Furthermore, the BASIC being distributed was not free of bugs, and he'd wanted to eliminate all the bugs before officially releasing the product.

Gates wrote an open letter to the hobbyists, which David Bunnell published in his newsletter for Altair users in February 1976. It began: "As the majority of hobbyists must be aware, most of you steal your software. Hardware must be paid for, but software is something to share. Who cares if the people who worked on it get paid?"

This software theft could deter talented programmers from writing programs for microcomputers, Gates added.

"Who can work for nothing? What hobbyist is ready to spend three years of his life programming, finding bugs, and documenting his program, only to have it freely distributed?"

Gates's letter was bold and to the point. But it was not favorably received. One computer club threatened to sue him for calling all hobbyists thieves. Gates received 300 letters in response to his open letter, but very few contained a check to rectify the situation. Most responded furiously, with faulty arguments, to say the least. They claimed that

1. BASIC was implicitly in the public domain
2. The hobbyists were altruists, not thieves
3. Without BASIC, their systems were almost useless

If the software necessary for running the computer was too expensive, the reasoning went, it was acceptable to copy it for oneself and others. Although totally illogical, such arguments have continued to plague software publishers to this day.

WORLD ALTAIR COMPUTER CONVENTION

In 1975, Altair sales reached $1 million. To capitalize on this instant success, Roberts thought the time was right for a three-day "worldwide" conference. David Bunnell, one of the first MITS employees, organized the event, held March 26–28. Almost immediately, the conference became a festival of microcomputing.

Gates made the first public speech of his career. Paul Allen, Ed Roberts, and Ted Nelson also spoke. (Nelson became famous in the late 1980s as one of the fathers of Hypertext, a system of creating multiple links among different types of information, much as the human brain does.) Discussions about new opportunities for microcomputers were carried on late into the night. Microsoft BASIC was often the subject of discussion, especially after Gate's "Open Letter to Hobbyists."

Despite all the hype, MITS had some enormous problems: The Altair did not work well and was having trouble keeping up with the growing competition. The IMSAI 8080 computer released in the summer of 1975 began overtaking the Altair's market. Other manufacturers such as Processor Technology and Cromemco entered the scene. Since Ed Roberts had excluded competitors from the Altair convention, Processor Technology rented a suite in the same hotel to display its reportedly reliable memory cards for the Altair. This incensed Roberts.

Roberts realized that history could repeat itself, bringing upon him crushing competition as in the early days of his calculator business. So when Pertec, a manufacturer of minicomputers and mainframes, approached him about buying out MITS, Roberts listened willingly, and negotiations soon began.

CONTINUING THE CRUSADE AGAINST PIRACY

In April 1976, Gates wrote a second open letter, which was also published in the Altair newsletter. He softened his initial position, but continued to condemn software pirating.

A Second and Final Letter:

Since sending out my 'OPEN LETTER TO HOBBYISTS' of February 3rd, I have had innumerable replies and an opportunity to speak directly with hobbyists, editors and MITS employees at MITS's World Altair Computer Convention, March 26–28. I was surprised at the wide coverage given the letter, and I hope it means that serious consideration is being given to the issue of the future of software development and distribution for the hobbyist. . . .

Unfortunately, some of the controversy raised by my letter focused upon me personally and even more inappropriately upon MITS. I am not a MITS employee and perhaps no one at MITS agrees with me absolutely, but I believe all were glad to see the issues I raised discussed. The three negative letters I received objected to the fact that I stated that a large percentage of computer hobbyists have stolen software in their possession. My intent was to indicate that a significant number of the copies of BASIC currently in use were not obtained legitimately and not to issue a blanket indictment of computer hobbyists. On the contrary, I find that the majority are intelligent and honest individuals who share my concern for the future of software development. I also received letters from hobbyists who saw the stealing going on and were unhappy about it, and from small companies that are reluctant to provide software because they don't think enough people will buy the software to justify its development. Perhaps the present dilemma has resulted from a failure by many to realize that neither MicroSoft nor anyone else can develop extensive software without a reasonable return on the huge investment in time that is necessary.

In his second letter, Gates also proposed certain solutions that could protect developers against pirating. He suggested, for example, that programs could be permanently stored in the computer's ROM (read-only memory), which is noneras-able. This would make it impossible, however, to correct bugs if they were found after the computer was sold to the customer. He also predicted that thousands of applications would be written in languages such as his BASIC. Gates ended by saying that he considered the pirating debate closed.

Among his other legacies, Gates will be noted for declaring the need for software protection in the early years of the industry. His actions contributed to the gradual acceptance of the idea that a software program is a creative effort and, as such, should be protected like a musical composition or a literary work.

MICROSOFT TAKES SHAPE

Gates could not find the time to write the DiskBASIC Allen wanted for the Altair because on top of his classes at Harvard, he was trying to get Microsoft off the ground. Determined that his company would provide BASIC for the top microcomputer manufacturers, he was writing most of the code himself.

When he wasn't studying or programming, Gates became a passionate spokeman for the new microcomputer era. He met with manufacturers and tried to convince them either to sell Microsoft BASIC with each of their computers or to build a computer around that language. When he encountered a company that had some reservations about the possibilities of the 8080, Gates often successfully persuaded them otherwise.

Despite his youth, Bill's salesmanship proved effective, even in the plushest corporate offices. Gates tailored BASIC to the needs of major companies, and consequently Microsoft's first orders came from such prestigious firms as General Electric, NCR, and Citibank.

Gates soon recognized he could not do it all alone, and began to build a programming staff. Microsoft's first employee was Marc McDonald, age 21, a former classmate of Bill's from Lakeside School. When McDonald joined Microsoft in April 1976, the company had no offices, so he worked at a terminal in his apartment. He improved BASIC 8080, with his boss checking each line of code he wrote.

New microprocessors were now appearing on the market. Motorola offered the 6800, and MOS Technology the 6502. Zilog released an 8080 clone called the Z80.

The next month, Bill Gates hired a second programmer, also a former classmate at Lakeside School. Rick Weiland was responsible for writing a BASIC and a COBOL for Motorola's 6800. He too worked at a terminal in his apartment. Marc McDonald, meanwhile, began working in the MITS offices on a DEC terminal in Paul Allen's division. Ed Roberts was not happy with this arrangement.

In August 1976, Gates recruited two other programmers, Albert Chu and Steve Wood, both 24 years old. Wood had seen the Microsoft job announcement posted at Stanford University, where he had just finished his degree.

Microsoft then leased its first offices—four rooms in downtown Albuquerque. Steve Wood arrived before the furniture. A meeting was scheduled with a representative from Hewlett-Packard about providing a BASIC, so Rick Weiland and Marc McDonald did everything possible to find furniture that very night. Gates supervised linking the terminals to the DEC PDP-10 at the public school in Albuquerque. In a few days, the office became an adequate workplace.

Steve Wood helped write FORTRAN, while Weiland ported BASIC to the MOS Technology 6502 chip. Meanwhile, Gates assumed the new company's necessary administrative duties. He wrote paychecks, filled out tax forms, managed the company's advertising, and marketed its products on the road.

In November 1976, Paul Allen resigned from MITS to join Gates at the helm of Microsoft. The company was beginning to take shape.

Bill returned to Harvard in the fall of 1976. But it was obvious he could not continue his studies and also manage his growing company. His priorities were clear. In December, he dropped out of school despite objections from his parents, and devoted himself fully to Microsoft.

William Henry, Jr., and Mary Gates were very disturbed by the direction their son had chosen, and even more worried that he might not complete his college degree. These parental concerns were understandable, considering that the microcomputer industry was still in its infancy and its viability was unproven.

5

Life at Microsoft

In the spring of 1977, Microsoft moved into formal offices on the eighth floor of Two Park Central Tower in Alberquerque. From the five offices in suite 819, the programmers had a commanding view of the city and a bright vision for the future of their company.

The staff at this time numbered six. Bill Gates and Paul Allen were the general partners; and they were assisted by programmers Marc McDonald, Steve Wood, Bob Greenberg, and Rick Weiland. Each devoted countless hours to improving BASIC, the language Microsoft was striving to put on every machine appearing in the turbulent microcomputer market.

With business activities and corresponding administrative duties expanding, it was time to hire a secretary. Miriam Lubow, a 42-year-old mother of four who had recently decided to go back to work, spotted a newspaper ad for a secretary at Microsoft. She applied for the job.

Steve Wood greeted Lubow when she arrived for the interview. On the phone, he had called himself the general manager, but in person, she began to wonder. He had a mustache and long hair, and he sat with his feet up on the desk throughout most of the interview. Wood told Lubow that they were looking for a versatile person who could do a little bit of everything. Despite the unorthodox business atmosphere, the offered salary was good, and the work seemed interesting.

Bill Gates's previous secretary had held the job two months. She was a slender young woman with long blond hair, and when Lubow saw her, she thought: "They'll never hire a woman my age. They're going to want the prettiest young woman they can find." The departing secretary's remarks were not very reassuring either. She made a point of warning Lubow: "I don't think you'll like it here. It's terribly boring."

That night, Miriam Lubow told her husband about her interview with Steve Wood. She explained that Microsoft had very nice offices, that they developed *software*—a term which was a bit enigmatic to the Lubows—and that they offered a very good salary. Yet she remained pessimistic about her chances of getting the job.

MIRIAM LUBOW DISCOVERS SOFTWARE

A week later, though, Steve Wood called and told her that if she was still interested in the job, she could start the following Monday. An excited Miriam accepted and told herself that sooner or later she would have to figure out what in the world software was. . . .

When Miriam met Paul Allen and the other employees on her first day of work, she asked them where the boss was. They answered that he was on a business trip and would be back in a few days.

Miriam soon began to wonder just what type of company she had signed on with. The doors to all the offices were left open, and computers were everywhere. As the programmers typed on their keyboards, they produced very long documents which piled up accordion-style on the floor. Every day around noon, Miriam was responsible for going to the computer center at the local school and getting *listings*. Eventually she made the connection: What the Microsoft programmers were typing ended up as these printed lists on the school's computer!

After her first few days at Microsoft, Miriam explained to her husband that *software* meant computer paper with lots of marks written on it. Having no better idea of what software was, Mr. Lubow did not contradict his wife.

One morning when Miriam was seated at her typewriter, a young boy entered the Microsoft offices. "Hi!" he said with a grin, and then walked right into the chairman's office and began working on the computer. Having received very strict instructions that no unauthorized person was to enter any room with computers, Miriam rushed into Wood's office, fretting that some kid had barged into the chairman's office. Not at all surprised, Steve responded tersely, "Oh yeah. That's no kid. That's our chairman."

"What? *He's* Bill Gates?"

"Yes."

Miriam returned to her typewriter somewhat disconcerted. Five minutes later, she went back into Steve Wood's office. "Excuse me, Steve, but how old is he?"

"Twenty-one."

Lubow realized that she was indeed working for a unique company. That evening, her husband advised her to make sure that Microsoft could pay her at the end of the month.

As time went by, she learned that Microsoft sold diskettes. She knew that there must be something valuable on those diskettes, but she still had difficulty understanding what was being magically created in those offices. The programmers typed all day in front of their computers. A mystery... When she tried to read what was finally printed on the listings at the school, she only became more confused. What was the significance of these strings of words that meant absolutely nothing to her? At the office, she overheard the strangest conversations. The programmers continually used technical terms like BASIC, FORTRAN, and RAM and jargon like, "My program crashed." She tried her best to grasp the meanings of these terms, the seriousness of their technical concerns, and the programmers' instructions to her about her duties.

She had no problem working with Gates though. "One thing that I always liked about him was whenever he asked you to do something, you always understood perfectly what it was he wanted you to do. He always took the time and the trouble to explain if you asked him a question. He could explain anything to you in your terms at your level," Lubow recalls.

She had to ask her boss many questions, but Gates was a patient teacher. "He never said, 'Oh well, that's too difficult for you, or too technical for you,' or anything like that. Never." Sometimes she relayed a question from a potential client to Bill, and then listened as he answered. Usually, Lubow saw the person in question enter the Albuquerque offices a few days later to sign a contract with Microsoft.

As she worked directly with Gates, Lubow realized that she was working with an extraordinary individual. He had an almost infallible memory and could immediately rattle off any telephone number she asked him. She saw him read a page and find a typo in an instant. He also showed a rare understanding of law. His two years of studies at Harvard and help from his father made it easy for him to grasp often disconcerting legal issues. Quite often, when his lawyer brought him a carefully drawn-up contract, Gates rewrote it entirely. When it came to selling BASIC to a prospective client, Lubow watched him negotiate like a seasoned expert.

Gates now drove a fast green Porsche 911, and Lubow regularly found speeding tickets for him in the mail. At times, she says, she almost expected to see the headlines of one of the local newspapers read: MICROSOFT PRESIDENT BEHIND BARS FOR SPEEDING.

Above all, Miriam Lubow saw her boss work very hard, seven days a week. Sometimes he went several days without leaving the office. When she arrived in the morning, she often found him asleep on the floor. Like a mother, she grew concerned when Bill skipped lunch and reminded him to eat. Sometimes, when he had guests, Miriam watched the passing hours and took the initiative to give him a call. "Bill, you ought to break for lunch because those people are probably hungry. It's already two P.M.!" After a few weeks, she realized that when Bill was alone, he simply forgot to eat. She therefore made it a habit to bring him hamburgers at lunchtime.

The Lubows began to gain a greater appreciation for what was happening at Microsoft. "After just six months," Miriam recalls, "we understood that great things were going to happen. It was inevitable, the way his mind worked." One day, Miriam Lubow's husband went to the office to tell Bill, "If you ever decide to go public, let me know."

Heads of large companies came to Albuquerque to meet Gates. Members of the East Coast corporate culture, they arrived in formal business attire, whereas Bill, reflecting both his youth and the informality of the Southwest, dressed casually. The contrast was often striking.

Gates usually met potential clients at the airport. When visitors asked Miriam Lubow ahead of time how they'd be able to recognize him, she'd answer: "Look for a 16-year-old blond kid, with glasses, who looks like he's spaced out, in another world. That's him!"

Two Park Central Tower was just a few minutes drive from the Albuquerque airport. When he left on a business trip, Bill would drive his old 1974 Porsche to the airport and let Miriam drive it back. However, he developed a habit of leaving as late as possible so as not to waste a minute more than necessary at the terminal. As a result, he often ran for planes just as the ground crew was about to push back the boarding stairway. If the plane was scheduled to leave at 10 o'clock, Bill left the office at 9:55 and devoured the distance, paying little heed to speed limits or red lights. It was a kind of game he played against himself. "I like pushing things to the edge. That's often where you find high performance." Finally, Miriam began to tell Bill that his departure time was 15 minutes earlier than it actually was so that she would not always be so anxious for him.

Miriam did most of the administrative work of the company, including payroll, bookkeeping, order taking, purchasing, and general typing. She also made sure that the programmers were working in the most comfortable environment possible. The only beverage available in the office at that time was coffee; one day, Marc McDonald asked if they could have Coca-Cola. Bill thought it was a great idea and sent Miriam out to buy some. She came back with a six-pack, and five minutes later, all six bottles were empty and the programmers were thirsty for more. Miriam was on her way out the door to buy another six-pack, but Bill stopped her and asked her instead to arrange for Coca-Cola to be delivered twice a week by the case. Offering free soft drinks (and later, milk and juices) to all employees became a company tradition.

Every night around nine o'clock, the janitors came to clean suite 819. One morning, Marc McDonald walked into his office and exploded with strong epithets, then approached Miriam with an accusing look and asked her if she had thrown out his program. She answered that she never threw their papers away, as a matter of principle. McDonald yelled that he had left a listing at the foot of his computer and that it had disappeared. Miriam then realized that the janitors had very professionally scooped up everything they found on the floor. McDonald lost many hours of work and had to start again from scratch. From that time on, the janitorial staff had express orders never to throw out anything that was not in the waste baskets, and they zealously complied. When empty Coca-Cola cans started piling up all over the offices a short time later, Miriam had to clarify to the janitors what was trash and what wasn't!

Miriam's baptism as a computer user came after a year with the company when the programmers showed her how to copy the contents of one diskette onto another. "We essentially had two products, BASIC and FORTRAN. So, depending on what the client wanted, I put a diskette into the machine, made a copy, and sent it out. I felt especially brilliant!"

BOB O'REAR AND THE MICROSOFT CULTURE

Bob O'Rear went to work for Microsoft on January 8, 1978. (He still works there.) His first assignment was to adapt Microsoft BASIC to the Tandy TRS-80. Then he devoted himself to writing mathematical functions for FORTRAN.

Bob found Microsoft to be very different from his previous company. Bill Gates and Paul Allen usually got to the office around noon, sometimes not until four in the afternoon, and worked late into the night, seven days a week. If a client meeting was scheduled for the morning, they would stay all night to be sure they were there on time.

O'Rear was a day person who liked to work normal hours, which seemed strange to the other Microsoft programmers. In the beginning, when he arrived at work around 9 A.M., he was surprised to find Bill asleep on the floor. His first reaction was panic. "Oh my God, he passed out! Call an ambulance!" However, he soon got used to stepping over a few bodies every morning.

And he eventually adapted to the pace in his own way. He started coming to work at 3 A.M., so his workday began just as the other programmers were finishing theirs. He also picked up the in-house custom of working barefoot. The programmers believed they needed to be as comfortable as possible in order to devote themselves fully to the strict discipline of programming.

Sometimes, however, their idiosyncrasies got them in trouble. One winter night at 4 A.M., Bob O'Rear was working alone in the office. He went down the hall to use the restroom and returned to find the Microsoft door had automatically locked behind him. There he was, standing barefoot in a corridor with no heat, in the middle of winter, unable to get back into his office. Fortunately, he had enough change in his pocket to use a pay phone in the building. He called and woke up his wife, and asked her to come get him.

The programmers worked at night as a matter of practicality. Microsoft was still developing its languages using the technique Paul Allen had used for the first Altair BASIC, simulating a given microprocessor on the PDP-11 at the Albuquerque public school. Because many users were simultaneously connected to the PDP-11 during the day and thus the computer was slower then, Microsoft programmers chose to work at night, when there was little demand, and writing programs became much more efficient.

6

The Microcomputer Market Blossoms

Toward the end of 1976, a dispute arose over the rights to BASIC. Since business was declining, Ed Roberts was trying to sell MITS to the California company Pertec. He also reneged on the terms of the contract with Microsoft, which stipulated that MITS had a nonexclusive right to use BASIC and would try to license the language to other manufacturers. In the discussions preceding the Pertec buyout, Roberts claimed BASIC as a definite asset of his company, saying he had paid the stipulated $200,000 in royalties to Microsoft and now owned the language.

On May 22, 1977, Pertec officially bought out MITS. At that time, Microsoft was engaged in talks with several companies, including Texas Instruments, about licensing BASIC. Pertec, however, took a different perspective and refused to grant a license of "its" BASIC to the other manufacturers.

Gates and Allen expressed their objection to Pertec officials, saying they would take the matter to court if necessary. The Pertec people were amused by the self-confidence of these "kids" and felt assured of winning any potential lawsuit with their battery of lawyers. They took on Microsoft's challenge.

One morning Paul Allen was served a summons to appear in court. He was told that for the duration of the legal battle, Microsoft would not be able to touch any money from the sale of BASIC 8080. Microsoft would therefore have to make do with income from the sale of more recently developed software: BASIC 6502 and FORTRAN. For the next six months, the company experienced financial difficulties. The problem became all the more troubling as competitors like North Star BASIC and Tiny BASIC appeared on the market. Gordon Eubanks (who became president of Symantec, a software publisher, in 1985) wrote BASIC E, which he put into public domain, authorizing anyone to copy it at no charge.

Although adroit in legal matters, Gates did not hesitate to ask for his father's advice on the matter. William Henry Gates, Jr., was glad to help. He gave wise counsel himself, assured Bill that his company would win, and found a talented Albuquerque lawyer to represent Microsoft.

The trial lasted six months, and at the end of that time, an arbitrator was appointed to the case. This was good news because it meant the matter would be quickly resolved. The normal legal process could have taken several years. "We were nervous," Paul Allen confided, hinting that it was not possible to predict how the arbitrator would interpret the law.

In December 1977, Microsoft won the case. The arbitrator was particularly harsh on Pertec and Ed Roberts because the initial agreements with Microsoft had not been respected. He called the situation the "ultimate case of business piracy," and ruled that MITS had the right to use BASIC, while Microsoft had the right to sell it as it wished.

After 1977, says Steve Wood, Microsoft never had to worry about money again.

SUCCESSFUL PIONEERS: APPLE, TANDY, AND COMMODORE

The Altair success of 1975 was history. The MITS machine was no longer selling, and Pertec soon experienced serious disappointments. When IMSAI tried to monopolize the microcomputer market with a more professional computer, it too was unable to produce high enough quality and was heading for bankruptcy. This was bad news for Microsoft, since IMSAI had just licensed FORTRAN and could no longer make the payments.

For the microcomputer industry to take off, more reliable machines were needed. These appeared in 1977: the TRS-80 by Tandy, the PET by Commodore, and the Apple II.

Tandy was known for its nationwide chain of Radio Shack stores, which sold a wide variety of electronic goods. One Tandy buyer tried to persuade John Roach, the marketing director, that the company needed to start making personal computers. He showed him a prototype he had built himself. Roach was convinced, but did not expect much from the TRS-80 in terms of Radio Shack's overall sales. He said he would be happy if Tandy could sell 3,000 computers in a year. He soon changed his mind, however: In the first month, they sold 10,000 TRS-80 computers!

The first BASIC for the TRS-80 was not Microsoft's. It was called Level I BASIC and was written by a young Radio Shack employee. Gates tried to convince Tandy that it needed a more professional language on its machine. Microsoft BASIC was renamed Level II BASIC for the occasion.

Commodore, a Canadian firm that had experienced difficulties similar to those of MITS in its original calculator market, also became interested in microcomputers. President Jack Tramiel hired Chuck Peddle, the engineer who had built the 6502 microprocessor at MOS Technology, to build a Commodore microcomputer. The resulting Commodore PET had 16K of memory, and included a keyboard and a monitor like the TRS-80. When the PET computer was introduced at the first West Coast Computer Faire in 1977, it was a tremendous success. Microsoft also provided the BASIC for this machine.

The Apple II, also introduced at the first West Coast Computer Faire, did not come with a monitor, but could be connected to a television set. It was a powerful computer which contrasted sharply with the amateur machines being offered by many other hobbyists-turned-manufacturers.

Steve Jobs had met Steve Wozniak at the Homebrew Computer Club. "Woz" was working for Hewlett-Packard and had been trying in vain to persuade the company to build a microcomputer. Wozniak's genius combined with Jobs's demanding nature gave birth to the Apple I. The two friends built the machine in Wozniak's Palo Alto apartment. Even before it was totally finished, the Apple I earned a reputation for reliability, a rare quality for microcomputers at that time.

The Apple II, introduced in 1977, ranked one notch higher on design. It looked much more professional than most machines available at that time, with its beige exterior and keyboard. It weighed less than 15 pounds, which made it easy to transport, and its price of $1,350 made it accessible to a broad public. Inside the Apple II were seven expansion slots, which allowed the user to increase its capabilities by adding up to seven expansion cards for graphics, printing, communications, and so on.

At that time, Jobs succeeded in convincing venture capitalist Mike Markkula to finance the Apple enterprise. Markkula, at age 34, was enjoying an early retirement after making his fortune on Intel stock. He invested $91,000 of his personal money in the new company and raised an additional $600,000. Apple set up shop in spacious offices in Cupertino, California. The company had all the ingredients for success, in terms of both the quality of its product and the company's financial base.

When the Apple II was unveiled at the 1977 West Coast Computer Faire, the Commodore PET stole its thunder. In June, however, the first Apple II ad appeared in *BYTE* magazine, and two-page spreads were regularly published in other computer magazines. Concurrently with these marketing efforts, the Apple II received much-deserved praise from journalists for being a computer that worked as soon as it was plugged in.

In the summer of 1978, a disk drive became available for the Apple II. Then in late 1979 came the release of a software package called VisiCalc, written specifically for the Apple II, which met the exact needs of many managers. Aggressive advertising by Apple and the presence of the Apple-based VisiCalc software led the Apple II to success. Apple II sales rode on the coattails of VisiCalc, which had proved to be the first immensely successful software application. Customers were entering computer stores saying that they wanted to buy VisiCalc and a computer that could run it, and they were walking out with an Apple II. The Cupertino manufacturer soon became number one in the microcomputer market and helped establish the credibility of the fledgling industry.

Apple was an obvious client for Microsoft, which had developed a version of BASIC for the 6502, the microprocessor used in the Apple II. In the fall of 1977, Microsoft granted Apple a license to BASIC.

OPERATING SYSTEMS AND LANGUAGES ABOUND

Computer software is a three-layer pyramid: The operating system is the base, the languages are the middle layer, and the application software is the top layer.

The operating system, the lowest layer of the pyramid, directly controls the microprocessor and related cards such as memory cards. All the thankless and behind-the-scenes operations of the computer take place on this level. When a user tells the computer to record payroll information onto a diskette, for example, the operating system finds the free space on the magnetic medium and then writes the data. The operating system is usually written in assembly language, a *low-level* programming language one step up from the machine instructions. It is very different from everyday English and requires advanced technical knowledge of the hardware.

An operating system is essential to the functioning of the computer. It establishes how data are handled when entered into memory (for example, from a keyboard) or when extracted from memory (for example, onto a diskette).

In 1977, creativity was rampant, and hardly a week went by without a new brand of microcomputer appearing. Each manufacturer entering the booming market was convinced that it had a better product than its competitors. As a result, computers often came with their own operating systems. Processor Technologies used PT-DOS; Intel offered ISIS; Apple, Atari, and Commodore also had their own operating systems.

Programming languages such as COBOL, FORTRAN, Pascal, and some advanced versions of BASIC—the middle layer of the pyramid—rely on the operating system to manage disk drives or other storage devices (such as cassette tapes or hard disks). These languages are called *high-level*, or *evolved*. Unlike assembly language, BASIC, FORTRAN, and COBOL allow the programmer to use instructions in a language similar to everyday English to control the computer. BASIC, for example, uses commands such as PRINT, READ, and WRITE (to write the data on a disk). A program written in a high-level language must be *compiled* to translate instructions such as PRINT or READ into code that the microprocessor can understand.

In a move to expand its product line beyond BASIC, Microsoft released FORTRAN in July 1977 and later COBOL and Pascal. These languages were more advanced than BASIC, and Microsoft chose to write them to run with the CP/M operating system.

Most application software is created using languages such as BASIC, COBOL, or Pascal. In this third layer of the pyramid, we find the programs for public use, such as games, word processors, and accounting packages. A person using application software does not have to worry about the operating system or the programming language. He just has to choose the options from a menu of simple terms such as "Print Document."

The plethora of operating systems available in 1977 and the corresponding lack of standardization hindered the expansion of the software market. Developers who wrote software for a given computer could not sell it for another machine because it would not run. Although Microsoft had successfully adapted its BASIC to many different machines, FORTRAN and COBOL were more sophisticated and could not be easily adapted.

Gates's DiskBASIC performed some of the functions normally handled by the operating system, but that was a special case. Microsoft's other language products were written for the CP/M operating system. When FORTRAN needed to read information from a diskette, for example, it transmitted this request to CP/M, which then located the information. For Microsoft's languages to be widely successful, CP/M needed to become the standard for microcomputer operating systems.

CP/M BECOMES THE STANDARD

CP/M was created by another Seattle native, Gary Kildall, who began working on it in late 1973. One year earlier, Kildall had seen an ad posted on a bulletin board offering a microprocessor for $25. He had always worked on large computers that occupied a whole room, so he thought the small chip with all its capacity was very exciting. He bought an Intel 4004 chip and, for fun, wrote a few short programs. But that chip was too limited for serious development.

Nevertheless, Kildall contacted Intel and became a consultant for them. When Intel released a more ambitious chip, the 8008, Kildall wrote a high-level language for programming it. Then Intel released the 8080 chip, which truly lent itself to professional development. This was the same microprocessor that MITS used one year later in developing the Altair.

Gary Kildall then set out to write an operating system for the 8080 microprocessor: CP/M, or Control Program for Microcomputer. CP/M could run on any computer with that processor. The 3K of code performed all the necessary operations for managing a disk drive. Kildall also developed related programs: a text editor, an assembly language, a debugger, and utilities for copying files from one diskette to another, printing a document, and so on.

Kildall began selling his operating system through classified ads in the *Dr. Dobbs Journal*. Then in 1976, he founded Digital Research (its original name was Intergalactic Digital Research) with the goal of selling his system directly to manufacturers so they could sell it with their machines. His first client was GNAT Computers, which bought the license to CP/M for $90. When Shugart introduced the first 5¼-inch disk drive for $390, CP/M took off. In less than a year, several dozen manufacturers had adopted this operating system, and Digital Research sold a license to IMSAI for a healthy $25,000. Kildall's company made $60,000 in its first year, and revenues steadily increased over the next five years.

A New York-based distributor, LifeBoat Associates, helped make CP/M the industry standard of the late 1970s. At first, LifeBoat was a club for CP/M users, then it began distributing software and publishing a catalog of CP/M software. Microsoft sold its FORTRAN and COBOL through that catalog. LifeBoat Associates is credited with truly getting the software market in motion.

The existence of a distribution channel for hundreds of CP/M programs helped give the operating system the leading edge in the market. Manufacturers such as North Star Computers and Processor Technology also adopted CP/M for use with their machines.

In 1977, Gary Kildall decided to further refine CP/M. He extracted a small section from the rest of the code and called it the BIOS, the basic input-output system. The BIOS was the part of the CP/M operating system consisting of drivers and other software designed to manage peripheral devices, such as the monitor, disk drive, or printer. The rest of the operating system could be used without changes on any machine. Only the BIOS needed to be rewritten for each different machine. Now CP/M could be easily adapted to many different kinds of computers.

When Gates and Allen chose CP/M for their FORTRAN and COBOL, they had providentially latched on to the emerging standard. This meant that a program written in Microsoft FORTRAN or COBOL could be sold for many different computers. In the late 1970s, industry leaders Apple, Tandy, and Commodore continued to use their own operating systems, but many other firms—including newly arrived competitors such as Zenith, Sharp, and Sirius—hopped on the CP/M bandwagon.

7

Kazuhiko Nishi Brings Microsoft to Japan

A JAPANESE ENTREPRENEUR

By 1978, Microsoft enjoyed undisputed domination of the market for microcomputer languages. Microsoft's sales for fiscal 1977 were $500,000. When large companies like Texas Instruments decided to enter the arena with their own microcomputers, they called upon Microsoft for its BASIC. Amid all the different computers and operating systems, Microsoft BASIC seemed to be the one standard element.

In 1978, Kazuhiko Nishi—called Kay by his friends—had two things in common with Bill Gates: his age (22) and his passion for personal computers. Long before they met, Gates and Nishi were travelling surprisingly parallel routes.

In 1973, Bill Gates was following in his father's footsteps, studying law at Harvard. In 1976, he dropped out of college and founded his own company. During that same period, Kazuhiko Nishi was enrolled at the prestigious Waseda University in Tokyo and was planning on a career in the private school owned by his parents. Two years later, he also dropped out of school and plunged headlong into microcomputing by becoming the publisher of a newsletter for diehard hackers. It was so successful that Nishi launched *ASCII,* a computer magazine. The ASCII Company gradually began to distribute software as well.

Nishi wanted to meet the author of Altair BASIC, whose reputation had transcended national borders. He picked up the phone and told the operator that he wanted to contact Microsoft in the United States. "You'll have to tell me what city," the operator said.

Nishi thought for a few seconds and remembered that MITS was located in New Mexico. He then asked the operator to look in the biggest city in that state, Albuquerque. Nishi obtained the number and called immediately. He asked to speak to the president, and Gates came on the line. Nishi explained that he was interested in BASIC and offered to send Gates a first-class plane ticket to Japan.

Gates felt an affinity for this young man who had also dropped out of college to delve into microcomputers. Nevertheless, he explained that he didn't have time to go to Japan. They finally agreed to meet at the next National Computer Conference.

A few months later, Nishi arrived in the United States and met Gates. They talked for eight hours and discovered that they had a common vision of a time when large companies would inundate the market with millions of microcomputers. Gates's dream was for Microsoft to be the number one publisher to meet the accompanying demand for software. Before parting, they both decided to immerse themselves in microcomputing issues and trends. Nishi offered to become the Microsoft representative for the Far East, and the two young men signed a one-page contract to formalize this arrangement.

NEC BUILDS A MICROCOMPUTER

When Nishi returned to Japan, he remembered having met a NEC Corporation executive named Kazuya Watanabe, who was interested in microcomputers. Nishi contacted him once again and persuaded him to go meet with Gates in the United States.

When Watanabe arrived at the Albuquerque airport, he was disconcerted by the two eager young men who picked him up in a Porsche. However, he liked their enthusiasm and the work Microsoft had already done for other companies. Upon returning to Tokyo, he gathered the leaders of NEC together and described a unique opportunity that could be theirs: to produce the first Japanese microcomputer. Watanabe announced that he was going to enlist help from Microsoft—a young company unknown in Japan—in designing it. For a well-established company like NEC to undertake this project when the Japanese personal computer market was in its infancy was quite a risk. "Microsoft played a big role in our decision-making," Watanabe told the *Wall Street Journal* (August 27, 1986). "I always felt that only young people could develop software for personal computers—people with no tie, working with a Coke and a hamburger—only such people could make a personal computer adequate for other young people."

NEC released its NEC PC 8001 computer in 1979. Success came quickly and benefited the Japanese firm as well as Gates and Nishi, who were invited to speak at Japanese computer trade shows and give speeches about the future of microcomputer technology. Very soon, the two became known as the whiz kids who had brought microcomputers to Japan.

But besides being technically astute and very persuasive, Nishi was brash and disrespectful by Japanese standards. He began spending money excessively on outrageous things in order to shock the traditional conservatism of the Japanese business world. He chartered a helicopter to travel to meetings and stayed in the most luxurious hotels. Nishi consistently challenged the established rules. He was even known to fall asleep on the floor during meetings with executives.

ONE OF THE FIRST PORTABLE MICROCOMPUTERS

In late 1981, Hitachi announced it was building a new type of liquid crystal display for up to eight lines of text and that it planned to mass-produce this product. This news struck a chord in Kazuhiko Nishi, who began developing the basic ideas for a portable computer that could truly be used professionally. He needed only to find an investor. Nishi's natural reckless enthusiasm did the rest.

In the first-class cabin of a San Francisco–Tokyo flight, Nishi found himself seated next to Kazuo Inamori, president of Kyocera Corporation, a large Japanese industrial ceramics concern. Nishi struck up a conversation with Inamori and shared his idea for a portable computer. Inamori was soon convinced that this was a once-in-a-lifetime opportunity and pledged Kyocera's support.

In January 1982, Kay walked into Bill Gates's office and unfolded a large drawing of a prototype for a portable computer with the Hitachi liquid crystal display. He told Gates that Kyocera was willing to manufacture the machine. After studying the plans, Gates concluded it was indeed a very interesting prospect, and he and Nishi set about designing the computer in detail.

In April 1982, Nishi flew to Fort Worth, Texas, to show a prototype of the new computer to Tandy/Radio Shack. He met with the vice president of the company, Jon Shirley, who later became president of Microsoft. Kay made a convincing presentation, and Shirley committed Tandy to marketing the new machine.

Thus Gates and Nishi developed one of the first portable microcomputers ever. Kyocera produced the machine, and three companies marketed it: NEC in Japan; Olivetti in Europe; and Tandy in the USA, which sold it as the Radio Shack Model 100.

GATES AND NISHI GO THEIR SEPARATE WAYS

Microsoft's partnership with Kazuhiko Nishi came to an end in 1986.

Bill Gates was having an increasingly difficult time balancing his friendship with Nishi and his frustration with Nishi's unpredictable decisions. Surprises came regularly. One day, Bill learned that Kay had spent $1 million hiring a special-effects expert to build a life-size electronic dinosaur for a television show promoting Microsoft software. This high-tech monster was to be displayed outside the Shinjuku train station in Tokyo's high-rent district. Gates sent a series of telexes to Nishi expressing his complete disagreement with this scheme. Gates felt the money would be better spent on more conventional promotions.

The last straw came a short time later. In 1983, while in the San Jose airport, Gates was paged for an emergency call. Nishi needed help. He explained that on a whim, he had bought $275,000 worth of stock in an American company that looked promising, and now the broker was asking him to pay up as soon as possible. Once again friendship prevailed, and Gates bailed Nishi out.

When Microsoft was preparing for its initial public offering, Gates offered Nishi a full-time position at Microsoft and generous stock options, but he refused. "Bill Gates demands 100 percent loyalty and demands being his subordinate. I'd be very happy to work with him, but I don't want to sell my soul to him."

In March 1986, the two men flew together from Sydney, Australia, to Tokyo. After 30 hours of exhausting discussion punctuated by heated arguments, they decided to go their separate ways.

Microsoft recruited Susumu Furukawa from ASCII Corporation (Nishi's firm) to head Microsoft's official Japanese subsidiary. This move cemented the rift between Microsoft and Nishi. "In the cowboy age, Billy the Kid can be a star. But Microsoft became an army, and Kay was still playing like Billy the Kid. Kay's not a general who can manage an army," Furukawa explained. Almost immediately, however, Furukawa hired 18 employees away from ASCII, a move that infuriated Nishi, who publicly railed against his former associate. Gates sadly shrugged it off. "The guy's life is a mess. He's worth negative half a million, and I'm worth X million—that's certainly seeds for bitterness," he told the *Wall Street Journal*.

"For a guy from Japan, Kay's more like me than probably anybody I've ever met. But he just went overboard."

8

Going Home

By the end of 1978, Microsoft had made its first million and doubled its sales over the previous year. The company had 13 employees, still based in Albuquerque. Early in the year, Microsoft released a fifth version of BASIC. Allen and Gates shared the executive tasks, with Allen supervising the development of new software tools while Gates took care of relations with manufacturers and managed the company's daily activities.

Many people in the microcomputer field encouraged Gates to move his company to California's Silicon Valley. The area had proved fertile ground for computer firms, particularly semiconductor manufacturers, ever since William Shockley founded Fairchild Semiconductor in 1955. In 1968, Robert Noyce left Fairchild and founded Intel. Within 11 years, some 3,500 manufacturing plants had grown up alongside the eucalyptus, sequoia, and palm trees in the 1,300 square miles of the verdant valley. Some of the largest computer companies—Intel, Apple, Fairchild, and Hewlett-Packard—were born in this region located just south of the San Francisco Bay. There were many millionaires under the age of 40. Toward the end of the 1970s, three to four new companies opened their doors in Silicon Valley each week.

Silicon Valley had several attractive features. Many high-tech companies were concentrated in one geographical area, and Stanford University and the University of California at Berkeley continually added talented new risk takers to the labor pool.

Paul Allen, however, was interested in returning to Washington. Gates was more or less indifferent, being primarily concerned with the growth of Microsoft and the development of increasingly sophisticated languages. Allen therefore decided to take advantage of his friend's strong family ties. He talked to Gates's parents and persuaded them to encourage their son to return to Seattle. Allen explains some of the other reasons behind the move:

> Our company kept expanding, but we were having a hard time convincing people to move out to Albuquerque because it's in the middle of the desert. . . . We were wondering, should we stay in Albuquerque or should we consider going to the Bay Area, where a lot was happening at that point, . . . or should we move back to Washington? I had been in Albuquerque three-and-a-half years at that point and I was getting kind of antsy to go back home. In the Bay Area, the amount of time people stay at jobs is not always more than a year or two, people do a lot of job changing, and we wanted more continuity than that. Seattle was where we were from, and we both missed seeing our families. After being in the desert for a while, you want to see trees and water again. We felt we'd have no problem recruiting people for the Seattle area because it's a nice place to live.

In the summer of 1978, Gates told employees of his intention to move Microsoft to Seattle. This was when Miriam Lubow discovered that Bill was a native of the Pacific Northwest. "But why do you want to leave Albuquerque, Bill?"

"I want to return to Seattle where my friends are and where there's water!" (One thing New Mexico couldn't satisfy was Bill's passion for waterskiing.)

Most of the employees moved to Seattle with the company, but Miriam Lubow stayed behind because her husband's business was based in Albuquerque. Before leaving New Mexico, Bill expressed his gratitude to her and encouraged her to join the others as soon as possible. "If you ever want to come back, there will always be a place for you," he promised.

In the meantime, Gates, Allen, and Steve Wood, who was still serving as general manager, wrote a letter of recommendation for Miriam. They said her duties included payroll, bookkeeping, purchasing, and order handling. A few years later, each of these functions became an entire department at Microsoft Corporation.

Microsoft rented its new offices in the old National Bank building in Bellevue, a suburb of Seattle. Once again, the offices were on the eighth floor, in suite 819. The move was scheduled for January 1979.

Marc McDonald and Paul Allen arrived in Bellevue in December so that the offices would be operational when the rest of the staff arrived. In the meantime, Microsoft acquired a DEC 20 computer, which was to be delivered by the end of the month. DEC, however, refused to extend credit to Microsoft on the grounds that the company was too small to be a good credit risk. Gates therefore had to withdraw $200,000 from the company account, dropping the balance by a third.

Soon all the employees had arrived in Bellevue. Gates, true to form, collected many speeding tickets on the drive from Albuquerque to Seattle. Now all they had to do was start recruiting in the area.

In absolute numbers, Seattle was not home to a vast number of programmers, but with Boeing and the major universities nearby, there were plenty of bright minds to attract.

Paul Allen says of Seattle: "It's the kind of environment where a large part of the year you're pretty much doing things indoors. We always used to joke about the fact that it was a conducive atmosphere to programming. You'd sit at your terminal and look outside at the rain." When it came to recruiting, the key words were aptitude and enthusiasm. "We didn't necessarily look for degrees and things like that,"

Allen says. "We did tend to hire people who loved to program. Formal qualifications were less important to us than enthusiasm and programming ability."

THE 8086

Intel had introduced a new chip called the 8086 in April 1978. It was a giant improvement over earlier chips in terms of performance and memory capability. With the 4004 in 1969, then the 8008 in 1972, Intel was targeting the household appliance market. After the unexpected success of the 8080 as a computer chip, Intel began serious development of a chip that could truly handle data processing. The Intel engineers designed the 8086 with the knowledge that the microcomputer market was beginning to boom.

The Intel 8080 chip used in the Altair and the IMSAI computers was an 8-bit microprocessor. (*Bit* is a contraction of *binary digit.*) One bit is the smallest unit of information that a digital computer can hold and it can take a value of 0 or 1. Digital computers use a binary numbering system, which consists of only 0's and 1's. It is a base-2 number system, meaning that each position has a value of a power of 2. The right-most digit has a value of 2^0, and the exponent increases by 1 with each digit to the left. The values of 2 are multiplied by either 0 or 1. So, for example, in binary mode, "1" means 1 times 2^0, which equals 1 times 1, or 1; "101" means $(1 \times 2^2) + (0 \times 2^1) + (1 \times 2^0)$, which equals $4 + 2 + 1$, or 7, and so on. An 8-bit chip can handle one 8-bit instruction at a time. It can also handle numbers from 0000 0000 to 1111 1111 (0 to 255). In order to represent normal letters, numbers, and symbols, certain conventions have been established. For example, ASCII (American Standard Code for Information Interchange) specifies that the letters A to Z are located between the binary equivalents of 65 and 90. Most software users never have to worry about these concepts, but they are essential to programmers.

The 8086 was a 16-bit microprocessor. It could handle numbers up to 1111 1111 1111 1111 (65,535) in one programming command. But that's not all. Eight-bit chips such as the 8080, the 6800, and the 6502 had a significant limitation: They could address only 64 kilobytes (64,000 bytes, or characters) of memory. This was a small amount, considering that memory must store the operating system, the application, and data managed by the application. A business letter created using a word processing program, for example, might occupy 2,000 bytes of memory. The 16-bit 8086 was attractive because it could address 1 megabyte (1 million bytes) of memory.

Intel presented its new 8086 chip to Microsoft, which showed definite interest in developing a BASIC for the new microprocessor. At that time, Microsoft had to decide between continuing to develop other languages for 8-bit computers or switching to 16-bit computers based on chips like the 8086. Gates chose the technological challenge, seeing an additional opportunity to position Microsoft as an industry pioneer.

"OK, we can write your BASIC in three weeks," Gates said.

The Intel representative was startled.

"Come on. Be serious. Do you think you could get it to us in nine months?"

Gates consulted with his associates.

"Actually, we can do it in three weeks."

Development of a BASIC for the 8086 began in the fall of 1978 and ended up taking six months. First, as had become the tradition, Microsoft developed a simulator of the chip on a DEC PDP-11. The BASIC was ready in the spring of 1979. Once again, Microsoft programmers had developed the language from start to finish without ever seeing the actual chip.

At the same time, another computer scientist was working on the 8086 in Seattle. Tim Patterson had just received his computer science degree from the University of Washington and had landed a job at Seattle Computer Products, a small local firm. Patterson became fascinated with the 8086 microprocessor and began building a card based on it. He then integrated the card into a microcomputer using the same bus as the Altair. (A bus is the path along which information is transmitted in a computer. It is an electrical or electronic connection between the cards that handle the speaker, the disk drive, etc.)

In May 1979, Patterson learned that Microsoft had moved to Bellevue, so he went and introduced himself to Paul Allen, asking if the company had developed a program he could use to test his machine. Programmers like Bob O'Rear were thrilled to meet Patterson. Since they still had not seen a real 8086 chip, they asked him to come immediately and test their BASIC 8086.

Tim Patterson drove across the bridge over Lake Washington to Bellevue, set up his computer, and installed Microsoft's BASIC 8086. One week later, BASIC 8086 worked with Patterson's card.

"It's really exciting," says Bob O'Rear, "when you develop something simulated for a long time and then actually put it on the chip that it's intended for. It's pretty exciting stuff the first time it comes up and actually runs."

A short time later, LifeBoat Associates invited Microsoft to share their booth at the National Computer Conference (NCC) in New York. Microsoft in turn invited Patterson to demonstrate BASIC 8086 on his computer.

When O'Rear arrived at the hotel near Central Park, the atmosphere was partylike. Bill Gates and Paul Allen were shooting off fireworks from the window of their hotel room. Microsoft employees rarely had the chance to take a break from work, but when they did, they played hard.

During the NCC, Tim Patterson became better acquainted with the Microsoft programmers. Their discussions turned to operating systems and file managers. Microsoft employees explained how BASIC used the file allocation table, which interested Patterson immensely because it related to his major concern at that time: writing an operating system specifically for the 8086.

After the conference, Microsoft hosted a party in one of its suites. Kay Nishi arrived in New York late in the evening along with other representatives from Japanese companies.

He hadn't reserved a room, so Gates had someone call the reception desk and ask them to bring up a few beds for the latecomers. When the bellboy arrived with seven beds, he asked Chris Larson from Microsoft, "Do you really need seven beds?"

Larson thought a moment and answered, "Uh, wait a minute—make that eight!"

In the end, 15 people slept in that suite, some on beds and others on the floor. After all, sleeping on the floor was nothing new to Microsoft programmers!

SOFTCARD FOR THE APPLE II

In 1979, Microsoft's yearly sales reached a new high of $2.5 million. Worldwide sales of Microsoft BASIC gradually climbed to 1 million copies. To Bill Gates and Paul Allen, the future looked bright.

Allen's group had developed numerous languages for the 8080 chip, and independent programmers had used those languages to write many applications. Allen, however, was feeling frustrated about what he called the tyranny of the hardware. He wanted Microsoft to tap into the Apple II software market, which they had not yet been able to do. Apple IIs, which were selling like hotcakes, used the 6502 chip and Apple's own operating system (an Apple tactic to develop user loyalty). Therefore, Apple IIs could not run Microsoft languages like FORTRAN and COBOL, which were developed for the CP/M operating system and the 8080 or Z80 chips. This frustrated other developers of CP/M applications as well, because they could not easily transpose their programs onto the best-selling personal computer.

Microsoft was considering developing a program to translate 8080 code into 6502 code, but Paul Allen had a much better idea. He wanted his team to develop a card (called Soft-Card) that would enable the Apple II to run 8080 programs.

Allen happened to know just the right person to lead this development: Neil Konzen, a Seattle high school student who had discovered computers when his brother bought an Apple

II. Neil had fun "disassembling" Microsoft's BASIC 6502 and adding features he felt were lacking in the original. After reading that Microsoft had moved to Bellevue, he called the company to introduce himself. Microsoft offered him an office and allowed him to look at the BASIC 6502 source code as often as he liked. Konzen appreciated the fact that Microsoft had gone to so much trouble for him, so he used his Microsoft office privileges to develop a BASIC program editor which later became a Microsoft product. Now Paul Allen offered Konzen a part-time job developing the software aspects of the SoftCard for the Apple II.

The SoftCard for the Apple II used a Z80 microprocessor and provided access to Microsoft BASIC, the CP/M operating system, and from there, to tens of thousands of software programs. Twenty-five thousand SoftCards sold in the first year. In all, SoftCard was installed on more than 100,000 Apple systems. It was so popular that in 1982 the Apple II became the personal computer with the broadest base of CP/M users.

A NEW TEAM MEMBER

In June 1980, Steve Ballmer, one of Bill's Harvard friends, joined Microsoft as assistant to the president. Prior to joining Microsoft, he had graduated from Harvard, spent some time in an MBA program (which he didn't complete) at Stanford University, and worked in marketing at Procter & Gamble. One of Ballmer's greatest feats at Procter & Gamble was redesigning the Duncan Hines chocolate cake mix box to sit horizontally instead of vertically. This took up more shelf space and literally crowded out the competition.

Microsoft was growing rapidly. Seeing the VisiCalc success, Bill Gates and Paul Allen began thinking that they should expand their activities beyond languages and try their hand at application software.

For the time being, no major manufacturer had yet decided to build an 8086 machine. Meanwhile, across the country in the Florida sun, something was brewing at IBM.

PART 3

THE IBM PC AND DOS

The software business is very American. The original technological advances were all made here. The largest markets are here. And the atmosphere that allowed it all to happen is here. That's how our original customers, including IBM, could be so open-minded about buying from a 25-year-old guy with a small company out in Washington. They may have thought it was crazy at the time, but they said, "Hey, if he knows so much about software, maybe he knows even more."

–Bill Gates in *Money* magazine, July 1986

9

Project Chess

As news of the success of Apple, Tandy, and Commodore reached IBM's top leaders in 1980, IBM began to take an interest in microcomputers.

The company, headed by chairman John Opel, was the uncontested leader in the computer world, with annual revenues of $28 billion. Venerated by some, feared by others, its nickname was "Big Blue" because of the thousands of managers who traditionally wore blue suits. IBM was so clearly the dominant leader that journalists described its competitors (DEC, Honeywell, Control Data, Burroughs, Data General, Wang, and Sperry) as "the seven dwarfs."

IBM formed several committees to study the possibility of entering the personal computer market. One group had proposed to Frank Cary, John Opel's predecessor, that IBM buy Atari. During the presentation, Cary had asked a key question:

"Is Atari the best?"

"No."

"Who is the best?"

"Apple."

"Why shouldn't IBM have the best?"

Since Apple was not for sale, IBM's thoughts turned in a different direction. Others suggested that since IBM employed several hundred thousand people, it would be easy to develop the specifications and software for a microcomputer internally.

Bill Lowe disagreed. In his proposal to the leadership of IBM, the lab director of IBM's system division stressed one point: Big Blue's size could be a hindrance when entering such a rapidly changing market sector. If this project was developed internally, it would take at least four years, which was the usual lag time from design to finished product. One of the reasons behind this delay was IBM's extensive quality assurance procedures. The world of microcomputers, however, was evolving far too quickly for such a delay: Only four years had passed between the release of the primitive Altair microcomputer and the sophisticated Apple II.

Bill Lowe's recommendations implied that the group responsible for this project needed to be able to stray from IBM's beaten path. The PC development team should include programmers and sales and marketing people, all of whom would have carte blanche to select outside suppliers for the hardware and software. The outgoing president, Frank Cary, cleverly asked about this modus operandi, "How do you make an elephant tap-dance?"

John Opel agreed to Bill Lowe's proposals. He too was convinced that the time was right to release a personal computer. For the "Project Chess" committee, Lowe carefully searched IBM's conservative ranks for people who showed some degree of creativity. Many of them already owned microcomputers. These "eccentrics" had endured teasing from their coworkers, who were immersed in the successful world of mainframes.

The members of the Project Chess team came together at Boca Raton, Florida, one of IBM's research and development centers. Leading the team was an older executive named Jack Sams.

Sams and his colleagues were humble enough to study the strategy of another winning company, Apple. Even though Apple was infinitely smaller than IBM, it had rapidly moved into first place in its field. Two lessons emerged from this study: Apple had encouraged software development by independent publishers, and had created an open architecture, thereby fostering the growth of a secondary industry. Many manufacturers had made a name for themselves by developing cards for the Apple II. The Project Chess team laid out its plan of action. IBM would follow the same steps that had made Apple so successful. Now they just had to convince IBM's top management, which was no small challenge.

BIG BLUE APPROACHES MICROSOFT

The Project Chess team studied the popular computers at the time, in particular the Apple II, the Commodore PET, and the Tandy TRS-80. One company kept popping up in their research, a software publisher named Microsoft. It seemed that this company's know-how was recognized in the realm of microcomputer languages. Microsoft BASIC had become the standard. Furthermore, Microsoft had seen its sales double every year since its inception. IBM was impressed.

Jack Sams called Bill Gates and explained that he wanted to meet with him to discuss a potential development project. Would it be possible to come in the next few days?

Gates was amazed to get a call from such an enormous company. Of course he would meet with Jack Sams. After all, he thought, IBM might be interested in Microsoft BASIC.

In July 1980, Sams and another IBM representative paid Microsoft a visit. Gates, Allen, and Ballmer even donned suits and ties for the occasion. The IBM people asked fairly general questions about personal computers and the languages developed by Microsoft. They played down their intentions: Officially, this was just a market study. Sams and his colleague then asked Gates to explain how Microsoft was able to develop all the software for a computer so quickly. The visitors from another corporate culture left with a terse, "Don't call us. We'll call you."

Gates and Allen had dealt with many representatives from other computer firms before. The microcomputer industry was still young, and composed of people who were fairly direct and open about their plans. IBM's hush-hush, cautious attitude seemed strange to them.

THE SECOND MEETING

In August, Jack Sams called Gates again to ask whether they could arrange another meeting. "How about next week?" Gates asked. "We'll be on a plane in two hours," said the IBM representative. Gates immediately canceled a meeting he had scheduled with Ray Kassar, the president of Atari. After all, Atari was big in the world of personal computers, but IBM was the largest computer manufacturer, bar none.

Gates, Allen, and Ballmer met with the IBM representatives. Right off the bat, Sams asked them to sign a statement saying they agreed to keep absolutely confidential anything revealed during the meeting. The text also stipulated that Microsoft would never be able to sue IBM in the future. The young men signed without hesitating, anxious to find out more.

"This is the most unusual thing the corporation has ever done," IBM's head of corporate relations announced. Bill Gates also felt that this was the strangest thing Microsoft had ever done.

Then the IBM representatives revealed the Project Chess plans. They wanted to know how they could quickly release a personal computer capable of running already-popular software. The code name for the computer was Acorn. Sams explained that he was convinced IBM needed to depart from its usual routines. The only way to bring a microcomputer to market in one year was to use a standard microprocessor such as Intel's 8080, and to rely on outside developers to provide the software. Then came the crucial question. If IBM gave Microsoft the specifications for an 8-bit computer, could Microsoft write a BASIC for the ROM (permanent memory)? If so, could they do it by April 1981?

Bill Gates responded affirmatively. However, he made it clear that he preferred a 16-bit microprocessor such as Intel's

8086 chip. The 8086 had enormous advantages over the 8080. Instead of 64 kilobytes, the 8086 had a capacity of 1 megabyte. It was faster than an 8-bit chip. Since IBM was targeting the business market, Gates insisted that the hardware be built around the 8086 chip.

Gates and Allen were convinced that the future belonged to 8086 computers, and Microsoft prepared itself accordingly. For almost two years, Microsoft had been learning about the new Intel chip, beginning, naturally, by developing a BASIC specifically for it. Then, in the fall of 1979, after an order from Convergent Technologies, Microsoft had begun developing an 8086 version of FORTRAN.

Sams and his companion listened to Gates's arguments. For the time being, the market belonged to 8-bit machines. Some manufacturers felt that the investment needed to switch to 16-bit computers was unjustifiably high. Gates, however, knew that a chip like the 8086 gave programmers the possibility of developing more ambitious software. He felt that IBM's entry into the realm of personal computers was the opportune time to launch a 16-bit computer. The Project Chess representatives decided to include Gates's analysis in the recommendations they submitted to IBM management.

At the end of the meeting, Gates signed a contract stating that he would provide IBM with a report describing the design of a computer able to run the languages developed by Microsoft. The men from Boca Raton returned to Florida with the outline of a construction plan for a 16-bit workstation.

At the same time, other IBM study groups were proposing solutions that would enable a microcomputer to emulate the instruction sets of IBM's large systems. The Project Chess team got the green light. Gates received an exciting phone call from Jack Sams: Chances were good that they could work together. Sams added that since there were so many issues involved, he was going to bring five IBM people to Microsoft to discuss technical, legal, and sales matters with the corresponding Microsoft people. That way, he said, they could cover four or five different areas at the same time. Gates was slightly disappointed, because he normally handled all these areas himself. When the five representatives from IBM arrived, however, Gates had lined up the same number of people, including a Seattle lawyer who had represented the company.

It was September 1980. Sams asked Gates and Allen whether Microsoft would be able to furnish not only the BASIC, but also a FORTRAN, Pascal, and COBOL. The BASIC needed to be ready by the following April. Gates explained that first they needed to find an operating system. BASIC was designed to run independently of any other software; however, Microsoft's current versions of FORTRAN and COBOL relied on the CP/M operating system.

KILDALL'S MISSED OPPORTUNITY

CP/M seemed like a reasonable choice for the operating system, since it dominated the market at that time. And there was a rumor that Digital Research, the developer of CP/M, was making good progress on CP/M-86, a version of CP/M for the 8086 chip.

When the IBM representatives asked Gates whether Microsoft could sell them CP/M, Gates picked up the phone, called Gary Kildall at Digital Research and said he was involved in a big deal with a very important client who wanted to meet with Kildall very soon. Digital Research Inc. was growing rapidly, and Kildall, age 40, was not particularly impressed with Gates's call. Gates frequently asked him to meet with manufacturers interested in CP/M.

When the IBM representatives arrived in Pacific Grove, Kildall was away on a business trip. Dorothy McEwen, his wife, met with the four IBM managers. Before beginning the meeting, they asked her to sign the same imposing nondisclosure agreement that Gates, Allen, and Ballmer had signed. She was concerned. The contract implied that it would be impossible to sue IBM even if ideas heard at Digital Research were later found in one of IBM's products. The IBM agreement, however, was merely a formality necessitated by unfortunate experiences in the past. The company had integrated a discovery made in its labs into certain products and had then been sued by a small company that had made a similar find around the same time. Nevertheless, Digital Research's legal counsel advised McEwen not to sign. It was a total impasse. IBM had no intention of entering into discussions without a signed nondisclosure agreement.

When Kildall returned from his trip and learned what had happened, he said he had no problem with signing the agreement. At that time, however, Digital Research was involved in serious negotiations with Hewlett-Packard and that opportunity seemed more lucrative than a possible job for IBM. Also, in its current form, CP/M was inadequate for the IBM PC. It had been designed for 8-bit microprocessors. Digital Research was in the process of writing CP/M-86 for the 16-bit 8086 chip, but was already one year behind schedule. Nothing indicated that it could be ready by April. In any case, Kildall didn't seem willing to commit the resources. There was no hurry. Kildall and his wife had been getting ready for a weeklong Caribbean cruise, so they decided to wait until after their vacation to make a decision.

The IBM representatives did not appreciate being put off. They pushed for Kildall's cooperation for a few days, but the two parties just didn't see eye to eye. And Kildall, absorbed in the work resulting from the success of CP/M, neglected to return IBM's call. Finally, the members of the Project Chess team returned to see Bill Gates.

MICROSOFT SEIZES THE CHANCE

Until 1978, Digital Research and Microsoft had had a tacit understanding that they would share the microcomputer software market. Digital Research would provide the operating system, Microsoft the languages. In 1979, however, Digital Research had broken the agreement by adding languages to its catalog. To counterattack, Microsoft had acquired the license to AT&T's UNIX operating system and had begun development in February 1980. And the rumor that Digital Research was trying to acquire a BASIC other than Microsoft's to sell with the CP/M-86 was driving the two companies farther apart.

Microsoft tried for several weeks, however, to convince Digital Research to participate in the IBM project. Microsoft wanted access to the CP/M code that Digital Research was developing for the 8086 so that Microsoft could adapt FOR-TRAN, COBOL, and BASIC to use with CP/M on an 8086 machine. Digital Research refused to provide the code, which seemed to confirm that in the long run, they did not intend to continue relying on Microsoft for languages. And since Digital also refused to sign IBM's preliminary agreements, it seemed that CP/M-86 was not destined for use on the IBM machine,

One memorable night, September 28, 1980, Gates, Allen, and Kay Nishi met in Gates's office. They discussed at length the possibility of designing the operating system for IBM themselves. They also discussed the obstacles. Microsoft was already swamped with work. There were certain risks involved: IBM worked with strict deadlines, and had reserved the right to cancel the deal at any time.

Nishi's impulsive personality, however, provoked the decision. He was the first to say, "Gotta do it! Gotta do it!" Gates recalls. "Kay's kind of a flamboyant guy, and when he believes in something, he believes in it very strongly. He stood up, made his case, and we just said, 'Yeah!' "

Gates and Allen then began to talk nuts and bolts. They envisioned an operating system that would take up 30K of memory. Microsoft did not have time to develop a system of that magnitude. It would be better to adapt an existing system. Then the name of Tim Patterson came to Allen's mind. Patterson had just finished creating an 8086 operating system for the computer he had built for Seattle Computer Products.

Seattle Computer Products could not sell Patterson's computer until it had an operating system. In April 1980, tired of waiting for Digital Research to release a version of

CP/M for the 8086, Patterson had decided to take matters into his own hands. He wrote an operating system which he named QDOS, for Quick and Dirty Operating System. Patterson was very familiar with CP/M; he wrote QDOS so that software written for the Digital Research system could be easily ported to QDOS.

Allen contacted Patterson in October 1980 and told him that Microsoft liked his DOS and wanted to sell it to computer manufacturers. Allen said that they already had an interested client, whom he refused to identify.

Microsoft paid Seattle Computer Products for the right to sell QDOS. Although the exact sum has not been revealed, indications are that Microsoft acquired QDOS for less than $100,000. The agreement provided for additional payments each time the license was granted to another manufacturer.

During the week after Labor Day, Gates and his associates worked on a proposal to convince IBM that Microsoft could develop the four languages IBM wanted *and* the operating system. In his letter, Gates made sure to include additional arguments in favor of an open architecture.

MICROSOFT BAGS THE CONTRACT

When Gates, Allen, and Ballmer flew to Boca Raton in October 1980, they prepared themselves for one of the most pivotal moments of their lives.

Upon arriving in Miami, Bill Gates suddenly realized that he had forgotten to wear a tie! Already late, they parked their rental car in front of a department store along the way and waited for it to open. Bill bought a tie, and they continued on to Boca Raton.

When they arrived at IBM, the three men from Seattle walked into a small conference room where 14 IBM technicians were waiting. During the meeting, Gates proposed that since the time limits were so tight, it would be better if Microsoft supervised the entire software development process itself. The experts from Boca Raton bombarded him with questions, which he fielded calmly and clearly.

Don Estridge, a tall, warm man, had been named head of Project Chess. He was extremely interested in microcomputers and had an Apple II at home. Bill Lowe had selected him because he combined eccentricity—by IBM standards, anyway—with a sterling reputation for company loyalty and self-control. Estridge and Gates hit it off.

During lunch, John Opel happened to be seated next to Estridge. When the question arose concerning Microsoft's developing the operating system for the PC, Opel asked about Bill. "Is he Mary Gates's son?" It turned out that John Opel and Mary Gates had served together for a long time on the board of the United Way. Another stroke of luck!

Microsoft and IBM signed their contract November 6, 1980. It stated that Microsoft would provide a specified number of software programs for the Chess machine, and that Microsoft would deliver these products a certain number of days after receiving the first prototype of Chess and a working joystick. The time periods ranged from 96 days for providing extensions to Microsoft BASIC, which would become part of the ROM, to 257 days for FORTRAN. The contract also specified the delivery deadlines for certain intermediary products, test programs, and documentation. Microsoft, in particular Gates, would work in conjunction with Estridge's team on designing the hardware. IBM also contacted Personal Software and asked them to adapt VisiCalc for its PC.

The IBM-Microsoft union was a major departure from IBM protocol. The industry giant with yearly revenues of $28 billion was asking a small firm with revenues of several million and a 25-year-old president to cooperate in a major new development effort. This collaboration was to have a significant impact on the future of both firms and the entire microcomputer industry.

First, Microsoft needed to expand the capabilities of its DOS. It was a huge programming task and the giant was in a hurry: The first version had to be ready for IBM by January 1981. Gates recalls that when IBM showed Microsoft the schedule for the project, they were three months behind before they had even started.

DEVELOPMENT BEGINS

IBM insisted that the personal computer project be protected by strict security measures. Gates set aside the most out-of-the-way room, at the end of a hallway in Microsoft's eighth-floor offices. The working conditions were far from ideal. The room was narrow, about nine feet by six feet, and had no windows or ventilation.

The office used for the development of DOS shared a wall with the offices of a stock brokerage firm. The IBM people were extremely worried about any information leaks and insisted that the office door remain locked at all times and that all equipment and documents having anything to do with Project Chess remain inside that room. IBM provided special safes for storing the documents and rushed an employee out to install them. IBM even asked Microsoft to install chicken wire on the ceiling to guard against invasion from the floor above, but Microsoft would not go that far.

Microsoft received the first prototype of the IBM personal computer during Thanksgiving weekend. Big Blue had finally opted for the Intel 8088 microprocessor instead of the 8086. The 8088 acted just like the 8086, but ran a little more slowly. It functioned like a 16-bit chip, but exchanged data with the outside environment in packets of 8 bits.

Bob O'Rear, in charge of the MS-DOS development, went right to work. The immediate challenge was to transform the rudimentary operating system purchased from Seattle Computer Products into a professional piece of software. (Patterson's QDOS was first officially called SCP-DOS, then 86-DOS, and was finally dubbed MS-DOS by Microsoft.) The specifications for the computer were not yet completely established, however, and the job was very tricky. Furthermore, Microsoft had not defined all the details of the operating system they were developing. Considering that IBM hoped to take delivery of the code in March, the project was extremely ambitious.

In the cramped, windowless office, O'Rear and Mike Courtney began writing software with a PC prototype that was as wide as a desk. They also used an Intel computer with a hard disk. The heat from the two machines caused the hardware to behave strangely. The two industrious developers endured this situation as best they could. IBM's requirement that the door remain closed at all times turned out to be impossible to fulfill. When Steve Ballmer would stop by to see how the development was going, he'd prudently close the door behind him on his way out. A few minutes later, O'Rear, unable to tolerate the heat, would reopen the door.

The biggest problem was reconciling the operating system from Seattle Computer Products with the BIOS that IBM was writing. To complicate things even further, Tim Patterson's DOS was available on 8-inch diskettes, but the IBM machine used 5¼-inch diskettes. Microsoft had to determine the format of the new diskettes, and then find a way of transferring the operating system from the old format to the new one. Other problems arose because of the manner in which data had been recorded on the 8-inch diskettes.

At Seattle Computer Products (SCP), Patterson was working closely with the Microsoft developers and making the changes they requested. He still didn't know who Microsoft's mysterious client was. One day, however, SCP received a strange phone call from someone at IBM who asked questions about the DOS. Somewhat surprised, the SCP people asked the caller to identify himself, but he only replied, embarrassed, "Oh, that's not important," and hung up.

Every day, packages were shipped between Seattle and Boca Raton. To speed communication, an electronic mail system was established between IBM and Microsoft. This was no small feat, since Seattle and Boca Raton are about as far apart as two cities can be in the contiguous 48 states. Messengers continually shuttled back and forth across the 4,000 miles, and Bill Gates frequently traveled to Boca Raton. He got accustomed to sleeping on the plane and then going straight to work. Sometimes he made the round trip in one day.

It had been one year since Gates had told Miriam Lubow, his secretary in Albuquerque, "I know that you're going to come to Seattle!" Time had proven him correct. She arrived alone in the winter, and was later joined by her family. "Once you have worked with Bill closely," Lubow says, "you just can't stay away from somebody like that too long. He has such an energizing, inspiring effect on people." Her first week there was not the best for showing off the area. The fog was so thick that an entire week passed before she realized that there were stores very close to her hotel.

Lubow had always known a Gates who dressed very casually. Then one morning she saw him come to work in a three-piece suit. She couldn't believe her eyes, but refrained from laughing. Ten minutes later, three men arrived dressed in jeans and tennis shoes and carrying large briefcases. Lubow almost didn't let them enter the offices, thinking they were door-to-door salesmen. When one man explained that they were from IBM, she was puzzled: Why were these people from such a serious company dressed so unconventionally? Suddenly, it hit her. The engineers from Boca Raton had adopted Gates's style, while Gates was trying to adopt theirs. When she showed the three visitors into Bill's office, they looked at one another in surprise, and then all burst out laughing.

HEAT AND HARDWARE PROBLEMS

Besides the stifling heat, the programmers faced another problem: The hardware was still not reliable. The Microsoft team sometimes spent hours looking for the source of a software error only to find that it was actually a problem with the hardware. The PC communication card would respond when it wasn't supposed to, or would put incomprehensible information into memory.

On January 5, 1981, Bob O'Rear wrote a letter to Lou Flashinski at IBM describing the magnitude of the problems:

Dear Lou,

Over the last several weeks, Microsoft has been diligently working to bring up 86-DOS on the prototype hardware. At first, the hardware appeared to be working satisfactorily, but as this effort proceeded it has become apparent that we do not have a sound system. From conversations with engineers at Boca, the problems appear to stem from the wire wrap prototype boards. It has been suggested that as the system heats up these wires can release contact and random problems occur.

Due to the nature of bringing up an operating system on a prototype machine, it unfortunately sometimes takes days to ascertain whether the problem lies with the hardware or software. Numerous of these type days have already been consumed, and although it is still possible to make the January 12 date for delivery of the DOS and standard BASIC-86, all slack time has been removed from the schedule.

Ken Rowe from the engineering group at Boca is to arrive tomorrow with new etched versions of the current wire wrap boards. Should these boards work reliably, I believe we can get the project back on track. Any further hardware problems, however, will mean certain slippage of an already tight schedule.

Sincerely,
Robert O'Rear, Project Manager

In February 1981, MS-DOS ran for the first time on the prototype. At that time, Bob O'Rear wrote to Pat Harrington of IBM, expressing his concern about the slowness of the computer.

We have run tests in house that indicate the prototype is no faster than an Apple II. . . . We are not sure that the machine has memory speed of the final version, but are very concerned because the first evaluation of the prototype by personal computer magazines will probably be of this nature. If we cannot surpass 8-bit processors, we'll receive poor first reviews.

A short time later, Don Estridge wrote a response to O'Rear's concerns.

Subject: problems with software/hardware.

It is my understanding that the problem items identified in your letter have been corrected. Please keep me up to date on any other areas of concern. Thanks for expressing your concern and commitment to meet the March schedule. As discussed in the February 10, 1981, telephone conversation, IBM will support that commitment by assuming full responsibility for developing the test suites for 86-DOS and BASIC-86 extensions, given the required documentation. To further support that commitment, IBM has asked Microsoft to recommend an alternative delivery date for the BASIC-86 extensions to allow Microsoft to concentrate its efforts on the March deliverables. Your expressed concern about the performance of the prototype machine is appreciated. IBM engineering has indicated to me that the performance of the final product will be consistent with the 8088 architecture.

Another hardware problem also slowed down development. IBM's BIOS could not transfer data beyond an address of 64K. When the DOS tried to write a piece of information at a higher address, the system crashed. It wasn't until April that Bob O'Rear's team discovered the source of this problem.

IBM readily offered needed assistance. The firm immediately took every hardware problem into consideration and responded quickly. When necessary, IBM sent engineers to Seattle to solve the problems pointed out by Microsoft. Nevertheless, Bob O'Rear finally wrote a letter explaining that 60 days had been lost before the programmers had a prototype that was truly functional. Furthermore, the card for the joystick didn't arrive until the end of February. As a result, BASIC fell behind schedule.

On March 5 and 6, Mel Hallerman and Dave Stuerwald from IBM met with Gates and O'Rear to determine what Microsoft could do to accelerate delivery of the software. They set a new schedule, to which Microsoft agreed. However, Gates and O'Rear made it clear that they could not meet even the new deadlines unless the hardware was reliable.

In April 1981, Tim Patterson left Seattle Computer Products and went to work for Microsoft. At last he found out who the client was. The impact of this news was sizable. Patterson realized that SCP was not big enough to handle this deal itself, and thought it logical that SCP had passed the baton to Microsoft.

As the project progressed, O'Rear and the other programmers often found themselves cramped together in the tiny room, working nonstop through the night. Neil Konzen joined them for a short time to program the graphics routines for BASIC. In addition to the development machine from Intel, the room now contained two prototypes. Each of these computers generated heat and the temperature rose as high as 100 degrees, which further diminished the reliability of the hardware. The programmers now left the door open all the time.

IBM inspectors were regularly sent to Bellevue to make sure that Microsoft was adhering to the established security measures. This kept the programmers constantly on the lookout. They developed a system: Other employees would run to the end of the hall and warn them each time someone from IBM arrived. One day, however, the alert system didn't work. An inspector from Boca Raton was surprised to find the door open and some parts of the computer sitting out in the hall. He called Steve Ballmer and demanded an explanation.

The Boca Raton team did not fail to remind Bill Gates of an unpleasant possibility: The project could be canceled at any time. If that happened, they threatened, they would call Microsoft and tell them to put all confidential materials in a box and send them to IBM. Microsoft did not need to be told twice. From that moment on, the security rules were respected to the letter. Also, the IBM surveillance system was reinforced.

As the months went by, the programmers grew tired of their intensive work regimen. When he wasn't programming, Bob O'Rear was dealing with about 20 people in Boca Raton. The stress was building. The only break the programmers took was one weekend when they flew to Florida to watch the launching of the space shuttle, despite vehement protests from Gates and Allen.

THE DOS IS READY

Throughout the development of the PC, Microsoft continued as a consultant to IBM. Bob O'Rear even offered advice on how to paint the machine.

On June 11, 1981, Microsoft sent a letter to IBM, this time concerning the minimum amount of memory a PC should have. IBM was planning to release its machine with 16K of RAM. Microsoft once again tried to persuade IBM not to worry about the extremely low end of the market, saying that Chess should have a minimum of 64K RAM and that the next version up should have 128K. Microsoft argued that it was very difficult for software to support many different hardware configurations. To launch COBOL, BASIC, and Assembler, a machine with at least 64K of RAM was needed. It would take at least a 128K machine to run PASCAL and FORTRAN. Furthermore, Microsoft convinced IBM to sell its computer with a disk drive and not to concentrate on cassette drives. To satisfy the demands of the client, Microsoft adapted its BASIC to accommodate a certain number of options that IBM felt indispensable, such as a joystick and a cassette drive. The manufacturer soon discovered, however, that the business market was not at all interested in those capabilities.

By mid-1981, Microsoft had 100 employees, with 35 of them contributing to the IBM project in some fashion. At IBM, 450 people worked on developing the PC. IBM's work methods greatly influenced the standards Microsoft later adopted. Because IBM subjected Microsoft's software to very advanced tests, according to Gates, the quality of the languages Microsoft offered for the 8086 was better than anything they had done for 8-bit computers.

In conjunction with the technical testing, which Gates described as draconian, IBM performed quality tests with "guinea pig" users. This enabled IBM to discover the most obscure bugs. Ordinarily, it would have taken several years of tests by end-users to get that far. After working with IBM, Microsoft changed its product quality evaluation systems, project planning, security conditions, and many other practices.

Microsoft, however, sometimes worried that IBM would abandon the entire project. The company was known for having developed many products that were never marketed. In June, *InfoWorld* published an article hinting that IBM was working on a microcomputer. When Steve Ballmer discovered that there had been leaks, he was furious with the magazine and worried about the potential reaction by Estridge and his colleagues. Microsoft, however, could not be blamed: The bustling activity in Boca Raton was what had attracted the attention of the press.

Microsoft continued to improve the PC software until the last minute. Version 1.0 of MS-DOS contained 4,000 lines of assembly language and took up 12 kilobytes of memory.

Finally, IBM accepted the operating system created by Microsoft, and MS-DOS became the official system of the IBM PC. Microsoft continued to improve BASIC, and Gates did not hesitate to work on it himself. He recalls adding features to BASIC up until the minute it was put into ROM.

Finally, one night in July 1981, Microsoft found out that IBM was getting ready to officially announce its personal computer. Gates and his team celebrated the occasion at an expensive Seattle restaurant.

The programmers still had to finish the compilers for the IBM PC Pascal, FORTRAN, COBOL, and Assembler, so the work started up again. In the end, Microsoft developed more than 250K of code for the operating system, the languages BASIC, Pascal, and Assembler 8088. The FORTRAN and COBOL compilers soon followed.

Now all they needed to do was wait for the verdict from the market.

10

The MS-DOS Crusade

IBM announced its first microcomputer on August 12, 1981. The news was reported in all the major publications the following day. The *Wall Street Journal* account began as follows: "International Business Machines Corp. has made its bold entry into the personal-computer market, and experts believe the computer giant could capture the lead in the youthful industry within two years." The prices ranged from as low as $1,565 for the basic 16K machine to as much as $6,000 for a fully loaded version with color graphics capabilities. Noting that the top-of-the-line models were likely to pose a threat to Apple, Tandy Radio Shack, Commodore, Hewlett-Packard, and other microcomputer makers, the reporter added that according to analysts, "IBM's equipment appears better suited than competitors' models to handling bigger tasks and presenting information in clear, well-defined images."

The IBM PC was built around an Intel 8088 microprocessor, which was faster than those used in competing computers, the writer explained. The software that could run on the new computer included VisiCalc—"a financial forecasting model marketed by Personal Software Inc."—the EasyWriter word processing program, three accounting packages from Peachtree Software Inc., and a communications link to databanks such as Dow Jones News and The Source.

The article reported that IBM would be adopting new marketing techniques by selling its computers through Sears, Roebuck & Co. and Computerland. Response from competitors included Tandy president John Roach quoted as saying, "I don't think it's that significant," while Apple president A. C. (Mike) Markkula reportedly welcomed the news because it would increase the microcomputer market for all computer manufacturers.

The IBM PC was available in stores two months later. The first model had just one disk drive and 64K of memory. The 320K computer with two disk drives would not be available until May 1982.

In the eyes of industry analysts, the IBM PC was a "third-generation" machine. The first generation was the Altair 8080 released by MITS in 1975, and several "copies" which were generally called S-100 machines, after the name for the Altair bus. S-100 computers were essentially for hobbyists. The second generation consisted of 8-bit, fully assembled computers such as those produced by Apple, Tandy, and Commodore. These computers came with BASIC in their ROM, a concept that IBM emulated. These computers led to the boom in a new category of software called "productivity software," of which VisiCalc is the best example. The third generation began with the IBM PC, a 16-bit computer supported by the number-one computer manufacturer in the world, and clearly aimed at the professional market.

Apple greeted this formidable competitor with courtesy and humor. In October 1981, it ran a full-page ad in the *Wall Street Journal,* with the headline "Welcome IBM. Seriously."

Welcome to the most exciting and most important marketplace since the computer revolution began 35 years ago.
And congratulations on your first personal computer.

By putting the power of a computer into the hands of individuals, it is possible to improve the way they work, think, learn, communicate and spend their leisure time.

Apple added that it hoped IBM would be a responsible competitor and would help distribute this American technology throughout the world.

BYTE published the first benchmark tests on the PC in its October 1981 issue. The writer expressed his surprise that IBM was using software suppliers who were already well established in the microcomputer industry, and that IBM was providing all the necessary information for other developers to write applications and for other manufacturers to develop peripherals. IBM had broken the isolation to which it had confined itself in the minicomputer and large-systems sectors. To outside observers, this was good news.

Better yet, the very serious and professional IBM offered a card for connecting a joystick to the PC! Without a doubt, as folksinger Bob Dylan had prophesied some 20 years earlier, "The times, they are a-changin'." To top it all off, the IBM PC did not cost much more than an Apple II Plus. "For those of us who dislike giants, the IBM Personal Computer comes as a shock," wrote the *BYTE* journalist.

I expected that the giant would stumble by overestimating or underestimating the capabilities the public wants and stubbornly insisting on incompatibility with the rest of the microcomputer world. But IBM didn't stumble at all; instead, the giant jumped leagues in front of the competition.

IBM, uncharacteristically open, said it wanted to favor outside development with no restrictions. Don Estridge announced that IBM was going to publish a manual with the complete specifications for what he already called the industry standard, for anyone who wanted to develop cards for the PC. He also said that IBM was open to proposals for software. Since IBM has always held to the principle of pushing its personnel to take more initiative, employees were encouraged to develop software in their spare time. If IBM decided to market the software, the authors of such products would receive royalties.

Microsoft naturally entered the software race. It immediately released MS-DOS, Assembler, BASIC, FORTRAN, Pascal, as well as two applications: an adventure game and a typing instruction program.

A competitor to MS-DOS quickly surfaced: Digital Research was working on a version of CP/M for the IBM PC. At first, it seemed that the CP/M-86 would be a threat to Microsoft's operating system, but this turned out not to be the case. Applications developed for CP/M on 8-bit machines could not run under CP/M-86. Thus MS-DOS and CP/M were in the same boat: New applications were needed to stimulate demand for either operating system.

Gary Kildall had good reason to be upset when he examined the published version of MS-DOS. Much to his surprise, it copied the system calls of CP/M. Tim Patterson had modelled his DOS on CP/M, and Microsoft had felt it wise to continue in the same direction. The reason was simple: The high-level languages written by Microsoft ran under CP/M, so basing the new operating system on CP/M made adapting computer languages to the new system much easier.

In the next issue of Microsoft's quarterly customer newsletter, Paul Allen openly championed this resemblance to CP/M, saying that maintaining compatibility with CP/M system calls made converting programs written for the 8080 and the Z80 into MS-DOS programs a fairly straightforward procedure.

CP/M compatibility became a major factor in the success of MS-DOS. As soon as the PC was released, Microsoft was able to offer a wide selection of programs for it. Some very popular CP/M programs, such as the best-sellers WordStar and dBASE, were essential for getting current users to latch on to the PC. They soon appeared in MS-DOS versions.

Kildall, however, did not see it quite that way. He viewed the close resemblance between MS-DOS and CP/M as outright theft. For a while, he even considered suing IBM.

Big Blue responded that it was unaware of this similarity between the two systems, and the two parties finally settled out of court. IBM agreed to offer the future 16-bit CP/M operating system by Digital Research with its PC. That way, it said, CP/M-86 and MS-DOS would be on equal footing. In actuality, however, this would not be the case.

At one time, IBM's official position was to not impose a given operating system for its PC. It would sell CP/M-86 or Softech Microsystems' UCSD p-System just as readily as MS-DOS. However, IBM's apparent openness was contradicted by one action: It changed the name of Microsoft's DOS to PC-DOS. The three magic initials had a certain pull. While some users may have been attracted to Digital Research's operating system, the price factor outweighed that attraction. CP/M-86 cost four times as much as MS-DOS ($240 versus $60). Gates understood that he had everything to gain by agreeing to rock-bottom prices with IBM, whereas Digital Research acted according to its dominant position and named a more prohibitive price. Finally, the release of CP/M-86 was late. IBM could not offer it until April 1982. That delay left the market wide open to Microsoft for more than six months.

Nevertheless, the trade press supported CP/M since it was the dominant system for 8-bit computers. The newsletter of Future Computing, a Dallas-based market research firm, baptized the IBM PC the "CP/M-player," insinuating that CP/M applications would soon be widely available. The July 20, 1981, issue of *InfoWorld* was very pessimistic about the future of MS-DOS. A front-page article noted that firms such as Xerox and Burroughs were already preparing stiff competition in the microcomputer market. "None of these firms share IBM's hesitancy to use Digital Research's CP/M as an operating system, so IBM may find itself with a competitive system, but little or no software to compel potential buyers," it concluded.

On the other hand, Microsoft received considerable support from LifeBoat Associates, the software distributor that had once been an ardent fan of CP/M. Tony Gold, head of LifeBoat, called the introduction of the IBM PC "potentially the most important event in the history of microcomputers." Another member of LifeBoat agreed that IBM had brought legitimacy to the personal computer because until then, the public had always seen it as just a toy for hobbyists. He added that MS-DOS had already become the industry standard for 16-bit computers. LifeBoat announced that it had begun negotiations with several suppliers of MS-DOS applications. LifeBoat itself had ordered 25 PCs in order to test the programs it received. Beginning in November 1981, it hoped to add about a hundred IBM PC-specific programs to its catalog.

There was some confusion at first over the name of the system for the PC. Microsoft called it MS-DOS. IBM named it PC-DOS, distinguishing it from MS-DOS by adding some IBM utilities. LifeBoat Associates distributed the system under the name Software Bus 86, or SB-86. Later, other manufacturers acquired the license and didn't simplify things any: Zenith called it ZDOS, while Compaq named it Compaq DOS. Eventually, Microsoft insisted that all manufacturers use the name MS-DOS. Only IBM refused.

THE PC'S IMPACT

The IBM PC further encouraged the proliferation of software. When 8-bit microprocessors dominated the market, there had been three categories of software suppliers:

- Creators of operating systems, such as Digital Research with its CP/M
- Suppliers of languages, such as Microsoft
- Applications developers, such as Software Arts (developer of VisiCalc) and MicroPro (WordStar).

Programmers often had to struggle to make the operating system, the applications, and the data and graphics fit into the available 64K of memory.

The PC's graphics memory was in the addressable space of the computer. Certain instructions from the 8088 could be used to produce animation effects on the screen. This, for example, made it easier for Gates and Neil Konzen to write demonstration programs with graphics for the IBM PC in a few hours one Sunday afternoon. With the Apple, on the other hand, it was very difficult to write programs with good graphics.

Microsoft established MS-DOS as the interface that made applications and languages independent of the hardware. In other words, a program written according to MS-DOS conventions could theoretically function on any machine supporting MS-DOS. This enabled Microsoft to offer its DOS to several hundred different manufacturers, who in turn were responsible for making the necessary simple adaptations to their hardware.

MS-DOS VS. CP/M

For almost two years after the release of the IBM PC, it was difficult to determine whether MS-DOS or CP/M would dominate the microcomputer market. Some software developers wanted to wait and see how the market would develop and which operating system IBM's hardware competitors would choose. Some publications, such as *Info World,* refused to take MS-DOS seriously. When the magazine selected the best products of the year in its January 1982 issue, nine out of the top ten products were CP/M programs. It wasn't until March 1982 that *Info World* consented to publish the benchmark test of an MS-DOS program.

Microsoft's evangelistic message, which it repeated over and over again, was that MS-DOS allowed easy adaptation of CP/M programs. Many CP/M applications had been written in high-level languages such as Microsoft BASIC, FORTRAN, or COBOL. All of these languages existed for MS-DOS, Microsoft explained, and it was therefore easy to transpose the CP/M applications onto the new operating system.

On the other side, certain other firms were pushing CP/M. In March 1982, Vendex Corporation adopted the idea of Microsoft's SoftCard—this time to the detriment of MS-

DOS. Vendex introduced Baby Blue, a card that would enable CP/M programs to run on the IBM PC!

Digital Research was also active during this time. The company managed to convince certain manufacturers to deliver machines with both the 8080 and the 8086 processors. That way, CP/M appeared as a better choice than MS-DOS, since the latter used a different file format.

MS-DOS CATCHES ON

Less than a year after the IBM PC was announced, a significant number of manufacturers were rallying behind MS-DOS, including Compusystems, IBM, Intel, SCP, Sirius, Tecmar, Victor, Wang, Zenith, Panasonic, Hitachi, and NEC. Microsoft was also negotiating with Sanyo, Toshiba, Texas Instruments, Commodore, Canon, and Sord, and most of those contracts came through.

As IBM continued to improve its PCs, Microsoft continued to improve its DOS. (See Appendix A.)

MS-DOS began to catch on more quickly beginning in 1983 when Lotus released a spreadsheet program which operated solely under MS-DOS. In just three months, Lotus 1-2-3 became the best-selling software package and the new standard for spreadsheets for 16-bit machines. This was a great boost to the market for MS-DOS machines.

As the years passed, the gap between MS-DOS and CP/M widened. By 1984, there was no longer any doubt about the dominance of MS-DOS. In December 1984, Future Computing published the results of a poll of 375 distributors. When asked "Which PC operating system do you use most?" 81 percent of those polled answered MS-DOS.

In June 1986, Microsoft announced that half its annual revenues—now estimated at $60.9 million—came from the sale of its operating system. This income established Microsoft's financial stability. By the end of the 1980s, 30 million MS-DOS machines were on the market.

Tim Patterson modestly believes that the IBM name was the determining factor in the success of the system. Bill

Gates, on the other hand, feels that the challenge was tough for Microsoft and that the presence of IBM was not in itself sufficient to establish MS-DOS as the standard. It also took a lot of hard work on Microsoft's part.

IBM PC-COMPATIBLES

Nineteen eighty-three was the year of the "PC-compatible": a microcomputer that uses the same microprocessor as the IBM PC, supports MS-DOS, and can run the same software as the PC.

Many major computer manufacturers—including Texas Instruments, Wang, Philips, NEC, ITT, Hewlett-Packard, DEC, and Olivetti—abandoned all hope of competing successfully with IBM and opted for compatibility. The French manufacturer Bull had not yet joined this group, but in France, everything was set for the release of a PC-compatible by the end of the year.

By 1984, however, compatibility had not yet been perfected, as clearly seen in Sanyo's MBC 550, Tandy's TRS-80 2000, and Wang's PC. Computer magazines published compatibility indexes based on test programs. At Comdex 1983, Sperry Univac proudly flaunted the fact that its Sperry PC was 98 percent compatible with the IBM PC. In the next few years, however, the differences among compatibles would become minimal if not imperceptible.

Hardware manufacturers could position their computers against IBM's by offering "extras." Extras could be speed, as in the PC-6300 by AT&T, more expansion slots for cards, as in the VP by Columbia Data Products, or portability, as in Compaq's PC.

Of all the compatibles on the market, the Compaq Portable was the biggest surprise. The founder of this Texas company, Rod Canion, had conducted a personal survey among IBM PC users to find out what aspects they would like to see improved. The consensus pointed to portability, so Canion lined up venture capitalist Ben Rosen, the investor who provided start-up capital for Lotus Development

Corporation, to finance the production of a portable PC. Compaq produced a very high-quality computer, which withstood the toughest tests: One employee had fun throwing it against a wall as hard as he could and then seeing if it still worked.

The Compaq Portable, released in January 1983, was so successful that in its first year, it brought the company a record $111 million in sales. It took Compaq only three years to make the *Fortune* 500 list. The previous record was held by Apple, which had taken five years to make the list.

One thing was certain: Almost 99 percent of the installed base of PCs used the MS-DOS operating system. At the end of 1983, 500,000 copies of MS-DOS had been sold, approximately 400,000 of them through IBM.

Digital Research's next entry in the operating system market was Concurrent CP/M-86, a multitasking version of its operating system. Multitasking allows a computer to carry out two or more tasks at the same time: for example, receive an electronic mail message, print a document, and work on a spreadsheet program simultaneously. CP/M-86 probably would have had a chance if some major publishers, such as Lotus, Ashton-Tate, or MicroPro, had decided to port their software to the system. But without 1-2-3, dBASE, and WordStar, multitasking was not very useful. Digital Research braced for some very difficult years ahead.

Since MS-DOS was firmly established, Gates turned his attention to promoting Microsoft's applications, including Multiplan, Microsoft Word, and Microsoft Chart. His message was crystal clear: Microsoft is "the name to buy in software."

FIRST APPLICATIONS: MULTIPLAN AND WORD

Most people are good at something. . . . Bill is distinguished by being good at more than one thing. It's a very rare combination. . . . Bill is a 10 on enough scales that he's one in a billion.

–Charles Simonyi, Microsoft employee since 1981

11

The Emergence of the Electronic Spreadsheet

At a computer conference in Boston in October 1981, Peter Rosenthal, representing Atari, played down the importance of the professional market for personal computers. A game like Space Invaders had sold 2.5 million copies, he noted, whereas the most widely used professional software, VisiCalc, had sold only 150,000. Rosenthal could not have foreseen the tidal wave that the IBM PC would unleash. Big Blue finished 1981 respectably, having sold 13,000 of its new personal computers. However, 1982 was shaping up even better for IBM. The Reagan administration granted much more freedom to big business than prior administrations had. In January, the Justice Department threw out the antitrust suit filed against IBM 13 years earlier. This was an immense relief for IBM: Under threat of dismantlement, the company had been forced to move slowly. Now that the danger was past, nothing stood in the way of an all-out conquest of the American PC market.

IBM built a new factory for automated mass production and lowered prices on all its products. Its direct competitors in the world of mainframes, such as Amdahl, maker of IBM-compatible computers, experienced a difficult year. Magnuson Computer Systems went bankrupt, and National Advanced Systems gave up trying to compete with IBM and turned to the Japanese. From then on, National Advanced Systems sold Hitachi hardware. In less than a year and a half, IBM stock rose 60 points, contributing to a rise in the Dow Jones Industrial Average.

The growing giant began adopting new tactics. IBM's use of an Intel microprocessor in the PC inaugurated a new strategy of relying on outside suppliers. And, at the end of 1982, IBM—a newcomer to buyouts—acquired 12 percent of Intel stock. IBM also bought stock in Rolm, manufacturer of state-of-the-art telephone exchange systems, and prepared to take its place in the telecommunications market alongside another giant, AT&T.

Even the most optimistic observers marveled at how well the IBM PC was taking off. Less than a year after its release, the computer reached monthly sales of 30,000. However, it was still too early to say that the game had been won. Other computers were also surprisingly well received, including the Osborne computer, released one month before the IBM PC. Adam Osborne believed that demand would be high for a portable CP/M computer with professional software. In one year, 100,000 Osborne computers were sold. Osborne, however, retreated just as quickly as it had advanced. The Osborne computer lacked one key ingredient: MS-DOS compatibility.

A YOUNG CHAIRMAN

In early 1982, Bill Gates appeared for the first time on the cover of *Money,* and Miriam Lubow made sure that every Microsoft employee received a copy of the magazine. She mentioned to Bill that she thought the photograph of him was wonderful. "Bill, did you see that? They really took a great picture! I really like it!"

"You think so? I look so young."

"Bill, you *ARE* young! What do you expect when you're only 27!"

In fact, Bill still looked much younger than his age. A few months later, he went out to dinner with a few employees, including Miriam. Bill ordered a beer and the waitress asked to see his ID. Miriam recalls: "We all laughed because they *always* ask him if he's over 21."

The young Microsoft chairman worked harder than ever. Eating hamburgers for lunch had become such a habit that he practically became addicted to them. One day Bill took his new secretary Linda out for her birthday with a few other Microsoft employees, including Miriam Lubow. They went to a posh restaurant where everyone ordered wine and the daily specials. Bill, however, ordered wine and a hamburger.

"He's having a hamburger?" thought Miriam. "But Bill, this is a nice restaurant. Why don't you order something different?" she urged.

In a mock whine, Bill responded, "But I *like* hamburgers!" (A few years later, Gates became a vegetarian, "as a random test of discipline.")

In mid-1981, Microsoft computerized its accounting on a small Tandy computer. Previously, Steve Wood's wife had kept the books manually. For a firm that was dealing with the likes of IBM, Microsoft's administration was still not very professional. And the absence of a financial consultant turned out to be costly for Gates: In 1981 he made $1 million, of which $500,000 went to taxes. He said he was too busy running the company to take time to shelter his income. His contribution as a taxpayer earned him a congratulatory letter from President Reagan—small consolation!

In May 1982, Microsoft was rushing to publish its first application, an enormous switch for a company that until then had concentrated primarily on computer languages. Gates had no time to focus on management, so in July 1982, he asked James Towne, a manager from Tektronix, to take the reins of Microsoft. Towne became the first president of the corporation.

Microsoft's first application, Multiplan, was a spreadsheet designed to compete with VisiCalc, the uncontested leader in software sales for all systems.

VISICALC: THE FIRST ELECTRONIC SPREADSHEET

VisiCalc was conceived in 1977 by a Harvard MBA student named Dan Bricklin. He was a 26-year-old programmer who had one foot in the 1960s while at the same time dreaming of starting a company and becoming successful in the business world. At Harvard, Bricklin encountered the many real-world business simulations used by the school to teach students about management. In resolving these practical business scenarios, he found that he was losing far too much time recalculating financial data by hand. To make his task easier, he wrote short programs in BASIC on the school's PDP-10. He realized, however, that there was no general computational tool for managers and financial analysts to use in solving everyday business problems, so he decided to write a program to automate those calculations.

Bricklin sought the opinion of several Harvard professors. His production and accounting professors were excited about his idea, but his finance professor said that it had no commercial future. Nevertheless, he encouraged Bricklin to talk to Dan Fylstra, who had just founded Personal Software, a publisher of software for home use. Fylstra sympathized with Bricklin and lent him an Apple II so he could develop a model of his program. The following weekend, Dan Bricklin invented the electronic spreadsheet.

Bricklin's program used a grid to reproduce an accounting worksheet on the computer screen. The rows of the grid were numbered, and the columns were designated with letters. Each cell formed by the intersection of a row and a column was identified by the corresponding number and letter—A1, B2, C4, and so on. The user could enter numbers or formulas into the cells. For example, ADD(A1..A4) in cell B5 told the spreadsheet to calculate the sum of the values in cells A1, A2, A3, and A4 and display the answer in cell B5. If the user changed the value in one cell, the program automatically recalculated all the values on the worksheet. The prototype took about 20 seconds to recalculate 100 cells.

Bricklin showed his program to a few friends, who encouraged him to continue his project, which he named VisiCalc. He then began working with Bob Frankston, a programmer he had met seven years earlier. Bricklin wrote the specifications of the software while Frankston developed it in assembly language. The two friends formed the company Software Arts, which held the rights to the program. They signed an agreement with Dan Fylstra for Personal Software to market VisiCalc.

In its first appearance in May 1979 at the West Coast Computer Faire, and a few months later at the National Computer Conference, VisiCalc evoked definite interest, but did not constitute major news. It was officially released in October 1979. Fylstra presented it to people at Apple, but they showed no immediate desire to promote the program.

Venture capitalist Ben Rosen saw the potential for this spreadsheet and praised VisiCalc highly in his investor newsletter. Public interest in the program then began to grow exponentially. Soon, VisiCalc was creating a market for microcomputers. Customers who wanted to use VisiCalc would go to a computer store and buy the program and a machine to go with it. Dan Bricklin's program was the first best-seller in personal computer software.

At first, VisiCalc ran only on the Apple II, and it had a tremendous impact on Apple's sales. In September 1980, the Cupertino manufacturer estimated that 25,000 Apple II computers (about one-fifth of all the Apple II computers that had been sold since 1977) had been sold primarily for using VisiCalc. Some likened the effect of this program to that of the Ed Sullivan show in the late 1940s, which was said to have triggered spectacular growth in sales of television sets.

Software Arts later adapted its program for other computers such as the TRS-80, the Atari 800, the Hewlett-Packard microcomputer, and the Commodore PET. In 1981,

IBM made sure to announce its PC in conjunction with a PC version of VisiCalc. Four years after its inception, Software Arts employed 125 people and had yearly sales of $10 million.

ELECTRONIC SPREADSHEETS ARE A HIT

By inventing VisiCalc, Dan Bricklin awakened a latent need in business. Managers the world over immediately recognized that this software had been designed for them. For a long time, they had had only two equally unattractive options when they needed help in calculating answers to business problems: Ask the computer services department to write a program on an IBM or Control Data mainframe, or do hundreds of operations with a calculator. Now, the VisiCalc spreadsheet enabled them to define their "model" and do all their calculations on an Apple II in their own offices.

VisiCalc, which came with all the standard accounting formulas, allowed users to run simulations and immediately observe how a change in one value would affect hundreds of other values. What would happen if salaries increased 5 percent while prices rose 1 percent? How would buying a machine to reduce costs in the long run affect profits? Each time, VisiCalc took the new data into account and generated a response. When managers discovered that there was a software tool that could help them make well-informed decisions, they quickly ordered a spreadsheet program and a microcomputer. VisiCalc, the top program in this category, sent sales skyrocketing not only for Apple but for the entire personal computer industry.

Electronic spreadsheets seemed destined for success. Since Software Arts had neglected to address the CP/M market with VisiCalc, another spreadsheet, developed for CP/M, soon appeared as well: SuperCalc. It was developed by Sorcim, a company whose name is Micros backward, and it too met with huge success. SuperCalc was bought a few years later by Computer Associates.

THE ELECTRONIC PAPER PROJECT

When Bill Gates and Paul Allen decided that Microsoft would start developing applications, creating a spreadsheet was a natural choice. The Electronic Paper project began in 1980.

The strategy Microsoft adopted to beat VisiCalc and SuperCalc was crucially important. Microsoft decided to create a spreadsheet that could be ported to as many different computers as possible, because at that time, it was impossible to predict whether the IBM PC architecture would become the industry standard. The public was enamored of several very different computers: the TI99 by Texas Instruments, the Osborne computer, and the UNIX computer by Fortune Corporation (this last manufacturer no longer exists). And some of Microsoft's clients, such as Zenith and Datapoint, were very interested in obtaining a spreadsheet for their own computers.

Also, the popular spreadsheets at that time ran on only one type of computer. For example, VisiCalc, written in assembly language, could not run under CP/M, and SuperCalc could run under only the Apple operating system. The path seemed predetermined. The Microsoft spreadsheet would be ported to all the operating systems on the market, including CP/M, Apple DOS, UNIX, and MS-DOS. To make its spreadsheet easier to adapt onto diverse platforms, Microsoft decided to develop it in C, a high-level language. With this strategy, Gates and Allen were sure of establishing Electronic Paper as the number-one spreadsheet for personal computers.

Microsoft hired Paul Heckel as a consultant to define the specifications for the new spreadsheet. He began by examining every last detail of VisiCalc and SuperCalc. Gates strongly disliked the "Battleship" style of notation used by VisiCalc, which called the cells A1, B2, C14, etc. In Electronic

Paper the columns were designated C1, C2, C3, etc., and the rows L1, L2, L3, etc. Cells were identified by combinations such as L1C1, L2C2, L14C3.

From the early specifications, a programmer named Mark Mathews created a prototype of Electronic Paper. Full development of what would become Multiplan was entrusted to a newly arrived master, Charles Simonyi.

Simonyi joined Microsoft on February 6, 1981, and became director of applications development. He enjoyed a remarkable reputation because he came from Xerox's Palo Alto Research Center (PARC). Top-notch developers greatly respected Xerox PARC because some of the most revolutionary concepts in computers emerged from there. These concepts appeared a few years later in Apple's Lisa and Macintosh computers, Digital Research's GEM software, and Microsoft Windows.

In the early 1960s, Simonyi had taught himself to program in machine language on a decrepit and elementary computer called Ural II in his native Hungary. His gift for programming led him to Denmark, then to the University of California at Berkeley, and finally on to a doctorate at Stanford University.

In 1972, Charles Simonyi was recruited to work at the Xerox PARC, where he began writing Bravo, a word processing program for Xerox's Alto computer. According to Simonyi, Bravo was the first WYSIWYG (what you see is what you get) system with a mouse interface, 11 years before the Macintosh.

Although Xerox successfully recruited talented people to venture into new domains, it failed to transform the intellectual gold mine in its laboratories into marketable products. One by one, the best engineers left the Xerox PARC, attracted by more practical ventures.

For Simonyi, the time to leave came in 1980. At lunch one day, a former PARC colleague, Bob Metcalfe, who had just founded 3Com, gave Simonyi a list of people to contact for jobs. The first name on the list was Bill Gates.

Simonyi met Gates and Steve Ballmer in November. After talking with them for five minutes, he was convinced that he wanted to work for Microsoft. "It was obvious to me that Bill knew what was going on." Out of courtesy, Simonyi went to a few other previously scheduled interviews. Each time, he was amazed at how different Gates's vision was from the others. Simonyi realized immediately that the software programs being developed by this young man from Seattle were destined to make a tremendous impact on the industry.

When Simonyi announced his resignation from Xerox, one of the secretaries asked him what company he was going to work for. When he said Microsoft, she was surprised, never having heard of it. He showed her one of Microsoft's newsletters. On the last page was a photograph of the chairman: Without his glasses, Bill Gates looked like a schoolboy sitting at his desk. The secretary started to laugh. "Charles, what are you doing? Here you are at the best research lab in the world!" She didn't want him to make a serious mistake by going to work with "those kids."

The first thing Simonyi did after joining Microsoft was try to recruit two of his former colleagues. One of them worked at Convergent Technology. On their way to the meeting, Simonyi and Gates opened the *Wall Street Journal* and discovered that Convergent Technology had just received a $1 billion order from AT&T. This was not exactly the best day to try to hire away a Convergent programmer, but they made their pitch anyway. Although Microsoft had already prepared a very attractive offer, including a high salary and generous stock options, the engineer was reluctant to leave and declined the offer. Simonyi's other friend also refused Microsoft's job offer. Simonyi was very annoyed. "It really bothered me to not be able to make them understand what an opportunity this was!"

MENUS IN MULTIPLAN

When Simonyi took responsibility for the Multiplan project (as Electronic Paper was now known), he inherited the study done by the consultant Paul Heckel. Since he was a new employee, he thought it best not to make drastic changes in what had already been established, and kept the L1C1 notation for rows and columns.

Simonyi did, however, have certain ideas about how to program. His pet project was menus. Menus, he said, were essential in keeping a user from feeling bewildered by a software program. He later explained this to *PC World* magazine (November 1983).

> I like the obvious analogy of a restaurant. Let's say I go to a French restaurant and I don't speak the language. It's a strange environment and I'm apprehensive. I'm afraid of making a fool of myself, so I'm kind of tense. Then a very imposing waiter comes over and starts addressing me in French. Suddenly, I've got clammy hands.
>
> That's probably the same feeling the bookkeeper gets when he or she sits down at a computer. . . . What's the way out?
>
> The way out is that I get the menu and point at something on the menu—I cannot go wrong. I may not get what I want—I might end up with snails—but at least I won't be embarrassed.
>
> . . . But imagine if you had a French restaurant without a menu—that would be terrible.
>
> It's the same thing with computer programs—you've got to have a menu. Menus are friendly because people know what their options are and they can select an option just by pointing. They do not have to look for something that they will not be able to find, and they don't have to type some command that might be wrong.

In the article, the *PC World* journalist teased about the fallibility of menus: "There are other possibilities. For instance, you could say, 'These are our three specials. If you would like to see more, ask your waiter.' "

Simonyi caught the joke:

> I don't want to go overboard on the analogy, but I know what you are driving at. When I got into the micro world, I realized that menu programs typically have many menus and that those menus are arranged in almost a maze-like fashion. It's a little bit like an adventure game. . . . Some of these programs have five, six, or seven menus, and to get from one menu to the other you press Control-C, for example. In fact, charts of

those menus are published with different menus connected by channels, like charts of North America as viewed by a sixteenth-century explorer. One almost expects a little dragon to pop up somewhere and threaten you if you go the wrong way. That is crazy stuff.

Simonyi defined a software element that would become famous: Multiplan menus. They appeared as two lines on the bottom of the screen and had self-explanatory names, such as Calculate and Print. When the user chose a menu command such as Print, Multiplan opened a submenu. The Escape key enabled the user to move back to the previous menu.

Other new features appeared in Multiplan. Multiplan allowed the user to consolidate several spreadsheets. For example, each of 12 monthly spreadsheets could be combined into one overall spreadsheet. Finally, to simplify writing formulas, Multiplan offered the possibility of naming a group of cells. The sum of sales could therefore be given a specific name, such as SUM(SALES).

Once Simonyi finished the product specifications, he passed the baton to the programming team: Doug Klunder and Bob Mathews, with occasional help from four other developers. Klunder had recently been recruited to Microsoft straight out of college.

According to the initial specifications, Multiplan was supposed to be ported to as many different computers as possible. In 1981, however, Microsoft's top priority was its relationship with IBM. Gates told the Boca Raton teams about the Multiplan project and listened carefully to their feedback. At that time, IBM was concerned about offering a range of software for its clients who had bought IBM PCs with 64K of memory. IBM had invested an enormous amount of money in advertising these limited-capacity PCs. Don Estridge and his team felt they had to keep the implied promise of software availability for that machine and thus insisted that Multiplan be able to run in less than 64K of memory. Microsoft acquiesced to its primary client. This limitation made the programmers' work much more complicated than expected. A few years later, this decision proved to be an enormous blunder.

RELEASE OF MULTIPLAN

IBM received the PC version of Multiplan in the spring of 1982. The spreadsheet had 64 columns and 256 rows, and required only 64K of memory. For obscure internal reasons, IBM delayed listing Multiplan in its catalog of application software. Officially, the division that received the software was putting it through a battery of rigorous tests in accordance with in-house policy. Doug Klunder was surprised, however, that he wasn't receiving any news from IBM about problems with Multiplan. Apparently, Big Blue did not perceive this spreadsheet as a major product, and continued intensively promoting the MS-DOS version of VisiCalc.

The first version of Multiplan actually released (in August 1982) was for the Apple II. Microsoft released a CP/M version a short time later.

Gates declared that anyone who had ever used a calculator could use Multiplan, positioning Multiplan as a second-generation spreadsheet. He tried to relegate VisiCalc and SuperCalc to the cobwebs.

The IBM version of Multiplan was published in October 1982. IBM marketed it directly. When it was finally released in its PC version, Multiplan had been in development and intensive beta testing for two years. In a beta test, users test the software in a real-world environment before it is officially released to market.

Jeff Raikes, who had left Apple Computer to join Microsoft in November 1981, was responsible for marketing Multiplan. (He looked so much like Bill Gates that some thought he must have been a clone.) Raikes organized the biggest advertising campaign Microsoft had ever conducted.

Multiplan received highly enthusiastic press reviews. *Software Review* gave it an "excellent" in all categories, congratulating it on being easy to learn, easy to use, and powerful. "Multiplan seems to have been designed with the sole objective of taking VisiCalc's place as market leader," the article said, concluding that it had all the necessary ingredients. In December 1982, the weekly *InfoWorld* named Multiplan "software of the year." In January 1983, Apple announced its official endorsement of Multiplan.

In January 1983, when sales of VisiCalc reached 500,000 copies, Software Arts experienced a serious setback. Fylstra's VisiCorp (the new name of Personal Software) was suing Bricklin's Software Arts over the rights to VisiCalc. Fylstra criticized developers Bricklin and Frankston for failing to release their spreadsheet sooner, thus leaving the field wide open to competitors such as SuperCalc and Multiplan. The legal battle between Software Arts and VisiCorp seemed advantageous to Microsoft as it launched Multiplan.

THE ARRIVAL OF LOTUS 1-2-3

Three months later, however, another spreadsheet stole the number-one spot from VisiCalc: 1-2-3 from Lotus Development Corporation.

Lotus was founded in 1982 by 32-year-old Mitch Kapor. Before focusing his attention on programming, Kapor was a fan of psychedelic rock music, and had worked as a disc jockey and later as a teacher of transcendental meditation (hence the name Lotus). In 1979, he had written two software programs for VisiCorp: VisiTrend, a statistics package, and VisiPlot, a business charting application. As stipulated in his contract, he received royalties of 33 percent from the sale of each program. Wanting to free itself from this costly agreement, VisiCorp offered to buy back the rights to these two programs from Kapor. He accepted their offer of $1.7 million.

Kapor was then ready for his next coup: a spreadsheet that translated numbers into graphs. He met Jonathan Sachs, a programmer who enjoyed working alone and loved to tackle challenging programming tasks. Sachs himself had an idea for a new spreadsheet and was looking for a partner to help him market it. Sachs and Kapor agreed on the idea of a spreadsheet in which numbers could be converted into graphs. Mitch Kapor founded Lotus in the belief that their program would be a record-breaking hit. Jonathan Sachs was not as convinced; however, he dedicated the next ten months of his life to developing Lotus 1-2-3 in assembly language for the IBM PC.

During that period, Kapor showed venture capitalist Ben Rosen a prototype of 1-2-3. Rosen, of Sevin Rosen Management, immediately saw the potential of this software and invested $600,000 in Lotus. They brought in other venture capitalists as well, and soon Kapor's firm had received almost $3 million in investments. Kapor allocated several million dollars—an unprecedented amount—for the advertising budget. He also made sure that his product received abundant press coverage. Laudatory articles appeared in the national financial press even before the spreadsheet was on the market.

Lotus introduced 1-2-3 at the November 1982 Comdex in Las Vegas. Charles Simonyi was there: "When I first saw 1-2-3, I knew that we were in trouble. That was pretty clear." Whereas Multiplan's capabilities were restricted because of the 64K limit required by IBM, 1-2-3 was aimed specifically at 256K machines and had a wealth of capabilities. It was extremely fast at recalculating and came with file management tools. Within the first few days after the introduction, Lotus received more than $1 million in orders.

Three months after its release in January 1983, 1-2-3 dethroned VisiCalc and settled into the number-one spot, where it remained almost continuously.

MULTIPLAN VS. 1-2-3

In February 1984, Microsoft released an expanded version of Multiplan PC, version 1.1, which could address all the memory in a PC and could therefore handle larger spreadsheets. Version 1.1 could run on almost a hundred different systems including the PC, the Apple II, the Commodore 64, the Osborne, the TI-99, the Rainbow-100 by DEC, the B20 by Burroughs, the Professional Computer by Wang, the JB3000 by National Panasonic, the Xerox 820, and several UNIX machines. Multiplan had been translated into more than a dozen languages, including German, Italian, Spanish, and French. It was even chosen as the spreadsheet for the John F. Kennedy presidential library because it was the only one that could run on the Datapoint 8645 used there.

Microsoft even produced a Japanese version of Multiplan. When Mitsubishi asked for a version of Multiplan for its 16-bit machine using CP/M-86, Microsoft made the necessary adaptations. Developing this version was no easy task, since the Japanese Kanji alphabet has more than 10,000 characters!

Microsoft thus achieved its initial objective of developing Multiplan for a wide variety of environments. Probably no other application has been adapted for so many machines. Many manufacturers sold Multiplan directly with their computers. In the meantime, however, Lotus 1-2-3, written specifically for the capabilities of the IBM PC, had made its assault on the market. IBM felt that 1-2-3 was doing for the PC what VisiCalc had done for the Apple II. By the end of 1984, the success of 1-2-3 was clear. Lotus Development Corporation took first place among software publishers with sales of $157 million, compared to $125 million for Microsoft.

Simonyi recognized that Microsoft had taken the wrong road, partly because of IBM's request for a program that could run in less than 64K of memory. "We were just working on the wrong problem all along." Simonyi regrets that Microsoft didn't foresee the rise in popularity of powerful machines with more memory and tailor its product to the high end, rather than sticking with the low end.

Microsoft adopted several strategies to help Multiplan compete with Lotus 1-2-3. In early 1984, it released "ready-to-use" models for finance and budgeting, and offered a tutorial program with its spreadsheet. As the years went by, however, the gap widened. While 1-2-3 consistently remained number one, Multiplan managed to stay in the top 30, but could not halt its progressive decline.

THE DEMISE OF VISICALC

In the fall of 1984, Dan Bricklin and Bob Frankston won their lawsuit against Dan Fylstra. VisiCorp was ordered to pay Software Arts $500,000 in damages and interest. Software Arts, however, was seriously weakened by having to spend so much time defending itself against VisiCorp. The arrival of 1-2-3 had dealt a harsh blow to VisiCalc, whose monthly sales fell from 20,000 in early 1983 to 2,500 in late 1984. At the same time, VisiCorp had not recuperated from the failure of the VisiOn program in which it had invested $10 million. VisiCorp went bankrupt in early 1985. At that time, Ashton-Tate, publisher of dBASE II, offered to buy battle-scarred Software Arts.

A few days before he was scheduled to sign the agreement with Ashton-Tate, Dan Bricklin ran into Mitch Kapor on a flight to the SoftCon conference. Kapor asked how things were going. "Could be better," Dan replied. The two presidents conversed, and Kapor ended up offering to buy out Software Arts. The acquisition cost $800,000, with Lotus absorbing a loss of $2.2 million. Such was the end of the firm that originated the most influential software idea in the history of microcomputing. Software Arts joined the long list of companies—including MITS, IMSAI, and Osborne—that began with a boom but could not sustain the momentum. Bricklin worked for a while as a consultant to Lotus before founding a new software publishing company, Software Garden.

According to Dataquest, the 1986 sales of 1-2-3 were three times as high as Multiplan sales (750,000 vs. 275,000). The Lotus spreadsheet sold its 2 millionth copy, while Multiplan had sold a total of about 1.2 million copies. That year, according to InfoCorp, 1-2-3 alone represented 17.6 percent of software sales for all systems in the professional sector. Lotus 1-2-3 eventually eliminated Multiplan in the American market, monopolizing 80 percent of all spreadsheet sales in the United States.

By the end of the 1980s, 1-2-3 had sold 5 million copies, setting a record that will be difficult to beat.

OBJECTIVE: EUROPE

Microsoft had not been completely wrong, however, in wanting Multiplan to be universally available. Although it lagged in the American market, it was enjoying extraordinary success abroad.

In the early 1980s, the Belgian firm Vector International represented the European interests of two software publishers: Microsoft and Digital Research. Vector was primarily active in promoting software by Digital, to the extent that in 1982, many European computer manufacturers had become interested in CP/M-86.

In the spring of 1982, Bob O'Rear was sent to Europe to take over Microsoft's affairs there. His first destination was the United Kingdom, where he discovered a unique market. The number-one-selling machine was designed by one of Her Majesty's subjects, Lord David Sinclair. Three hundred thousand Sinclair computers had been sold, which was three times the number of Commodores and ten times the number of Apples or Tandys. Bob O'Rear dug deeper in his study. As in the United States, Apple's domination in Europe appeared unshakeable. Apple held 50 percent of the market, followed by Commodore, with 30 percent. IBM had not yet arrived.

O'Rear won an early victory with Victor, a British computer manufacturer with a CP/M-86 license, when he managed to sway the firm over to MS-DOS. In France, he met with manufacturers such as Bull, R2E, and Léanord to extol the virtues of Microsoft's operating system. At the same time, he supervised the translation of BASIC manuals into French and German.

In August 1982, Jeff Raikes crossed the Atlantic to take charge of promoting Multiplan in Europe. He landed in Calais with a female friend and rented a car. Five minutes down the road, they suffered an accident, and Jeff's companion was hospitalized. Things were not starting out well for the spreadsheet in France. However, there was a double happy ending. Jeff Raikes and Bob O'Rear took the train from Calais to Paris, where they met Joachim Kempin of Apple.

(Kempin joined Microsoft a few months later to oversee the establishment of the German subsidiary.) Kempin signed an agreement specifying that Multiplan would be sold with the Apple II. A few days later, Jeff Raikes proposed to his girl-friend while she was still in the hospital.

Work soon began on adapting Multiplan to the various European languages, and Charles Simonyi, Doug Klunder, and the other programmers discovered some peculiarities of that continent: Different countries used different methods of indicating decimals, had different monetary symbols, and used a different format for dates. Furthermore, some lan-guages had a wealth of accents on their letters, such as the French é, à, and ô.

Bob O'Rear realized that Europe was not a single entity, and therefore Microsoft could not handle all its European business from a single headquarters in a London suburb. He determined that there were three major markets to cover: Germany, France, and England. Bill Gates agreed on the need to open a subsidiary in each of these three markets, so Microsoft hired the recruiting agency MARLAR to find three European bosses.

BERNARD VERGNES AND MULTIPLAN'S EUROPEAN SUCCESS

In December 1982, Jean-Paul Cruchot, a headhunter for MARLAR, contacted Bernard Vergnes, the marketing direc-tor for a European subsidiary of a minicomputer manufac-turer named ModComp. Cruchot had a job he wanted Vergnes to consider, but the only job description he had was a half page indicating that the potential employer was a micro-computer company. Vergnes was politely reserved. "You know, I'm not sure that I'm interested in this."

When Cruchot then explained that the company made software, Vergnes bluntly refused. "There's no need to go any further."

The headhunter insisted. "Wait—this is a very interesting opportunity."

"Tell me the name of the company," Vergnes demanded.

"Unfortunately, I can't reveal that at this point in our discussions."

"In that case, we'll drop it."

"OK, OK, I'll tell you the name. It's Microsoft!"

Vergnes remained silent for a moment and then responded, "I've never heard of it."

"Listen, Scott Oki, director of Microsoft's international operations, will be in Paris Saturday morning. Will you agree to meet with him?"

"Well, why not?"

Vergnes made it painfully clear to Cruchot that his meeting with Microsoft had little chance of amounting to anything. When Vergnes returned to his office, however, he flipped through his collection of *Zero 1* and *Monde Informatique* magazines, two of the top computer weeklies in France, and ran across a series of articles in which Microsoft was depicted as a huge success in the United States. Although he was still hesitant about a career in microcomputers, which was still a minuscule market in France, Vergnes's attitude began to change noticeably.

Vergnes met Scott Oki and Bob O'Rear at the Club Med hotel in Paris. The two Americans were surprised that Vergnes knew a great deal about Microsoft, and Vergnes was impressed by the enthusiasm of the two negotiators. He envisioned the possibility of re-creating the excitement he had felt in the opening stages of minicomputer development in the early 1970s.

Scott Oki, however, was apprehensive about Bernard Vergnes. Could a hardware man take on software? How would a minicomputer specialist handle microcomputers? Accustomed to dealing directly with large clients, would Vergnes be able to adapt to a retail distribution market? Excited by the challenge, Vergnes had an instant comeback for each of these concerns. Software? He had been selling it for ten years at ModComp. As for the rest, he recognized that he did not have direct experience in the field, but it seemed simple to him. He even explained how to approach the

French market. Vergnes was drawing on the memory of a conversation he had had with another defector from mini-computers, Jean-Louis Gassée. When Gassée had created Apple's French subsidiary, he had explained in great detail to Vergnes how he handled retail networks.

Oki sized up the candidate. Here was a Frenchman who spoke fluent English, seemed to understand software, and had good ideas. He asked whether Vergnes was willing to go to the United States to meet the directors of the company.

In January 1983, Vergnes met with Bill Gates, James Towne, Steve Ballmer, and Scott Oki. Gates looked as young as he had in the photos Vergnes had seen, and fit the intelligent, open-minded image portrayed in the press. Vergnes heard some of his own values echoed in Gates's philosophy, including a commitment to a high degree of integrity in professional relations. "I immediately felt at home in this company, which is respected for what it does and says, and which has a very positive and direct attitude. The kind of corporate culture Bill desired exactly matched my personal feelings on the subject." Microsoft decided to make him an offer, which Vergnes said he would consider. Oki was shocked to see him hesitate. Gates and Towne pressed harder, but could not get a firm commitment. Vergnes left for Paris saying that in the meantime, he was willing to help them if they needed him.

The following Monday, Carl Stork from Microsoft was in Paris to discuss the establishment of a French subsidiary with their lawyers. Vergnes was invited to the meeting, and he gradually began to intervene on behalf of Microsoft. He even interviewed potential candidates and hired two, including Michel Lacombe. Little by little, he was swayed by the responsibilities entrusted to him. (Lacombe became the CEO of Microsoft France in May 1989, and Vergnes was promoted to Microsoft Corporation's vice president for Europe.)

Microsoft France opened its first office on May 2, 1983. The company started out in a 450-square-foot room permeated by the smell of rancid meat at a refrigerator company located in Les Ulis, an industrial area south of Paris where a large number of computer companies such as Bull and Compaq are located. The French subsidiary took charge of relations with computer manufacturers such as Bull and Groupil. Vergnes and Lacombe also spent their evenings and weekends rereading and correcting the translation of the Multiplan manual.

The French version of Multiplan was released for the Apple II in September 1983. Jean-Louis Gassée of Apple was an enthusiastic promoter of the software. At the same time, IBM decided to introduce its PC in France and offered three software programs including Multiplan (under the IBM label). The PC version with the Microsoft label appeared in April 1984. Microsoft also released a version for Victor computers, then the most popular manufacturer in France after Apple.

Most French PC users discovered the electronic spreadsheet through Multiplan, which rapidly became the number-one software program in France. By early 1985, sales of Multiplan in France had risen to 28,000 copies.

Lotus arrived in France a year later and discovered the problems with internationalizing software. The company decided to wait until version 2.0 before offering a French version. However, when the French version of 1-2-3 was finally released in November 1986, it was too late. Multiplan had already been in France three years.

The June 1987 Faulkner report summed up the standings, noting that Lotus 1-2-3 held 80 percent of the American market for spreadsheets, while Multiplan had only 6 percent. Multiplan, however, was well established in other countries. It controlled 60 percent of the German market, ahead of 1-2-3, and 90 percent of the French market.

At the end of the 1980s, 1-2-3 had sold 150,000 copies in France, to Multiplan's 300,000. Despite three shifts in positioning, Lotus could not conquer the French market. In some areas of France, the name Multiplan became synonymous with the word *spreadsheet,* and people were heard to ask, "Which Multiplan do you use?" to which a few responded, "Lotus 1-2-3."

When American software publishers traveling in Paris asked what software was number one there, they were always surprised to hear the name Multiplan. They usually responded with, "Multi-what?"

FOR EXPORT ONLY

Multiplan 2.0 for the PC came out in October 1985. One of the new features was support for a mouse. It was followed by Multiplan 3.0 in January 1987. This was a multiuser version which was very fast at recalculating, and which could handle eight spreadsheets simultaneously. Overall, Multiplan 3.0 was twice as fast as the previous version.

Microsoft's marketing team debated whether to launch Multiplan 3.0. They thought the program had reached the end of its career, and wondered whether they could continue to market it in the United States. They decided to keep Multiplan primarily because it was so successful overseas.

Multiplan was doomed in the United States because it had initially aimed at the wrong target. Bill Gates, however, evidenced a rare capacity to analyze his own mistakes and set about to reproduce the conditions that had led to his competitor's success. Microsoft's counterattack in the spreadsheet market was to come in 1985 under the name Excel.

12

Microsoft Word

By 1983, more than 2.9 million people were using computers, up from just 300,000 in 1980. In 1982, sales of IBM PCs surged ahead of Apple, Tandy, Commodore, and DEC computers. In 1984, when IBM released the PC XT with a hard disk,[1] sales of PCs soared even higher. The gap between IBM and microcomputer manufacturers offering a different standard was widening to the point that only Apple was able to remain in the race.

MS-DOS was now available for more than 60 computer systems. Manufacturers, accepting the inevitable, were touting the "IBM compatibility" of their products, offering machines that could run software written for the PC. In reality, however, full compatibility had not yet been achieved, causing substantial frustration for users.

For software publishers, the PC was a godsend. Users spent $1 billion on software in 1982. Future Computing, the market research firm, predicted that sales would double during the course of the year. As a direct result of hardware

---

[1] A disk drive with a built-in, permanent disk that could hold 10 megabytes, or 30 times more memory than a diskette. Hard disks that appeared in late 1984 could hold 20 megabytes. By the early 1990s, the standard PC hard disk could hold up to 320 megabytes.

sales, the market for IBM PC software exceeded, for the first time ever, the software market for competing systems.

It was a euphoric time for IBM. The company piled up success after success, total revenues reached a new record of $34 billion, and Big Blue had already captured 20 percent of the U.S. market for professional microcomputers. Apple, in contrast, was stumbling, having just experienced its first failure, the Apple III.

THE CLUB OF FIVE

Four software publishers dominated the market in 1983: VisiCorp, Microsoft, Digital Research, and MicroPro. Lotus soon joined this quartet.

In 1983, VisiCalc was still the best-selling application software, with 500,000 copies sold. It had brought its maker, Software Arts, over $10 million in revenues. However, Lotus 1-2-3 was crowding VisiCalc out of the winner's circle. It was so successful that by 1983, Lotus Development Corporation became the number two software publisher, just behind Microsoft. The public particularly liked the spreadsheet's recalculating speed. In order to get the best performance on an IBM PC, 1-2-3 developer Jonathan Sachs did not hesitate to modify the MS-DOS operating system wherever it was found to be too slow. Bill Gates did not particularly appreciate the appearance of such "hardware-dependent" applications. He felt it was unwise for applications to interface directly with the hardware instead of calling on the services of MS-DOS, because they ran the risk of not functioning on new configurations.

Throughout the evolution of PCs, however, 1-2-3 was unchallenged. In fact, it became one of the standard programs for testing other computers for IBM compatibility.

Other than Apple, with its own operating system, Digital Research dominated the non-IBM microcomputer market. It expected to reach sales of $40 million by 1983, but instead, continued to lose ground to Microsoft. Digital Research's CP/M-86 operating system for the IBM PC was released too late. In the summer, Yates Ventures, a market research group based in Los Gatos, California, estimated that the total installed base of CP/M on 16-bit machines was 500,000. DOS surpassed this figure with 550,000 PC-DOS operating systems installed on the IBM PC and 100,000 MS-DOS systems installed on compatible computers.

The price of its system put Digital Research at a disadvantage early on. CP/M-86 sold for up to eight times more than DOS, yet there were no functional differences to justify such a huge price disparity. Digital Research adopted several strategies to try to catch up to Microsoft's uncontested lead in the market. First, it dropped the price of CP/M-86 by a factor of four. Then it tried to convince a number of manufacturers to adopt CP/M-86 as the standard for their personal computers. DEC, Televideo, Hewlett-Packard, Data General, and Honeywell complied, but decided also to offer MS-DOS for their computers. The die was cast: DOS would dominate. This became clear when Digital Research began secretly developing application software for DOS. Ironically, CP/M-86 was praised by experts as superior, and had the advantage of being available in a multi-tasking version. Users, however, preferred DOS because it was faster and more user-friendly.

By 1983, Microsoft BASIC had sold more than 1 million copies and had brought in $15 million in sales. The company was hoping to soon reach $50 million in overall sales, by adding a complete range of applications to its computer languages and MS-DOS. Bill Gates explained to *Business Week* (May 9, 1983) that Microsoft's goal was "to be a one-stop supermarket for the [personal computer] software of the future."

Business was great for the software genius, both professionally and personally. In fact, the gifted programmer-turned-company-chairman was making some of the best investments of his life at that time. In the early 1980s, Gates had staked $40,000 on technology stocks he thought were undervalued, including Apple stock. His portfolio rose to $1 million in the following years. With those profits, he bought a $780,000 house overlooking Lake Washington, with a 30-foot-long indoor swimming pool.

JON SHIRLEY LEADS MICROSOFT TO MATURITY

Gates was not happy, however, with James Towne, the president he had hired a year earlier. He felt that Towne was not enthusiastic enough to manage Microsoft during this exciting phase. Towne's nonchalance earned him a dismissal from Gates just 11 months after taking the post.

Now Gates chose the man who had launched the TRS-100 (a portable computer designed by Microsoft on Kazuhiko Nishi's initiative and then marketed by Tandy; see Chapter 7): Jon Shirley, a vice president from Tandy. The constant growth of Tandy was attributed to this 45-year-old executive, whose reserved demeanor concealed an unparalleled tenacity and organizational sense.

Shirley arrived at Microsoft to find a company whose sales were doubling yearly, but whose catastrophic administrative situation drastically needed change. Steve Ballmer, Gates's college friend, was struggling to handle accounting, recruitment, and several other functions. Despite his good intentions, personal charisma, and boundless energy, Ballmer was having trouble keeping the Microsoft ship from running aground. Finances were in a state of anarchy. The director of computer services continually wondered what equipment he could acquire. Certain software was not being produced quickly enough to satisfy demand, and management was not being informed. Shirley also discovered that the accounting was handled on one of the small Tandy microcomputers he had been making previously! The accounting software was far from adequate for handling the accounts of a nearly $50-million-a-year company, and none of the necessary controls for soundly managing a rapidly growing enterprise were in place.

Once he recovered from the shock, Jon Shirley began to put some order into the organization. He hired a financial director, drew up rules about filling out administrative forms, and ordered a central computer to manage inventory and accounting records. Steve Ballmer was named head of marketing.

In an interview shortly after his appointment, Shirley described his function as freeing Bill Gates to work as much as possible on research and development. Shirley's marvelous execution of his task largely contributed to bringing Microsoft to maturity.

On the personal level, Shirley was a fanatic for delegation. He believed that the only way to build a large company was to train excellent managers. At the Microsoft annual meeting, he formulated his vision of the ideal employee, declaring that Microsoft employees were the type of people "who make things happen."

WORDSTAR: THE FIRST SUCCESSFUL WORD PROCESSING PROGRAM

In April 1983, Microsoft launched its second application: a word processing program designed to steal WordStar's dominant position.

The word processor is an immense time saver for anyone who creates text. Instead of reproducing typed text directly onto a sheet of paper as a typewriter does, the word processor uses computer technology to record the text in memory and on disk. Users can then modify and reformat the text and print it at will. Numerous text changes can be made in memory and then saved to disk without the user having to retype the entire document, thereby saving time and eliminating much frustration.

The first word processing software was released on dedicated word processing machines at the end of the 1970s. Tens of thousands of secretaries were trained on IBM's Visiotext word processor or equivalent machines by Wang, Lanier, and CPT.

In 1978, Seymour Rubinstein, foreseeing the imminent failure of IMSAI, left that microcomputer manufacturer and founded a software publishing company called MicroPro. He hired a programmer who wrote WordMaster, a microcomputer-based text editing program designed for software developers. Rubinstein invested his last dime in this program, and on the eve of its introduction, with no money left to pay for a hotel, he slept in the subway.

Fortunately, WordMaster took off immediately and brought in tens of thousands of dollars for MicroPro. Rubinstein and his colleague, encouraged by the warm reception, then began developing a word processing program for the public at large. WordStar was released in mid-1979 and easily became the leader. Some journalists called this program the cash cow of the CP/M world. (There was no CP/M version of the other early best-seller, VisiCalc.)

When the IBM PC was released, MicroPro began to convert its software, which was originally developed in Assembler 8080 for 8-bit computers, so that it could run on the new 16-bit processors. The result was a version of WordStar that acted the same on the IBM PC as it had on CP/M computers. WordStar's popularity in the CP/M world quickly transferred into the IBM world. In 1982, MicroPro announced that it had sold more than a million copies of its word processing program.

WordStar had a significant drawback, however—its complexity. Simple tasks like deleting text or saving to disk involved difficult combinations of keystrokes. To delete a line of text, the user had to simultaneously hold down Ctrl, Q, and Y. Ctrl, K, and D saved a document to disk. A user had to memorize about 30 such combinations to become proficient at WordStar.

Some WordStar users began to show signs of impatience. Here and there, articles appeared indicating a market for a word processing program that would deliver users from Ctrl-QY and other confusing procedures. A *Softalk* editorial published in October 1983, for example, said that having to use such complex methods to manipulate text hindered free flow of thought.

MICROSOFT CHALLENGES WORDSTAR

Microsoft took all these factors into consideration in designing its competitor to WordStar. In the process, Charles Simonyi introduced several unusual concepts in this product, which was originally called Multi-Tool Word.

WordStar had been written in assembly language. In contrast, like Multiplan, MSWord (as it came to be known) would be developed in C, a high-level language. It would have the same interface as Multiplan, and many commands would be the same as those used in the Multiplan menus. And, of course, it would be written for MS-DOS.

Word was to be the first word processing program to display boldface, underlining, italics, subscripts, and superscripts on the screen. The screen could be divided into several "windows," so that a user could have several documents open at the same time. Word also stored deleted text in a "wastebasket" so a user could reinsert accidentally deleted text back into the document. One particularly innovative feature of Word was the mouse, a small pointing device connected to the computer. When rolled along a desktop, it moves a small arrow pointer on the computer screen. The mouse enables users to point to text and then delete, change, or make insertions.

WordStar required the user to format each document separately. Word, on the other hand, would offer style sheets, which stored certain character and paragraph formats and could be applied to any document. For example, the user could create a style sheet called Letter and apply it to a number of business letters to produce a common format for all company correspondence.

Microsoft designed Word to handle the proportional fonts used on laser printers, which had just appeared on the market. Programming this feature into Word was extremely complex, especially for such a small market, but Gates insisted, foreseeing the growth in importance of those printers in the near future. He knew that if Microsoft didn't include this feature in Word from the outset, later modification would be extremely difficult. Word thus was to be the first software program that could produce documents of almost typeset quality. It was designed to drive not only laser printers but also typesetting systems.

Finally, Word would not sever all ties with the past or the present. It was designed to be able to read (and therefore modify) files created with WordStar.

Once the Word specifications were defined, Simonyi began development in mid-1982 with the help of programmer Richard Brodie.

Multi-Tool Word was introduced at the spring 1983 Comdex in Atlanta. The word processing program with a mouse surprised those in attendance. In June, the magazine *Softalk* published its first impressions of a prerelease version of the software, giving it high marks.

A NEW NAME AND A NEW MARKETING STRATEGY

Microsoft modified the product name in summer 1983. Originally, Bill Gates, Charles Simonyi, and Jeff Raikes were planning to create a family of products named Multi-Tool, Multiplan being the first. To continue that line, the word processing software should have been called Multi-Word. A database was in the research stage, which they planned to call Multi-File. Then they discovered that some of these names were already trademarked, so they chose the name Multi-Tool Word. Rowland Hanson, the new communications director, was not thrilled with these long names. He proposed a much simpler solution. "Look, just use Microsoft. Just call them Microsoft Plan, Microsoft File, Microsoft Word." This struck Gates as a great idea. Public opinion surveys showed that the name Microsoft was still relatively unknown, especially compared to Apple. The new naming strategy would simplify the product names and boost the company's recognition.

To promote its new software, Microsoft retained the services of a San Francisco advertising agency, Doyle Dane

Bernbach. This was a departure from the past, when consumers learned about new software from product tests published in computer magazines. If they wanted to find out more, they had to go to a distributor for a demonstration.

In a new tactic, Microsoft decided to distribute 450,000 demonstration diskettes, accompanied by a 12-page tutorial book. The free demo diskette would have all the characteristics of the program except that it would not allow users to save or print files.

The magazine *PC World*, directed by former Altair newsletter editor David Bunnell, became the means for distributing these diskettes. Bunnell was preparing a special edition on the 1,200 top software programs on the market. His original idea was to include in each magazine a diskette containing 4 or 5 programs from various software publishers. *PC World* would bill each publisher for a percentage of the diskette production costs based on the amount of room its program occupied.

The first company *PC World* approached was Microsoft. Jeff Raikes in Microsoft marketing was so taken with the idea that he decided to appropriate the whole diskette, even though the bill would be $350,000, more than 40 times the usual price for a full-page ad ($8,000).

Microsoft communications director Rowland Hanson completely agreed with Raikes. His previous job as marketing director for Neutrogena had acquainted him with this type of promotion. He likened offering the demo diskette to the common practice in the cosmetics industry of offering free samples, which he knew from experience was a highly effective way to develop a faithful clientele. Hanson saw the tremendous potential of this sales technique in the world of software. It was crucial, he believed, for customers to be able to judge a product's usefulness for themselves.

Microsoft and *PC World* originally planned to place a diskette in each copy of the special edition. But they were afraid that some diskettes might be stolen off newsstand shelves, so they decided that only the 100,000 *PC World* subscribers would receive the diskette in the special edition.

The targeting was perfect, since a study had revealed that 95 percent of the subscribers to that magazine owned IBM PCs running DOS.

Microsoft and *PC World* knew that diskettes are fragile and sensitive to electric charges, heat, and humidity. Just bending one can render it unusable. Therefore, they tested 17 different protection methods. Finally, to remove any temptation to postal employees to snatch the gift for themselves, they decided to wrap the special edition of *PC World* in a hard plastic, which also kept it from being bent. When all was said and done, *PC World* received complaints on only 1.5 percent of the diskettes distributed, whereas David Bunnell was expecting to face a replacement rate of 10 percent.

The 464-page special edition came out in November 1983. The cover title "1,200 Programs for the IBM PC" was followed by a long list of the best-sellers: VisiCalc, WordStar, dBASE, 1-2-3, SuperCalc, and so on. The bottom of the page read, "Free Microsoft Software Demo Diskette Offer."

The 100,000 subscribers found the demo diskette inside the magazine. Newsstand readers found a subscription offer for 14 issues and a free Word diskette. This was how Microsoft intended to distribute their remaining 350,000 diskettes. Jon Shirley made a point of telling the press that Microsoft was positioning itself as a friend to the consumer. Now users could try out Microsoft Word in the comfort of their own home or office.

Microsoft invested huge sums in launching Word. The *PC World* promotion was only the beginning. Microsoft also planned an advertising campaign to capitalize on the media aspect of the diskette-in-a-magazine scheme. Many newspapers had commented on that tactic, calling it a first.

WORD: PROS AND CONS

Word was officially released November 15, 1983. It required 128K of memory and sold for less than WordStar: $475 with the mouse or $375 without.

Within four weeks of the *PC World* promotion, Microsoft had delivered 18,000 copies of Word. Though this early response was satisfactory, it was far from the flood they had expected. Consumers seemed to be withholding judgment.

The benchmark tests of the software had begun to appear in October. Opinion was divided. The October 1983 issue of *Softalk* had good things to say about Word, judging it the first word processing program able to get the most from 16-bit machines like the IBM PC. The November issue of *PC World* also gave it a favorable review, saying that Microsoft Word was "comparable or superior to [WordStar] in power and innovation," and that it was "a dramatic and obvious improvement in performance compared to WordStar." The March 1984 *Sentinel Star* went one step further in its appreciation. The journalist said that although he had tested a dozen word processing programs, Microsoft Word was the first that convinced him to give up his all-time favorite, WordStar. *PC Magazine* was more subtle. The author of the February article felt that Word was an incomplete product, but that it had the necessary ingredients to beat WordStar.

In contrast, the March 1984 Seybold report, a market analysis newsletter, was harshly critical, recommending against using Word because it was too difficult. *Business Computer Systems* (August 1984) said that Word "showed impressive power but contained some bugs and was disturbingly complex." The most severe report came from a computer consultant writing in the May 1984 *Personal Computer Age*. He explained that one of his clients had bought Word because of all the glowing reports in magazines. After his purchase, however, the client called the consultant several times a day to ask about problems he encountered with Word. Not accustomed to this word processing program, the consultant decided to study it. In the article, he said he could not recommend Word in its present form and advised readers to wait six months or a year for Microsoft to fix all the bugs.

The journalists seemed to diverge on one point: Was Word easy or difficult to learn? *Softalk* and *Popular Computing* said that it was easy to learn Word quickly. The March 1984 issue of *Life Insurance Selling* heartily recommended buying Word and no other word processing program, declaring that the basics of Word were easy to learn, and that the program was powerful enough to draft complex proposals with the help of the manual.

Business Computer Systems said, however, that "users with moderate word processing requirements might be better off with a product that does less, but is easier to learn and use." The June 1984 issue of *PC World* advised beginners to stay away from Word. The irate consultant writing in *Personal Computer Age* complained that Word's commands were complex and illogical, and judged it even more difficult to learn than WordStar.

Word did not elicit general enthusiasm. It was instead a highly controversial program that did not go unnoticed. In the first year, it performed modestly in terms of sales.

WORD 1.1

Over the course of 1984, Microsoft published two intermediary versions of Word. Version 1.1 released in April, supported cards that displayed up to 43 lines on the screen, instead of the usual 25 on an IBM PC. It offered a mail-merge feature which allowed the user to do mailings using an address file created in dBASE II.

Word 1.15, delivered in October 1984, doubled the speed of certain operations. In response to the criticism about the difficulty of learning Word, Microsoft added an interactive tutorial program that guided the user step by step through the software in 30 lessons.

At Christmas, Microsoft ran another promotional campaign. Anyone buying Word before December 31, 1984, would receive a free spell-check program.

WORD 2.0

Word was just not taking off, though. It was too original and not yet reliable enough to convince consumers. In an InfoCorp survey detailing sales of word processing programs throughout the world in early 1985, Microsoft did not make the top ten. WordStar continued to dominate the market, with 24 percent of sales and 290,000 copies sold in 1984. AppleWriter was close behind, with 22 percent and 254,000 copies sold. Further down the list was the very simple pfs:Write by Software Publishing, with 8 percent of the market and 92,000 copies sold. Word failed to make the expected breakthrough.

Gates says about Word: "You really have to blame us for not making a better manual and for not making it easier to get into the power. As far as power goes, this product was fantastic, but as far as ease in getting started, we didn't do as good as we should have." Gates noted that when Word was initially released, the mouse was considered a negative factor. Microsoft discovered that this hurt their sales, so they stopped selling Word and the mouse in the same package.

Version 2.0, which came out in February 1985, supported the Hewlett-Packard LaserJet printer and included an interactive tutorial program. Although a big improvement over the first attempt, it was still not completely finished. A reviewer writing in the May 21, 1985, *Seattle Post-Intelligencer* complained that the spell-checking and word-count features—missing from Word 1.0 and now present in version 2.0—were inconvenient because they weren't integrated into the program. This meant that to correct a document, users had to stop writing, save the document to disk, and then call a separate program. The tutorial was considered a notable improvement. "Despite the scope and number of its options, Word is a breeze to learn, thanks to an extraordinary interactive tutorial on disk," said the June 17, 1985, *InfoWorld* critique. The reviewer in the June 25, 1985, issue of *PC Magazine* agreed, saying, "The Learning Word disk tutorial is one of the best we've seen. The tutorial also makes good use of graphics to heighten and maintain user interest."

A minor controversy broke out over a system message found by some programmers when they explored the code for Word. They said it warned them of an internal security violation and then threatened to trash the disk program. After displaying the message, Word generated a series of terrible sounds from the disk drive. Fortunately, the threat of trashing the disk was not carried out. Nevertheless, Jeff Raikes had to issue a statement explaining that the company had not been aware of the activities of one apparently overzealous programmer.

Although Word had not yet conquered the market, the program was attracting a base of users ready to defend it as their favorite product. The *Seattle Post-Intelligencer* kept the trend going. After publishing the lukewarm article about Word, the editor-in-chief received voluminous mail from Word fans who came to its defense.

WORDPERFECT TAKES FIRST PLACE

Once again, however, Microsoft was beat out by another software publisher, WordPerfect. The Utah company avoided showy promotional campaigns. Their supreme weapon was service, service, service. Microsoft was at a loss to confront this competitor who attacked the market so differently.

The WordPerfect company was founded in 1979 by Bruce Bastian, who was a student at the time, and Alan Ashton, his computer science professor. They first wrote their word processing program for the Data General minicomputer and then adapted it to the IBM PC. With virtually no promotion budget, Bastian and Ashton enlisted students to distribute it. Bastian and Ashton performed all the tasks of running the company, even mailing the diskettes to the clients themselves. Above all, they established a reputation for incomparable service. They followed up on every call to the company until the caller was completely satisfied. The bare-bones advertisements they placed in computer magazines featured a photocopy of a check showing that they were paying large amounts to the phone company to assure free telephone support to customers. In the process of marketing their product, the two friends built the philosophy that would become the cornerstone of their company.

Initially, the growing success of the program went virtually unnoticed. Then WordPerfect made the hit parade of the 30 best-sellers of Softsel, a major software distributor, and sales continued to climb. WordPerfect finally arrived at the number two slot, just behind the seemingly immovable Lotus 1-2-3. InfoCorp listed the top word processing programs for 1986 as follows: 1. WordPerfect (31 percent); 2. WordStar (16 percent); 3. IBM VisiOn (13 percent); 4. pfs:Write (12 percent) and Multimate (12 percent); 5. Word (11 percent). In October 1987, WordPerfect took the number one spot on the Softsel list.

Unlike Word with its flashy media-supported entry into the marketplace, WordPerfect—the word processing program that managed to overtake WordStar—methodically built a reputation through word-of-mouth advertising and the company's strong service policy. To this day personal computing continues to produce such surprises.

VIVE LA FRANCE

Once again, the French subsidiary of Microsoft succeeded in mass marketing a product from the home office that had not become a leader in the United States.

Since Word 1.0 had not met with great success in the United States, the product arrived in France in the fall of 1984 with a mixed reputation. WordStar was omnipresent in France, and its primary competitor was Textor, a French product developed by Jean-Pierre Lorthiois, president of the Talor company. IBM was pushing its own product, the PC version of VisiOn.

Bernard Vergnes and Michel Lacombe devised a completely original marketing strategy. To get distributors to sell Word, Microsoft France decided to train them en masse: "We believed that in our field, which involves selling technical products, we had to acquire a 'market share' of our partners' minds," Lacombe explains.

The subsidiary inaugurated a plan: a Tour de France to retailers. Lacombe and three colleagues piled into a Renault 505 station wagon with several PCs and boxes of documentation. They drove at night and demonstrated Word's capabilities during the day. They contacted every French software distributor, regardless of size. To encourage them to attend the demonstrations, the invitation stated that distributors would receive a free program at the end of the training. The operation was costly in terms of both money and energy, but it introduced Word and the name Microsoft to the far reaches of France.

The second line of attack was to link Word closely with the new laser printing technology. Michel Lacombe came into contact with Hewlett-Packard early in the February 1985 PC Forum. The American giant was preparing to introduce its LaserJet, so it made sure that all retailers exhibiting at that conference had a LaserJet in their booths. Microsoft France furnished copies of Word to all retailers and trained the demonstrators how to use it with the laser printer. The operation was immensely successful.

The third strategy was to convince printer manufacturers to help promote Word. Lacombe explains what they did: "When a client would go to a retailer and ask to see how Word worked with a printer, in 95 percent of the cases, the distributor would not be able to answer the question. We visited all the printer manufacturers and sold them on the idea of a Microsoft Word binder with several pages of printing samples." Thousands of retailers received these catalogs, which were paid for by the printer manufacturers.

One morning, Bernard Vergnes arrived at the office very upbeat and called his colleagues together. "I think we're winning!" The previous day, during a reception, he had run into Thierry Lorthiois, the Textor developer, who was in a bad mood because he was beginning to notice the seductive effect that Word was having on Textor customers.

WORD 3.0

Although the early versions of Word were not entirely satisfactory, Word 3.0, released in April 1986, was closer to the refinement expected by the U.S. market. One of its major advantages was a highly sophisticated online tutorial that enabled a user to learn the program's functions without using the manual. This time, the problem of learning Word was resolved brilliantly. The program was so well received that in 1986 it became Microsoft's best-seller and the fifth-best-selling software program in the United States.

During a trip to the United States, Michel Lacombe discovered that the Word 3.0 destined for the French market was not of the same high quality as the American version. The French version did not include the tutorial. Angered by this news, Lacombe visited Bill Gates immediately and explained, "We have been bending over backwards to promote Word and we can't go any farther if you don't help!" Lacombe's complaints were heard, and the French adaptation was redone so that it was at the same level as the American original. "We obtained a product far superior to our competitors'. I was so convinced that we decided to raise the price," Lacombe says.

Two years of promotions proved fruitful. The success of Word 3.0 in France was phenomenal: In 1987, it became the most widely sold program in France. According to Intelligent Electronics, sales rose to 28,700 copies compared to 10,300 for IBM VisiOn, 7,000 for Textor, 3,800 for WordPerfect, and 3,300 for WordStar.

MICROSOFT IS NUMBER TWO

In early 1989, Dataquest estimated that in the previous 12 months, 937,000 copies of WordPerfect had been sold, compared to 650,000 copies of Microsoft Word. Even if

Microsoft's performance was more than respectable, the gap between it and its primary competitor seemed difficult to close. Despite its unrivaled success in the European spreadsheet and word-processing markets, Microsoft could not conquer first place in America. That opportunity would come on the Macintosh.

WORD FOR THE MAC: GETTING IT RIGHT

For the first few years after the Macintosh was released, Apple included its MacWrite word processing program with each machine. At first, users were very enthusiastic about it, but they soon ran up against the limitations of the program: MacWrite could not handle documents over eight pages long, such as a lengthy report, books, or film scripts.

At the first all-Macintosh exhibition (*MacWorld* Expo), Microsoft announced the first version of Word for the Mac. MacWrite users were excited because the program, which Microsoft said would soon be available, could process long documents. But fall arrived and there was still no Word.

The Microsoft Word developers could not meet their initial deadlines. The version finalized in September 1984 was thought to be too slow, and subsequent revisions introduced bugs that further delayed the release by four months.

In fact, there was no practical need to rush. Since Apple was offering a free word processing program with the Macintosh, developers were discouraged from targeting that market niche. In November 1984, there were 200 applications available for the Macintosh. Except for Microsoft Word for the Macintosh, however, there were no other word processing programs in store.

In the meantime, Apple released a new version of MacWrite that could handle documents up to about 50 pages long. The first version submitted for evaluation by journalists was full of annoying problems. Error messages occasionally appeared on the screen and frightened verbose writers. These messages sometimes warned that any text that had not been saved would be lost, because the only way out was to turn off the machine and then reboot. Sometimes, paragraphs disappeared without warning. While waiting for a more reliable product, writers took out their old copies of the original MacWrite and used it, even with its file-size limitations.

In December, Microsoft released a beta version of Word to a number of businesses for intensive testing. Although it was only a preliminary version, the product carried the name Macintosh Word Version 1.0. More than 100 companies tested the program. Then some began distributing pirated copies of the program. As with BASIC for the Altair, some users just could not wait any longer for a powerful word processing program. The situation was all the more problematic because the version had a major bug: The last line of text in a document was often erased. Microsoft also had to grapple with the problem of pirating. And since it was not perfect, the product was greeted with negative publicity. One morning, Microsoft got a phone call from a distributor in Michigan: Students from a nearby college wanting to buy a Mac 512K had come to the store with a pirated copy of Word Mac to see how it would work on that machine!

Word for the Macintosh was finally released in January 1985, much to the delight of many impatient Macintosh users. MacWrite users were pleasantly surprised. They could use Word to read MacWrite documents without changing formats.

The April 22, 1985, issue of *InfoWorld* gave Word for the Macintosh high marks, but had some reservations about its stability. Word would satisfy the need for more power, features, and increased document size, but the gain in muscle was not without drawbacks. Although the magazine generally liked Word for the Macintosh, it found that the first release (version 1.00) had a surprising number of bugs and lacked some key features.

Another evaluation, published in the April 30, 1985, issue of *PC Magazine,* had few kind words for this MacWrite competitor. Writer Kaare Christian criticized the Macintosh version for being too different from the PC version. "Word on the Macintosh lacks many features that contributed to the PC version's success. The Macintosh version lacks style sheets and lacks a spelling checker. I wouldn't recommend mixing PCs and Macs in one environment while expecting everybody to be able to use Word fluently on both machines. Their layouts are too different. I am an experienced PC Word user, and I was surprised at how long it took me to adapt to Macintosh Word." Christian concluded that Word for the Macintosh offered few improvements over MacWrite, and since the latter was free, advised against buying the new product.

But Word received positive reports in other publications, such as the March 1985 *MACazine*. "It's a joy to write a review of an excellent program, although it is difficult not to sound like an ad for Word. I have used Macintosh Word daily for more than six months, and even in its rough pre-release versions, its advantages over MacWrite were obvious. Now that it is a polished product, it is an absolute pleasure to use."

In June 1985, Microsoft published a revised version of Word which was supposed to be free of the bugs that users had found.

WORD 3.0 FOR THE MAC

On October 27, 1986, Microsoft announced Word 3.0 for the Macintosh. (Microsoft skipped version 2.0.) This time, major improvements were evident. Standing on the stage of the Guggenheim Museum in New York, Bill Gates introduced his new "document processor." He had carefully chosen the term to clearly differentiate his product from "word processors" such as MacWrite. Habits are hard to break, however, and when Gates was describing the advantages of Word, he could not avoid calling it "the fastest word processor ever on a personal computer."

Among the distinguishing characteristics of this version of Word for the Mac was its ability to display two pages in the print preview format. Word 3.0 also supported PostScript, the language used by the Apple LaserWriter. Word 3.0 also included style sheets and a spelling checker.

Microsoft began shipping Word 3.0 on January 29, 1987. In the meantime, the Macintosh had changed a great deal. The Mac Plus had earned Macintosh more acceptance as a tool for business. As a result, the price of the "document processor" was readjusted to conform with Word for the PC: It doubled, from $195 to $395.

Aldus PageMaker, a desktop publishing program for the Macintosh that had appeared two years earlier, enabled users to create professional-quality printed documents when linked with a LaserWriter. In the April 1987 issue of *Personal Computing*, however, Jack Bell said that Word easily provided the sophisticated functions needed for a business report and many other projects, so PageMaker was no longer necessary.

Once again, though, computer magazines reported certain bugs. In 1988, Stewart Alsop dedicated a column in *Info World* to this subject, saying he was surprised that Word had survived these bug rumors so well. At that time, Word for the Mac was selling 20,000 copies a month.

Meanwhile, other software companies were working to port their word processing programs to the Macintosh as well. When WordPerfect released its Macintosh version in 1988, however, it was too late. That year, according to Dataquest, Microsoft Word for the Mac sold 250,000 copies and became the number-three-selling word processor for all categories combined, behind the PC versions of WordPerfect (937,000 copies sold) and Microsoft Word (650,000).

In March 1989, Microsoft published version 4 of Word for the Macintosh. Word had become so popular that 100,000 users purchased the new version immediately upon release. By the end of 1990, Microsoft Word had made *MacWorld's* monthly top ten list of best-sellers 69 times, and was comfortably lodged in first place.

PART 5

MICROSOFT EXCELS ON THE MACINTOSH

"A lot of what you see is a reflection of Bill himself.
He has this ability to have the big picture,
yet also pay great attention to detail."

Jeff Raikoo, Microsoft employee since 1981

13

The Macintosh: A Friendlier Computer

The Apple II and the IBM PC greatly helped change computers' image as intimidating and confusing. VisiCalc and Lotus 1-2-3 showed that a computer could offer vast practical benefits to the average business person. WordStar and Microsoft Word made computers more approachable as the means of efficiently producing reports, letters, and other important documents. However, an enormous chasm still separated the average person from the high-tech realm of computers.

The mid-1980s saw a drastic change in the design and packaging of computer hardware. A compact beige box began to appear in offices, universities, and homes, revolutionizing the way people worked with computers. It was called the Macintosh.

The Apple Macintosh computer was unlike the PC, the Apple II, or any other earlier micro, mini, or mainframe computer. A typical new user could learn the MacWrite word processing software in a matter of minutes. Whereas users of MS-DOS, dBASE II, and WordStar had to type obscure commands, with the Macintosh mouse, users could point to small pictures (icons) that clearly depicted the function they wanted. For example, to delete a file, the user pointed to the file icon and dragged it to an icon of a trash can.

Bill Gates and Apple cofounder Steve Jobs shared a common vision for computers that were more user-friendly and more practical in improving people's daily lives. The key, they believed, was the graphical user interface. PCs running MS-DOS at that time had a text interface, meaning that they communicated with the user by means of letters, numbers, and punctuation marks. The Apple Macintosh's graphical user interface, in contrast, displayed pictures on the screen. All data were drawn dot by dot on the screen. The basic philosophy behind this interface was the assumption that it is much easier to learn from pictures than from words. People of many different nationalities could more readily recognize a picture of a trash can and understand its function than they could the English word *erase*, for example.

The Macintosh was the first computer with a graphical user interface to meet with overwhelming success in the media and in the marketplace.

THE ORIGINS OF GRAPHICAL USER INTERFACES

In the early 1960s, George Evans and Ivan Sutherland, working on mainframe computers, conducted valuable research into the use of computer graphics. In his dissertation, Sutherland described the basis for a system he called Sketchpad. He argued that if a computer could display images rather than text, it would be a big step forward in computer usability.

A few years later, Douglas Engelbart of the Stanford Research Institute (SRI) developed Sutherland's work and came up with the idea of windows. In "classical" computer science, one program took up the entire screen. With the interface defined by Engelbart, several documents could be displayed on the screen at the same time, each appearing in a separate window. The user could use a mouse (invented by

Engelbart) to point to the document he or she wanted to work on. When the user pushed this small object along a flat surface, a pointer moved on the screen. The NLS computer developed at SRI was the first computer to use the mouse as a tool for pointing to information.

THE STARS OF XEROX PARC

In the early 1970s, Xerox opened a research center in Palo Alto, California, near Stanford University. The Palo Alto Research Center became known simply as Xerox PARC.

Xerox wanted PARC to be a place where creativity flourished freely, so engineers had great latitude to let their imaginations run wild, particularly in developing new approaches to computers. This invitation to discover new technologies attracted some very gifted minds to the PARC, including Charles Simonyi, Alan Kay, David Liddle, and Larry Tesler.

These researchers, continuing the work of Evans, Sutherland, and Engelbart, created Smalltalk, a new language that differed from others at that time because it allowed several windows to be superimposed on the screen. The windows could then be selected and moved with a mouse. Each program in a window ran concurrently with the others. When the mouse pointed to one of the windows, that window would be displayed on top of the others and the corresponding program could receive data.

The first version of Smalltalk was tested on the Alto, a research prototype computer by Xerox. The Alto operating system worked in bit-map mode, which meant that it continually redrew the screen dot by dot. Certain areas on the screen would react when the pointer was moved onto them. This is how menus were displayed on the screen. The Alto was undeniably easier to use than any conventional computer. To choose a command, the user took the mouse, pointed to the window of choice, and highlighted an option on the menu.

In 1981, the work at Xerox PARC led to the creation of the Star, which was even more sophisticated. The Star introduced another important concept: icons. Whereas most computers required the user to type commands at the keyboard, the Star displayed small pictures symbolizing objects and actions. The user manipulated these to perform the desired task. To ascertain the current time, for example, a user simply moved the pointer to the clock icon. Or, if the user wanted to erase a file, he or she used the mouse to drag it over to the trashcan icon.

At Xerox PARC, the creators of icons developed some of the most revolutionary concepts in computers, giving the machines a new look. Xerox was clearly paving the way for the computers of the late 20th century. The company, however, failed to capitalize on its discoveries and take the necessary steps to produce a microcomputer for the public.

When Xerox decided to market the Alto in 1977, it was aimed at a select clientele: The price was $20,000 to $30,000. Some Altos were installed in the White House, the Senate, and the House of Representatives. Three and a half years went by before the release of the Star workstation, which was geared for wider distribution. Its price of $16,595, however, once again made it a rare jewel for only a privileged few.

One by one, the high-profile programmers left Xerox PARC to build elsewhere what they had developed in Palo Alto. Throughout the 1980s, Apple, Microsoft, Atari, and Digital Research gladly appropriated discoveries from Xerox PARC.[1]

Many important figures in the personal computer world came from Xerox PARC. Alan Kay, considered the creator of windows and pull-down menus, left Xerox PARC for Atari and later went to work for Apple.

Larry Tesler brought his PARC knowledge to Apple in 1980, where he designed the Lisa computer. He was joined by Tom Malloy, who wrote the Lisa word processing program. And Jef Raskin, who attended many PARC conferences, later initiated the Apple Macintosh project.

Bob Metcalfe created the Ethernet standard that allows several networked computers to exchange data. In 1979, he

---

[1]It wasn't until 1989 that Xerox announced that its discoveries had been patented in 1981.

founded 3Com to market the cards that allowed the creation of PC networks.

John Warnock founded Adobe Systems in 1982. He revolutionized the publishing world with an important new concept called desktop publishing. Adobe's PostScript language became the standard behind-the-scenes language used to communicate with laser printers.

Robert Carr, who had worked on the Xerox Star and Smalltalk, created Framework, a popular software program in the mid-1980s that was published by Ashton-Tate.

Dave Liddle went to work for IBM, where he helped design the Office Vision system introduced in June 1989.

JOBS DISCOVERS THE GRAPHICAL USER INTERFACE

In December 1979, Steve Jobs visited Xerox PARC and was astounded by what he saw. When he realized the extraordinary range of visual effects that could be created with Smalltalk, he asked, "Why aren't you doing anything with this? This is the greatest thing! This is revolutionary!"

Steve Jobs saw what Xerox could not: the social and commercial implications of the PARC discoveries. He ran up against the inertia of the Xerox management, which simply did not realize the treasures it had in its laboratories.

Jobs returned from Xerox PARC convinced that he had just seen the computer of the future. One of the projects under way at Apple was the Lisa. Jobs reoriented the design of the computer to make it a graphical machine which integrated the basic concepts of Smalltalk.[2]

Seven months after his visit to Xerox PARC, Jobs hired Larry Tesler, the programmer who had demonstrated Smalltalk for him, and put him in charge of applying the characteristics invented at the PARC to the Lisa. Bill Atkinson

---

[2] In the book *Programmers at Work,* by Susan Lammers, Jef Raskin contradicts this version. He says it was he who initiated changing the Lisa computer into a graphical machine and that Jobs was against it at first, and against the Macintosh, but later changed his mind.

helped write the graphical user interface of the new computer. Jobs was then removed from responsibility for the Lisa project, which was assigned to a former Hewlett-Packard engineer, John Couch.

Jobs then took charge of another experimental project: the Macintosh. He put all his effort into developing a machine that he felt would change the way millions of people worked. He gave free rein to his perfectionist mind and tried to get the most from those who worked under his strict orders.

THE DEVELOPMENT OF THE MACINTOSH

A few months later, QuickDraw, the software that drew the Mac's graphical interface (of icons, menus, and windows), was operational.

In March 1981, Jobs was invited to the Ben Rosen Conference in Michigan, where he spoke about his vision of the future of computers and hinted that his Cupertino firm was moving in the direction set by Xerox PARC. Bill Gates attended that meeting and was electrified by the Apple founder's speech. It matched his own convictions about software presentation. After the conference, the two men talked fervently about the merits of graphical user interfaces and discovered that they were in complete agreement. While Jobs had hired Larry Tesler away from the PARC, Gates had just recruited Charles Simonyi. Microsoft had already begun to research how to design software for the Xerox Star. At the end of their conversation, Jobs encouraged Gates to come see what was shaping up in Cupertino.

At the end of the summer, Gates met with Jobs and Jef Raskin, head of the Macintosh project.[3] Jobs and Raskin wanted to use the Motorola 68000 microprocessor, a very advanced 32-bit chip. This was not too much power for a computer whose screen had to be continually redrawn. Gates immediately grasped the potential impact of the Macintosh and was convinced that he needed to invest in

---

[3]According to Gates, the Macintosh was really Raskin's project.

that machine. Jobs was conscious of one thing: The best-looking computer in the world would only be as good as the range of software that could run on it. The impact of VisiCalc on sales of the Apple II testified to this truth. Encouraged by the way he and Gates saw eye to eye, Jobs asked him to help launch the Macintosh by beginning immediately to develop applications for the new computer.

Upon his return to Seattle, Gates put Charles Simonyi in charge of creating the necessary tools for writing Mac software. Simonyi met with Robert Bellevue, the technical director of the Macintosh division, and Andy Hertzfeld, the designer of the Macintosh logic architecture. The three men exchanged ideas at length on how a standard software interface should be designed and what tools Apple should furnish to help in programming applications.

Simonyi wrote a two-page action plan for what he called the Apple IV. From that time on, Microsoft programmers worked closely with their counterparts at Apple. They were involved in defining certain aspects of the Macintosh interface such as the dialogue boxes and the horizontal scroll bars in the windows. Simonyi's team helped with debugging and suggested additional features.

Gates and Jobs signed a contract specifying that Microsoft Multiplan, Chart, and File would be shipped with the Macintosh. The contract stated that Microsoft would not publish software with a graphical user interface until at least one year after the first delivery of the Macintosh. Gates added a clause indicating that that date could not be later than December 1983.

MULTIPLAN FOR THE MAC

Since Simonyi had worked on similar projects at Xerox PARC, he was on familiar turf. When he originally designed PC Multiplan and PC Word, he envisioned that one day, those programs would be converted to run under a graphical user interface. This vision was reinforced by the news that Apple was already developing a graphical interface machine.

He therefore made sure that Multiplan and Word could be easily adapted to a graphical environment at a later time.

The Macintosh prototype arrived at Microsoft in the summer of 1982. Since Multiplan had been originally written so that it could be easily adapted to all kinds of different computers, it was the first program adapted to the new machine. The Multiplan code, written in C language, had been translated into an intermediary code called p-code, which was then entered into an interpreter that adapted it to a given operating system such as CP/M, MS-DOS, or AppleDOS. Neil Konzen was assigned to the Macintosh project to write the interpreter for converting p-code into Macintosh machine language.

Simonyi had done a good job. Though Multiplan and Word had been written to run with a textual interface on the PC, they included many features that were easy to adapt to a graphical interface. The submenus displayed by these programs worked like dialogue boxes. Adapting these programs was therefore surprisingly easy: Neil Konzen's interpreter mechanically translated the p-code with few problems.

According to Simonyi, translating Microsoft Word PC into the Mac version took only a few days. Once translated, however, it caused great problems for the Microsoft developers because the graphical operating system of the Macintosh worked very differently from the PC's operating system.

THE APPLE LISA

In Cupertino, the team working on the Lisa computer was making faster progress than the Macintosh team headed by Steve Jobs. Jobs had bet $5,000 that he would be the first to have a finished product, but had to pay up to his colleague John Couch.

The Lisa, introduced in the press in January 1983, represented the first time the Xerox Star and Smalltalk discoveries had been integrated into a computer for the general public. During the Lisa introduction, Steve Jobs spoke in lofty terms, calling that day the beginning of the software revolution.

In May 1983, a new president was chosen to lead Apple. John Sculley arrived in California preceded by his reputation as head of PepsiCo. By associating the image of Pepsi with a youthful lifestyle, "the Pepsi Generation," Sculley had succeeded in making competitor Coca-Cola's image look old. Jobs looked forward to the possibility of repeating this tactic in the Apple-IBM rivalry.

Apple, however, suffered its second failure with its first graphical computer. (The first failure was the Apple III, which was released in 1980 and was then rejected by the market for insufficient reliability.) Despite its technological innovations, the Lisa was not selling. Few managers were willing to shell out $10,000 for this dream machine. Jobs had wanted to sell it for two to four times less, but management had decided otherwise. Apple shipped as many Lisa computers in the month of July 1983—the first month it was officially marketed—as Xerox did Stars in 19 months, but this was small consolation. Apple had hoped to sell 50,000 Lisas in the first year, but only sold around 20,000.

Sales of the Apple II enabled the firm to stay afloat in 1983: More than 100,000 of these classics sold in one month. Apple did $1 billion in business, thanks primarily to the original model, which Steve Wozniak continued to improve.

FRICTION REGARDING MACBASIC

In the meantime, relations between Apple and Microsoft grew strained. According to an account in the *Wall Street Journal* (September 25, 1987), the issue of Apple's MacBASIC created a rift between the two firms. In 1985, shortly after becoming chairman, John Sculley wanted Apple to develop MacBASIC. He hoped this computer language would have the same igniting effect on the sluggish Mac market that Microsoft's BASIC had had on the Apple II market. Bill Gates, however, was strongly opposed to this plan, and threatened to revoke Apple's license to the BASIC for the Apple II, "unless Mr. Sculley killed MacBASIC and signed over to Microsoft the rights to the MacBASIC name." Sculley made the painful decision to comply. With morale already low at Apple, this move led several key software engineers to resign in disgust. "He insisted that Apple withdraw what was an exceptional product," recalls Bill Atkinson, an Apple software engineer. "He held the gun to our head."

Apple was quick to respond in kind to Gates's coup. A few months later, Jobs told Gates that he thought it unwise to ship programs like Multiplan, Chart, and File with the Mac. Gates was persuaded, and that contract was voided. Gates later discovered that Jobs had decided to bundle two Apple programs, MacPaint and MacWrite, with the Macintosh. He was furious.

LAUNCHING THE MACINTOSH

The Macintosh was introduced on January 24, 1984.

In the space of two years, IBM had captured 30 percent of the personal computer market and had allowed Apple only 21 percent, but Steve Jobs was convinced that the Mac would change Apple's market share. After a memorable speech in which he spoke of his fear of seeing Big Blue rule the micro-computer market alone and impose the methods it had used to conquer the mainframe computer market, Jobs unveiled the Mac. "I would like to let the Macintosh speak for itself."

A voice spoke from the small beige box: "Hello, I am Macintosh. . . . I'd like to share with you a maxim I thought of the first time I met an IBM mainframe: Never trust a computer you can't lift!"[4] The public then got a glimpse of the machine's operating system: The screen simulated a desktop with files and documents on it. Clicking with the mouse on a document "opened" the document and made it appear in a window.

The Macintosh had two standard software programs: MacWrite (for word processing) and MacPaint (a drawing program). MacPaint, written by Bill Atkinson, was very easy to use. With the mouse, the user could select basic shapes

---

[4]Jeffrey S. Young, *Steve Jobs: The Journey Is the Reward* (Glenview, Ill.: Scott, Foresman, 1988), p. 335.

such as a rectangle or a circle and stretch them to the desired size. To fill in the shapes, the user could choose from a wide variety of patterns.

MacWrite, written by Randy Wigginton, was also impressive for its simplicity and user-friendliness.[5] Clicking and holding down the mouse highlighted text, which could then be cut from the document and pasted elsewhere in chunks of any size. Bold type and italics were visible on the screen, which looked like a white page. Compared to WordStar for the IBM PC, MacWrite clearly represented a new generation of software.

The Macintosh was built around a 32-bit chip, the Motorola 68000, and had 128K of memory. At just under $2,500, it was much more affordable than the Lisa.

Bill Gates was an ardent fan of the Macintosh. At the time of the Macintosh announcement, he was bold enough to predict that in 1984, half of Microsoft's revenues from applications would come from programs written for the Mac.

MacBASIC and Multiplan for the Macintosh were released at the same time as the new computer. This was when the media learned that Microsoft had been working with Apple for two years on developing software for the Mac.

Gates predicted that Microsoft would soon release other software for the Macintosh, including Microsoft Chart, File, and Word. Microsoft intended to sell its Macintosh software at a relatively low price: $200 maximum. In contrast, PC software usually cost around $400.

Steve Jobs allocated an advertising budget of $15 million to launch the Macintosh. Thanks to a well-run marketing campaign, the Macintosh quickly became known throughout the world as a revolutionary computer that broke with the past. It took off immediately: 70,000 were sold in the first 100 days and 250,000 by the end of the year.

---

[5]Wigginton, one of the very first Apple employees, collaborated with Gates on writing BASIC for the Apple II. Later he developed the spreadsheet Full Impact, marketed by Ashton-Tate in 1989.

14

The World's Greatest Spreadsheet

In September 1983, Microsoft executives faced up to the facts: Lotus 1-2-3 was firmly entrenched in first place, with sales so high that it was unrealistic to think that Microsoft could catch up in the near future, even with an improved version of Multiplan, since it was designed in a completely different vein from 1-2-3.

Gates decided to try something new for Microsoft and organized a three-day off-site retreat.

A small, carefully selected group met at the Red Lion Inn in Seattle: Charles Simonyi; Jeff Raikes and his assistant Jabe Blumenthal from marketing; and Jeff Harbers, Bob Mathews, and Doug Klunder were among the programmers present. Gates told them that they were there to brainstorm about how to make "the world's fastest spreadsheet."

IDEAS FOR ODYSSEY

The question elicited a flood of new ideas. Everyone had his own idea about how Odyssey—the code name for the product—should function. Should they keep some aspects of Multiplan or stick as closely as possible to 1-2-3? Gates thought that recalculating speed should be a top priority. Jeff Raikes thought they should offer the capability of creating custom formulas that could be used within a spreadsheet. Someone raised the possibility of developing the spreadsheet in a graphical interface such as Macintosh or Windows, but not everyone favored that idea. The programmers' ideas were compared to the results from surveys of Multiplan and 1-2-3 users.

The group discussed a broad range of questions. Some programmers thought they should adopt the Lotus 1-2-3 (A1, B1, etc.) mode of numbering cells rather than the L1C1, L1C2 system used in Multiplan. Gates disagreed. He personally hated the way VisiCalc and Lotus worked. Since the public preferred the Lotus system, however, he finally conceded that the choice of modes should be left up to the user.

Lotus 1-2-3 had popularized the concept of "macros." Instead of typing a series of strokes on the keyboard, the user could execute a small program made up of the initials of the keys in question. Only relatively advanced users could write macros in Lotus 1-2-3. Gates thought that BASIC should be part of the new spreadsheet, but Doug Klunder felt that the macro language should be similar to the commands in the Odyssey menus. Odyssey would also include a new feature: Macros would be automatically recorded when the user typed on the keyboard.

For three days straight, the small group haggled over which features should be included in the new product. Each ardently defended his point of view and rained insults down on the others. Sometimes they could not hear themselves speak amid the shouting. Eventually, however, they put the specifications of the ideal spreadsheet on paper, and defined the major concepts.

One of the major concepts was "intelligent recalculation." When the user changed a value in VisiCalc, Multiplan, or 1-2-3, those programs would recalculate the entire spreadsheet. Odyssey would recalculate only the cells directly affected by the update. This simple improvement would make the recalculating speed far faster than that of 1-2-3.

The Lotus spreadsheet required a user to point to each row by number, one by one, in order to graph the data. Odyssey would automatically draw a graph as the spreadsheet itself would deduce the coordinates to be represented.

Like Multiplan, Odyssey would allow linking between several spreadsheets. Ideally, however, it would be able to display them simultaneously. Once again the idea of developing for the Macintosh was raised and then dismissed.

At the end of the meeting, Doug Klunder offered to write a summary of everything that had been said in those three days. Two weeks later, he presented a 20-page report on all the areas of agreement. Now they just needed to iron out the details of what would later become Excel.

WHERE TO BEGIN

Usually, Charles Simonyi and a few other developers wrote the design rules for a software product. For Excel, Bill Gates thought it wise to give that responsibility to a marketing person, who by definition would be closer to the end-users and their concerns. (Later, Microsoft created the position of program manager, the person responsible for writing the software specifications.)

Jabe Blumenthal seemed cut out for that job. Hired by Microsoft in 1982, he had worked on marketing Multiplan. To position that spreadsheet amid its competitors, he had studied the details of VisiCalc, SuperCalc, and 1-2-3, which he knew best of all. Blumenthal was put in charge of writing the design rules for what would become Excel. He was assisted by Doug Klunder, the head programmer for the spreadsheet.

It was finally decided that Excel would be developed in text mode on the IBM PC. Its interface would be very similar to Multiplan's, although many characteristics of 1-2-3 would also be incorporated, such as business graphics (bar charts, pie charts, etc.), a database, and macros. At the same time,

Blumenthal and Klunder discovered Framework, a new program by Ashton-Tate. It held amazing treasures: Robert Carr, its designer, had succeeded in defining an interface like Smalltalk's within the text mode of the PC screen. Jabe and Doug studied Framework for some time and were very impressed with its programming language, called Fred. They decided to use it as a model in designing the macro language for Excel.

When all was said and done, very few revolutionary characteristics were incorporated into Excel. It took most of the strong points of other spreadsheets and integrated concepts that were popular at the time, such as intelligent recalculation. Together, however, all the options selected for Odyssey/Excel produced a very ambitious spreadsheet.

Doug Klunder plunged into programming the spreadsheet. Thrilled with the scope of this project, he spent most of his days at Microsoft writing the program, particularly the internal routines. He had help from Jeff Harbers and Mark O'Brien, who worked on the user interface.

The development of Odyssey/Excel was supposed to take six months. By January 1984, the spreadsheet portion was practically finished, but developing the graphics and the links between spreadsheets still remained. Doug Klunder said the initial deadline would be difficult to meet and told Gates it would be better to delay the release of Odyssey until fall so that they could polish it.

A NEW DIRECTION: EXCEL FOR THE MAC

In late February 1984, shortly after the Macintosh's debut, Bill Gates learned that Lotus was devising a Macintosh product called Jazz.

Integrated programs were the latest development in software. Several publishers thought they should carry the idea of Lotus 1-2-3 further and offer a broad range of functions in one product. In the PC world, Ashton-Tate had released Framework and Lotus had introduced Symphony. Jazz was another all-in-one product. It combined five functions: a spreadsheet, a database, graphics, word processing, and communications.

This news precipitated a change in direction that had been anticipated for several months. Microsoft's marketing staff concluded that it was impossible to beat 1-2-3 on the PC, since American business was adopting that program as a standard. That spreadsheet alone brought in more revenue to Lotus than Microsoft earned from its entire line of products. One solution would be to fight the battle on another front: Macintosh.

In Gates's eyes, the choice of the Mac platform was justified for several reasons. First of all, he was convinced that the future belonged to graphical user interfaces. Although Gates toyed with the possibility of developing Excel under Microsoft's graphical user interface for the PC, Microsoft Windows, he realized that this environment was not yet mature enough to handle such a powerful program. If they developed Excel for the Macintosh first, the experience they gained would pay off later when they developed graphics applications on the PC. Second, Gates learned that Apple was about to release the Macintosh 512K, which would be powerful enough to support a spreadsheet like Excel.

The decision to port Excel to the Mac was made March 5, 1984, by Bill Gates, Jabe Blumenthal, and a few other programmers. Doug Klunder was not involved in that decision, for reasons which are still unclear. When he learned of the new direction for the project, he took it badly.

Klunder was informed about the change in the orientation of Excel by chance, through a memo from a technical writer. Klunder had to go see Gates to find out what was going on. Gates explained to him that for a few weeks, he had been thinking of porting Excel to the Macintosh and that he had discussed this with several marketing people. Klunder did not understand why Gates had not informed his key developer on this project and expressed his bitterness at having spent six months working day and night on a product, only to see it canceled. "Bill just screwed up from a human management point of view. I was killing myself on Excel. Basically, I *was* Excel."

Klunder also felt that Gates had made an unwise decision. He thought Excel had a good chance of beating 1-2-3, which was still a young program. He considered resigning on the spot but instead informed Gates that he would continue working on Excel for nine months, and would then leave Microsoft.

Jabe Blumenthal went to work redefining the Excel specifications for the Macintosh. He had the help of Mike Slade, who was named Excel product manager for marketing. They incorporated certain proven ideas from Multiplan Mac into Excel, in particular, a display in which spreadsheet lines and columns were clearly marked on the screen by a grid of dotted lines.

A short time later, Blumenthal and Slade attended a trade show where Mitch Kapor, president of Lotus, proudly displayed Jazz to the public. The two Microsoft employees stood in front of the Lotus booth and began scribbling notes about everything they saw: menus, commands, screen presentation, etc. The Lotus demonstrators did not appreciate Slade and Blumenthal's presence and tried to get them to leave. However, Mitch Kapor, a developer at heart, was very magnanimous. Blumenthal and Slade explained that they liked what they saw and wanted to know more. Kapor agreed to answer the questions of his competitors, who took full advantage of this opportunity. "How do you link the spreadsheet window to the graph? How do you handle the scrolling on a spreadsheet?" The Lotus president had no idea that Microsoft was writing a rival program on the Macintosh, so he did not hesitate to reveal a few company secrets. The two Microsoft employees feverishly scribbled down all this valuable information. Back in Washington, Blumenthal used some of the good ideas from Jazz in Excel.

Doug Klunder went back to work and continued adapting Excel for the Macintosh. In December 1984, Mac Excel was almost at the same stage as the PC version had been nine months earlier. Some new concepts were added to the spreadsheet, such as the ability to zoom in on a particular window so it filled the whole screen. Excel also included the ability to design a spreadsheet layout, which allowed users to produce professional-quality reports, the first time a spreadsheet offered that capability.

One of the most popular features of the program was added almost by accident. The printer for the Excel programmers was in a separate room, some distance from where they worked. The developer writing the printer code grew tired of running back and forth to the printers every time he tested what he had written, so he decided to write a small program that would let him see on the screen exactly what would be printed. This print preview feature turned out to be so helpful that he showed it to Jabe Blumenthal, suggesting they add it to the program. Blumenthal was skeptical at first, but the programmer insisted, saying that the feature had saved him lots of time. Jabe consented and included it in the product. Users liked this feature so much that it was soon found in many different kinds of programs.

APPLE ENDORSES JAZZ

In November 1984, Lotus officially announced Jazz. John Sculley spoke in glowing terms of the advantages of the program and its importance for graphics-based operating systems, saying that Jazz was a very important product for Apple's strategy and that it opened new markets for the Macintosh. Steve Jobs was so enthusiastic about the program he publicly declared that Jazz would run on half of all Macintoshes.

Lotus invested considerable sums in introducing Jazz. A large-scale marketing campaign was planned in order to position the integrated software as the ultimate program for the Macintosh. The release of the program was scheduled for the end of March 1985.

Microsoft's marketing staff had prepared a response to Jazz: a Macintosh utility called Switcher, developed by Andy Hertzfeld. It took up 20K of memory and enabled a user to run four applications simultaneously and to move freely between them. Microsoft promoted the idea that Switcher enabled users to build the integrated program of their choice by selecting the applications that they wanted to use simultaneously.

JOBS DOUBTS EXCEL'S POTENTIAL

Microsoft finally decided on the name for its Macintosh spreadsheet code-named Odyssey. The names NumberBody, Mister Spreadsheet, Plan 3, Champagne, and Lever were passed over for a much more distinguished name: Excel. According to Bill Gates, "Inside Microsoft, Excel is viewed as a very successful name. It was smart to make a clear demarcation between Multiplan and Excel, even though it's an evolution in some of the code."

Once the Excel project was far enough along, Doug Klunder followed through on his decision and quit in January 1985. Before leaving, he made several videotapes to explain how Excel worked. He promised to never again set foot in the Microsoft office. After failing to find another job in the area, he left for California, where he took several odd jobs.

In the meantime, Microsoft recruited a programmer from Wang to work on Excel. He was not efficient enough, however, and the project was not making progress. Furthermore, no one could find the videotapes Klunder recorded.

When Microsoft showed Excel to Steve Jobs for the first time in January 1985, he disagreed with their decision to develop a super-spreadsheet. "You guys are crazy! Jazz will be *the* Macintosh program. It will be on every desk with a Mac!"

Jobs tried to convince Jeff Raikes that Excel needed a word processing element. Gates, however, disagreed. He believed it was better to offer a dedicated product like Excel that could satisfy advanced users, rather than an integrated package in which all the modules were at an intermediate level. Jobs considered Excel's macros another bad decision, saying that Macintosh users would never use macros.

Gates did not heed Jobs's recommendations, holding fast to the initial vision. He believed the Macintosh was geared for a market that was not very different from the PC market. A high-level spreadsheet could re-create the VisiCalc/1-2-3 scenario for the Mac and plant it firmly in the business marketplace.

Fortunately for the Excel project, Doug Klunder had his luggage stolen while on the road in California. He was completely broke. Microsoft seemed to be the best answer, so he returned to Seattle. "Thank God, Doug is back," said a relieved Jabe Blumenthal. Klunder properly completed Excel. He improved the intelligent recalculation and the "undo" option. Overall, he was responsible for almost half the program's code. "Excel is definitely my baby," he says.

JAZZ IS LATE

In March 1985, Lotus announced that Jazz would be two months late. This was the first time the Boston software publisher was unable to meet an announced release date, and it dampened the initial enthusiasm over the product. Mitch Kapor justified the delay by saying his programmers were working hard to make the program as stable as possible.

The delay was bad news for Apple, because it was counting on Jazz to lend legitimacy to the Macintosh and open the doors to businesses with the power of the Lotus name. At that time, there were almost 500 programs available for the one-year-old computer, but as yet no best-sellers. Many potential buyers were awaiting the release of Jazz to decide whether they wanted a Mac.

For a few months, Apple had been going through hard times. After a blazing start, the Mac phenomenon slacked off a bit. Jobs's dream machine had represented 14 percent of microcomputer sales in April 1984, but Macintosh sales had not significantly increased since then. In December 1984, the Mac held only a 7 percent market share. Distributors could not move their inventories, so orders fell.

Despite the success of the Macintosh, 75 percent of Apple's revenues still came from sales of the Apple II. The Apple II team was beginning to resent the fact that the Macintosh captured most of the media attention, thanks to Steve Jobs's efforts. Some members of the Apple II group resigned, following the lead of Steve Wozniak.

THE EXCEL INTRODUCTION

A few days before Excel was introduced, a rumor appeared in the press that Microsoft was about to release a spreadsheet for the Macintosh, but Microsoft officially denied it. When journalists received the invitation to a Microsoft press conference at which Steve Jobs would be present, they bombarded the Bellevue offices with questions. When the name Excel came up, the official response was, "We cannot confirm or deny the existence of a product by that name."

The secret of the Excel development had been so closely guarded that even Lotus executives learned of it only a few days before the official announcement. The shock was sizable.

Mitch Kapor kept a calm facade when asked about this unexpected competition, saying it was wrong to position Excel as a competitor to Jazz because it didn't have a word processing feature or a database, and it wouldn't be available until the end of the summer. Excel, he said, was more like 1-2-3 than like Jazz. He predicted that Excel would have little impact. In fact, at that time, Kapor believed that integrated packages represented the future of software, and his vice president, Jim Manzi, had to fight to keep 1-2-3 from being removed from the shelves to make room for Lotus Symphony.

Excel was introduced to the press May 2, 1985, three weeks before the planned release of Jazz. The press conference took place at the Tavern on the Green restaurant near New York City's Central Park.

Jabe Blumenthal and Mike Slade wrote the script for the demonstration Bill Gates was to give. Blumenthal and Slade would type on the keyboard, and a large screen would project what was being displayed on the Excel screen, while Gates commented on what the program was doing.

The software was still being updated daily. On the evening of May 1, 1985, the Microsoft team arrived in New York with the latest available version.

When they arrived at the Tavern on the Green, Jabe, Mike, and Bill rehearsed the finely honed script, which had worked perfectly just one week earlier. This time, however, it didn't. Excel crashed a few seconds into the rehearsal. Jabe and Mike tried modifying certain key sequences, but the program crashed in other parts of the script. The version of Excel they were supposed to demonstrate the following morning was totally unpredictable. They called the home office to find out from the developers what was wrong. "Bill was ranting and raving, pacing back and forth. He was trying to learn his script, but the demo kept crashing. He was yelling at us, and we were yelling at him," Jabe recalls.

Finally, Blumenthal discovered that he could get a more or less stable script by avoiding certain key sequences. The demo finally worked two times in a row, so they decided to leave it at that.

Jon Shirley opened the press conference the following day saying he was satisfied by Microsoft's performance on the Macintosh: Microsoft had sold at least one program for every Mac sold throughout the world. He added that Multiplan for the Macintosh had sold 100,000 copies.

Bill Gates was extremely nervous during his demonstration. There were several points in the script where Excel could have crashed, which would have been disastrous in front of the press. At the crucial point where Excel was most likely to crash, Gates hesitated, as if expecting the worst, but the worst didn't happen. He grew more confident and resumed speaking at his normally quick pace. Says Blumenthal: "We pressed the magic key, and it worked."

The question of the recalculating speed was brought up. Gates answered with ease, saying that Excel would surprise even the most demanding users. He explained that they had designed new methods, and that Excel recalculated only the formulas directly affected by an update.

Steve Jobs attended the press conference as planned, in order to show Apple's official support. Since spokespersons for the Cupertino firm had always maintained that Apple openly supported Jazz, everyone was anxious to see what Jobs would say. He made a public reversal, surprising more than one observer in the room. After saying he thought a war was heating up between Lotus and Microsoft, he embarked on a string of personal considerations which seemed to indicate his preference for the future. He began by saying Excel would take part of the pie away from Lotus 1-2-3, and then explained that it was better to have a high-powered spreadsheet than a multipurpose program. The problem with integrated software, Jobs said, was that it was almost impossible for it to offer the best version of each program. He called most integrated software packages "compromises." Though he didn't explicitly mention any names, everyone recognized that he was referring to Jazz. Later, Jobs moderated his endorsement of Excel in response to a question about whether Apple still believed in Jazz. "There is a market for an integrated package with a certain amount of power." Gates, seated next to him, smiled faintly.

Just before the close of the press conference, one journalist asked the question everyone had been waiting for: "Are you going to develop a version of Excel for the PC?"

Bill Gates was walking on eggshells. He knew it would be difficult to get an Apple endorsement if he declared unequivocally that Microsoft would develop a PC version of Excel. His response was thus fairly vague.

"This is an issue of leadership. Apple has taken the leadership in this technology. Eventually, however, all technology becomes available to all people," he said, implying that there would be a graphical user interface on PCs and therefore a reason for having a PC version.

Jobs cut him off. "Yeah, and someday we'll all be dead!"

Laughter filled the room. Gates waited for the noise to die down and said with a mischievous grin, "Not IBM!"

An article published May 3, 1985, in the *Journal American* (a Bellevue, Washington, daily) said that in addition to bringing Microsoft "a ton of money," Excel could "save Apple Computer from financial ruin by turning the Macintosh into a viable business computer."

The Excel introduction provided needed encouragement for Apple. A few days prior to the press conference, John Sculley had announced that Apple was taking steps to reduce spending and was revising its sales forecasts due to the apathy of the market. Seventy-five employees at the manufacturing plant in South Carolina were laid off. In prior months, Apple had laid off a record 1,500 people, mostly temporary employees. It had cut its advertising budget to under $100 million, less than the previous year's. Manufacturing had shut down for a week in the spring to enable Apple to reduce its inventory. Production of the Lisa computer was cancelled. And in June 1985, Apple underwent a major reorganization, which prompted Steve Jobs to resign immediately.

Nevertheless, there were no signs of immediate relief for Apple. Excel wasn't expected on the market until September, and Microsoft was not known for being punctual. At Comdex/Spring in Atlanta, May 6 to 9, Excel received much attention and piqued the interest of many attendees. Two weeks later, on May 27, 1985, Lotus released Jazz. Early press reviews were mixed.

When asked by *InfoWorld* writer Tom Maremaa in the May 27, 1985, issue wheether Excel was in direct competition with 1-2-3 or Jazz, Gates responded with an elegant understatement:

> What is the most successful business program? 1-2-3. That is the state of the art in numbers solutions, and it is a very fine product. Now, the Mac plus Excel is the state-of-the-art numbers solution.
>
> We don't believe in the Jazz philosophy that you take all your uses—words, numbers, database, and the resources of the machine—and spread them in five different directions. So there is a significant compromise.

Lotus's philosophy is an all-in-one philosophy. Just give the guy one piece of software and all the other software companies are out forever.

Gates also believed that Jazz was similar to Symphony, which was generally considered difficult to learn. As a result, Gates said, the market would soon discover that Jazz was not as easy to learn as other Macintosh software. Furthermore, Microsoft had a response to Jazz's multiple capabilities: By bundling Switcher with Excel, Microsoft enabled users to obtain a similar set of capabilities as Lotus's integrated package (when combined with Microsoft Word, for example), but at a slightly lower price.

PROMOTING EXCEL

On September 30, 1985, Microsoft released Excel for the Macintosh 512K.

Microsoft went all out on advertising. The first medium they used was radio. On October 15, Excel commercials were broadcast in Boston, Chicago, Dallas, Houston, Los Angeles, New York, Philadelphia, Seattle, San Francisco, and Washington, D.C. Microsoft carefully selected stations that targeted business-minded audiences. When possible, the Excel spot followed a news story about business or finance. The message was broadcast 83 times in L.A. and more than 40 times in Boston, Dallas, and New York that day.

The radio ad, written by Keye Donna Pearlstein, Microsoft's advertising agency at that time, began with dramatic, military-sounding music. Then a solemn voice spoke:

Today, October 15, 1985, marks the introduction of Microsoft Excel for the Macintosh, an event that will put unprecedented power in the hands of anyone who wants it.
MAN (interrupting): Uh, wait just a minute here.
ANNOUNCER: Microsoft Excel is the most formidable spreadsheet ever to run on a personal computer.
MAN: Uh. . . .
ANNOUNCER: This spreadsheet is linked with an extraordinary graphics program and a highly capable data filing

application to create an extremely potent, yet simple to use, package.

MAN (interrupting): Excuse me.

ANNOUNCER: What is it?

MAN: You mean just *anybody* can walk in off the street and buy Microsoft Excel software for their Macintosh?

ANNOUNCER: Yes.

MAN: No special permits?

ANNOUNCER: No.

MAN: No minimum age?

ANNOUNCER: No.

MAN: Even though Microsoft Excel can give you the drop on your associates and blow away your competitors?

ANNOUNCER: Correct. Anyone can buy it.

MAN: That doesn't seem right somehow.

ANNOUNCER: No one ever said it was fair.

(The music comes and goes.)

ANNOUNCER: Microsoft Excel for the Macintosh. The most powerful financial analysis tool ever put on a desk. We trust you will use it responsibly.

MAN: I'm sorry, I can't promise that.

(The music rises and then stops.)

Microsoft placed ads in computer magazines and in publications such as the *Wall Street Journal* and *Venture*. In addition, Microsoft trained 1,500 Apple distributors throughout the United States.

Beginning January 20, 1986, Microsoft offered Mac Multiplan users a special Excel price of $200 instead of $395. That same month, Apple released the Mac Plus, which had 1,024K of memory. Now Excel could create spreadsheets of up to 750K.

EXCEL BEATS JAZZ

In the beginning, Microsoft's marketing division set a relatively modest goal for itself of selling one copy of Excel for every three copies of Jazz sold by Lotus. Most users favored the integrated package. Goldman, Sachs & Co. believed, for example, that the Lotus product was going to dominate the market because it was aimed at a wider user base. Very soon, however, Excel squarely beat Jazz.

Microsoft tried to portray Jazz as the Macintosh version of Symphony. The reasoning was simple: Symphony was much less successful than 1-2-3. Once that was established, it was easy to present Excel as the Mac version of 1-2-3. "It was such an easy message to understand that we got a lot of acceptance," says Jeff Raikes.

Furthermore, Jazz was being criticized on several points. First was the absence of macros, which was all the more surprising since macros had contributed substantially to the success of 1-2-3. The designers of the integrated program felt that macros were not appropriate in a Macintosh program because they might intimidate novice users who, according to Lotus, were the target group for the Macintosh. Second, Jazz could read spreadsheets in Lotus format, but it could not write spreadsheets in Lotus format. Excel was a better choice when it came to porting 1-2-3 files to the Macintosh. Third, Jazz was too slow—also surprising since 1-2-3 had built its reputation on speed. Ironically, Microsoft's Excel was much closer to the spirit of Lotus's 1-2-3 than was Lotus's Jazz.

By February 1986, Excel's victory was obvious. *InfoWorld* published the results of a survey of Macintosh distributors. Microsoft took 50 percent of December sales with Multiplan, Word, and Excel. Excel was the number-one-selling Mac software, with 36 percent of the market; Lotus Jazz had only 9 percent. A Future Computing survey of 4,000 computer stores indicated that Excel sales grew from November to December (from 4,404 to 6,196 copies), whereas Jazz sales declined (from 3,558 to 2,637).

By April 1986, Jazz had sold around 42,000 copies since its release, according to Future Computing. This group added, however, that Excel sales were twice as high as Jazz's between December and February. Others estimated the ratio to be three to one. Overall, revenues from Jazz made up only 5 percent of Lotus's income. To try to regain some market share, Lotus lowered the price of Jazz from $595 to $395, but to no avail.

The October 20, 1986, *Seybold Outlook on Professional Computing* published this sentence on the first page: "A year ago, the competition for boss spreadsheet of the Macintosh was between Lotus's Jazz (which arrived first, by several months) and Excel. That contest is clearly over." The Seybold report noted that Excel boosted Macintosh sales.

> Once businesspeople saw that, contrary to some popular notions, a powerful, full-featured spreadsheet program tailored to the Macintosh environment was available, a significant number of them may actually have bought Macintoshes for the purpose of spreadsheet work. Prior to the release of Excel on the Macintosh, people who needed to do heavy spreadsheet work may only have considered an IBM PC type of personal computer.

Some of the most noteworthy praise came in the November 10, 1986, issue of *InfoWorld*. "After being loyal and dedicated 1-2-3 users for several years, we've just recently converted all our 1-2-3 files over to Excel. It's that good." Peat, Marwick, Main & Co. installed Excel on 10,000 Apple Macintoshes.

At the beginning of 1987, when Dataquest published the figures for the 1986 market for Macintosh spreadsheets, the gap was unprecedented. Excel, with 160,000 copies sold, represented 89 percent of sales. Jazz had captured only 6 percent of the users, with 10,000 copies sold. (In fact, Jim Manzi, president of Lotus, stated in 1989 that Lotus had had more copies of Jazz returned than it had sold, referring to pirated copies.) Other programs were responsible for negligible market shares.

MICROSOFT TRIUMPHS IN THE MAC WORLD

Thanks to Excel and Word, Microsoft became the number one software publisher in the Macintosh world. InfoCorp attributed half of Macintosh software sales in 1986 to

Microsoft. In June 1986, when *MacWorld* published its list of best-selling Macintosh programs, Microsoft dominated the list with Excel in first, Word second, File third, and Multiplan fifth.

In 1987, Excel sales continued to expand at the expense of Jazz. While the ratio between Excel and Jazz was still three to one in terms of installed base (254,812 vs. 71,305), it was five to one in terms of sales for the year (123,462 vs. 24,650). The InfoCorp report said 1.25 million Macintoshes were in use by the end of 1987.

Excel 1.5 appeared in May 1988. It enabled developers to create complete applications in which the spreadsheet was totally transparent.

Excel 2.2, released May 1, 1989, broke the 1 megabyte memory barrier. Now spreadsheets could extend to up to 8 megabytes. Two competing spreadsheets had also appeared: Wingz by Informix and Full Impact by Ashton-Tate. Microsoft Excel, however, remained in first place. The research firm Stratagem attributed an installed base of 715,000 copies to Excel, compared to 30,000 for Wingz and 27,000 for Full Impact. To try to catch up, Informix and Ashton-Tate launched promotions allowing Excel users to switch to their spreadsheets. A Macintosh version of 1-2-3 was announced in September 1987, but was later scrapped.

Doug Klunder said that as time went on, he became increasingly proud to have developed Excel. But he continued to believe that it would have been wise to release it first for the PC.

> I didn't think that moving to the Mac was the correct decision. Looking back, I'm still not sure. It was certainly extremely successful on the Mac, but we also gave Lotus two more years to get entrenched on the PC. I think Excel could have gone up pretty strongly against 1-2-3. It was certainly a stronger program than 1-2-3, and at that time, 1-2-3 had only been out about a year. If we had stayed on the PC, we would have had

Excel out probably that fall. So, I'm not convinced in terms of sheer numbers whether that was the correct decision.

Excel, however, made Microsoft number one in the realm of applications for the first time. Microsoft had won such a decisive victory over Lotus that for years, Lotus stayed out of the Macintosh world. One important lesson came out of this experience: Microsoft's strength lay in graphical user interfaces. From there, the road to victory in the PC market was clearly laid out.

PART 6

WINDOWS

We worked like dogs on Windows.

–Neil Konzen, long-time Microsoft employee

15

Long-Awaited Windows

Microsoft's next task—transforming MS-DOS into a graphical user interface—was similar to the alchemy of turning base metal into gold. The goal was to change a monochrome, arcane, text-based environment into a multicolor, user-friendly, elegant, graphics-based environment.

Several other firms also attempted the feat, none of them knowing the pitfalls they would encounter along the way. This project proved to be the toughest undertaking in Microsoft's history and reached fruition only because of Bill Gates's tenacity and perseverance.

The IBM PC had imposed a standard hardware architecture and a standard operating system on the PC industry, but standards did not extend to PC applications.

The most popular software programs for the PC were completely different from one another. Adept WordStar users, for example, could not benefit at all from their WordStar expertise when they tried to use dBASE, Multiplan, or 1-2-3. Each of these programs' methods for cutting and pasting text or printing a file was unique.

Nor did standards exist for how applications communicated with printers. An Epson wire-matrix printer, an Apple

LaserWriter, and a Hewlett-Packard LaserJet all required different intermediary programs (called drivers) that enabled them to receive data from an application. When a customer buying a word processing program opened the box, he or she found a dozen diskettes, only one of which contained the actual program. The other diskettes adapted the program to a printer. The same was true, though to a lesser degree, of monitors. Sometimes, a user had to spend 20 minutes installing a word processor for the appropriate monitor and printer.

To address this inconvenience, Gates envisioned placing a layer (temporarily called the Interface Manager) between MS-DOS and applications to record the system's particular type of printer and monitor. Applications would then rely on the Interface Manager for this information, and this new layer would "protect" users from having to work directly with DOS, which was too complicated for the average user.

The second function of the Interface Manager would be to place a graphical interface on top of MS-DOS and bring uniformity to all applications that run under it.

DESIGNING THE INTERFACE MANAGER

The Interface Manager project, begun in September 1981, led to a new generation of more intuitive software for the PC.

Apple had designed its Lisa and Macintosh computers from the outset to work in graphics mode. The basic IBM PC, on the other hand, was designed to work in text mode. It could only display certain characters in certain places on the screen like a traditional typewriter. Only the color monitor could run graphics software, because images on the color monitor were drawn dot by dot (called bit-map graphics), so it could display drawings or pictures.

Gates set certain conditions for the Interface Manager:

- It had to be independent of the hardware.
- It had to work in graphics mode.

- It had to support WYSIWYG (what you see is what you get: What appears on the screen looks exactly like what is printed) applications.
- It had to standardize the appearance of applications.

In the early specifications, the Interface Manager was to look like Multiplan with an alphabetical list of commands at the bottom of the screen. In 1982, however, Microsoft opted for pull-down menus and dialogue boxes like those on the Xerox Star and the Macintosh. The Interface Manager would also be able to display several documents simultaneously in separate windows on the screen.

VisiCorp had already been working on a similar graphical user interface for DOS for two years. It announced VisiOn at the Fall 1982 Comdex. Bill Gates asked Charles Simonyi to attend the Las Vegas show to see what the program was like. On the outside, it looked very much like what Microsoft was doing.

In January 1983, during a personal computer conference, Gates hinted that Microsoft was developing a tool comparable to VisiOn and that it would ship before VisiCorp's product. In a few weeks, Microsoft got a prototype of the Interface Manager to run on a PC. The mouse was added for moving windows and selecting options from menus.

Microsoft still needed to find a name for this product. In May 1983, Jeff Raikes suggested the name Microsoft Desktop. In keeping with the tradition of Microsoft's other products, however, a simpler name won out: Microsoft Windows.

A much tougher competitor than VisiCorp—Big Blue—was also looming on the horizon. For several months, market analysts had been speculating on whether IBM would release its own interface manager. IBM had relied on Microsoft to provide the basic software for its PC. Past experience suggested, however, that IBM would want to recoup part of the pie by taking future software development into its own hands. In fact, IBM announced that it was going to publish TopView, another graphical interface designed to sit on top of DOS.

To meet the IBM challenge, Bill Gates implemented a survival strategy: He turned to the manufacturers of IBM-compatibles. Compaq, Zenith, Tandy, and others did not want IBM to monopolize the development of standards. Gates tried to convince these firms one by one of the Windows opportunity, thus isolating Big Blue. IBM did not yet fully appreciate the kind of competitor it faced in Bill Gates. Throughout Microsoft's history, Gates has never hesitated to forge the necessary alliances to benefit his company. Some have called this opportunism, others call it vision.

In October 1983, VisiCorp proudly announced it would begin shipping its windowing environment to the 30,000 customers who had already put in orders. There was still no news of Microsoft Windows. Then Quarterdeck, a new software publisher, announced its own windowing environment called DESQ. Bill Gates was angry about not being the first to release a product. To lessen the impact of VisiOn and DESQ, he decided to announce Windows to the press two weeks later — a hasty decision that the company bitterly regretted for years to come.

WINDOWS ANNOUNCED

It was a time of extravagant announcements and lofty promises. In light of the rumors about TopView and the actual arrival of VisiOn, Gates believed it was necessary to make a big impression. On November 10, 1983, in New York, Microsoft officially announced Windows, "a graphical user interface to cover DOS." Gates declared that by the end of 1984, Windows would be operational on more than 90 percent of all MS-DOS computers. He said that with Windows, users would finally be able to take their program and place it in any system, without having to worry about compatibility problems.

The Apple Lisa, released in January 1983, had popularized the idea of the desktop. The screen simulated a manager's typical work space with stacks of files. On the Lisa screen, windows were stacked haphazardly on top of one another, wherever the user placed them. Microsoft chose to display "a well-organized desk," with windows lined up neatly across the desktop.

For several months, people had been talking about integrated software, a new breed of software combining several functions in one program. The leader in this group was 1-2-3, and Lotus was preparing to publish Symphony, a program that took the same idea one step further. Ashton-Tate was also rushing to release its own integrated package called Framework. Gates explained to the press that Windows was different from integrated software. An integrated program is just a limited number of applications and does not allow interaction with other programs, Gates said. Windows, on the other hand, contains no applications. It is an environment that sits on top of the operating system. Gates claimed that Windows would integrate more than 90 percent of all MS-DOS programs.

This was an exaggeration. Windows could launch DOS programs such as 1-2-3 or WordStar. But after launching the program, Windows disappeared from the screen to allow room for the program in question. Such "classic" programs could not run under Windows. In fact, Gates had gone on the road, as in the days of MS-DOS, asking developers to write new programs specifically for Windows.

Some of the more notable software publishers who rallied around Windows were Lotus, Ashton-Tate, Software Publishing, Software Arts, and Peachtree, a publisher known for its business management software. Microsoft said it was going to modify Multiplan and Word so that they too could run under Windows.

Of all the support Microsoft received from publishers, Lotus's was the most appreciated, since Lotus was the largest supplier of software for IBM and compatible PCs. Lotus was enthusiastic about the potential of the windows environment; its chairman, Mitch Kapor, said Lotus would use Windows as the basis for an entirely new family of products. Officially, however, there were no plans to port existing products 1-2-3 and Symphony to Windows.

To market observers, it looked as if Microsoft was trying to take control of the PC environment, which at the time was controlled by IBM. In the past, Big Blue had never hesitated to change its hardware or software standards whenever such a move would eliminate the competition. Manufacturers of IBM-compatibles saw Windows as their long-awaited opportunity to escape IBM's yoke. Several of these manufacturers announced their support for Windows, including Compaq, Hyperion, Texas Instruments, Hewlett-Packard, Eagle, Zenith, Burroughs, and DEC. By early 1984, the list had grown to 24 in all, including Data General, ITT, Tandy, and Wang.

IBM was of course not on this list. A few days after the Windows announcement, Big Blue signed a distribution agreement for VisiOn. This was just one more tactic designed to signal Gates that IBM did not appreciate what Microsoft was doing.

AN INFAMOUS DELAY

The Windows development team, led by Scott MacGregor, experienced unprecedented problems. It was the first time a software publisher had taken on such a vast project, and the complexity had been thoroughly underestimated. Nineteen eighty-four arrived, and Windows was still not ready. Microsoft now claimed it would be out by the end of the first quarter.

Big Blue took advantage of this situation to go one step further in its alliance with VisiCorp. IBM distributed Calc and Graph from the VisiOn family under its own logo. Steve Ballmer, however, told *Electronic News* that IBM's signature on a distribution agreement was not enough to ensure the success of a product. Bill Gates ventured to predict that the true response to VisiOn would be called MS-DOS 3.0. This self-proclaimed miracle product was announced as a multitasking version with graphics, icons, mouse support, and a window manager. However, none of these characteristics were actually found in DOS 3.0. The promise was not feasible with the technology available at the time.

IBM continued to distance itself from Microsoft. A few weeks later, it chose to market a UNIX from a publisher other than Microsoft. And market analysts interpreted IBM's continued work on TopView as its ultimate attempt to break with Microsoft.

At the end of February 1984, 300 representatives from major software publishers and computer manufacturers attended a Microsoft conference in Seattle to hear the latest news about the graphics environment. Each participant paid $500 to attend, only to be disappointed. Microsoft could not yet give the developers the technical information they needed to begin writing applications. The Seattle firm pushed back the Windows release date to May. It was also rumored that Microsoft would try to port Windows to XENIX, a multitasking operating system.

A WEAK RESPONSE FROM COMPETITORS

The impact of Microsoft's delay was somewhat offset by the fact that VisiOn sales were disappointing. One reason for the lukewarm reception was that VisiOn required a hard disk, something few PCs had at that time. The major factor, however, was that VisiOn was a closed system. Windows allowed users at least to launch DOS best-sellers like 1-2-3, Multiplan, and dBASE, but VisiOn could run only programs written specifically for it.

VisiCorp had spent three years and $10 million developing VisiOn and had rewritten the software from scratch three times. However, users soon discovered that it was not the technological miracle they expected after such a long and costly development process. To write applications for VisiOn, software developers needed to invest about $20,000 in a VAX or DEC minicomputer. Furthermore, the mini had to run UNIX, a forbidding operating system. Therefore, at the outset, VisiOn buyers had to be content with three programs offered by VisiCorp: the VisiCalc spreadsheet, the

VisiWord word processor, and the VisiGraph graphics program. This wasn't enough to satisfy the public. VisiCorp cut the price from $495 to $95 one month after releasing VisiOn in an effort to hold on to its customers.

IBM finally decided to promote its own solution. TopView also handled windows and supported a mouse. It let the user run standard DOS applications such as dBASE; however, only certain programs—such as the IBM Family Assistant—could run simultaneously in the windows and allow cutting and pasting between applications. In contrast to the Windows graphical user interface, TopView ran in traditional text mode.

In May 1984, Quarterdeck officially launched DESQ, a windowing environment capable of running several DOS programs. MicroPro expressed interest in this system. DESQ, however, also received a lukewarm response, partly because it was very complex to use. DESQ was a commercial failure. A few years later, Quarterdeck succeeded in rereleasing it with the name DESQview, an environment that sold more than a million copies.

A fourth competitor entered the game, Digital Research. This firm saw launching a graphical user interface as a perfect opportunity to take its revenge on Microsoft for MS-DOS's victory over CP/M. While Windows looked similar to the Macintosh environment, Digital Research's GEM appeared almost identical, because it was more directly inspired by the concepts defined at Xerox PARC. Like the Macintosh, GEM used overlapping windows, but GEM could launch only one application at a time, whereas Windows could launch several.

MORE DELAYS

May 1984 came and went. The release of Windows was officially rescheduled for the end of August. Microsoft attributed this delay to certain pilot users' requests for changes, particularly in the screen presentation.

In July, Jon Shirley found himself faced with the difficult mission of communicating this delay to the press. He assured journalists that Windows was Microsoft's primary project and that the company remained firmly committed to it. He added that the development kits had been shipped to programmers in May and that many hardware manufacturers had received the information they needed to adapt Windows for their computers. Microsoft decided to organize an apology tour to officially announce the delay to manufacturers.

Meanwhile, VisiCorp was in bad shape. To get out of its rut, it sold the VisiOn rights to Control Data. It was also fighting a losing battle in trying to acquire exclusive rights to VisiCalc from Software Arts. VisiCorp eventually went out of business.

THE REORGANIZATION

The Windows delay was symptomatic of a bigger problem: Microsoft lacked strong organization within its development department. It had taken a year for those in charge of Windows, from Gates on down, to truly grasp the scope of the project and its difficulties. For example, Windows required too much memory to be adapted to 256K PCs, which were the most widely used on the market.

Jon Shirley concluded that Gates's effectiveness was diluted because he was was trying to oversee too many different functions. All the development divisions were his responsibility, and Gates had a habit of launching projects that were never finished. Programmers were often pulled from one team and put on another, and Gates would sometimes change product specifications suddenly. Shirley thought it best to put an end to this atmosphere of instability.

During the month of August 1984, Microsoft's activities were reorganized around two principal focuses: the operating system and business applications. Steve Ballmer took charge of the systems division, and Ida Cole, former marketing director at Apple, was recruited to head the applications division. Each of these divisions had its own technical and administrative teams.

This reorganization freed Gates to devote himself to what he did best: design future products. His role was limited to defining software products at a very abstract level and determining the direction for development.

In August 1984, Neil Konzen joined the Windows programming group and was given responsibility for the user interface. He disagreed with Scott MacGregor about what had been done up to that point and redefined many of the internal routines of the product in order to facilitate programming applications. One of his objectives was to make it easy to adapt Macintosh software to Windows.

At that time, Microsoft still thought it possible to deliver Windows in two months. In October 1984, however, instead of releasing Windows, Microsoft announced the release was rescheduled for June 1985.

The new Windows product manager, Leo Nikora, had to explain the reasons for this delay to the press. The basic problem was that Windows took up too much memory and was too slow. Nikora said Microsoft had set overly ambitious goals in light of the capacity of the 8088 microprocessor. To meet those goals, they would need to redesign certain parts of the product from scratch.

This tarnished Microsoft's image and the difficulties were quickly seized upon by critics. Esther Dyson of Venture Holdings told *PC Week* that she believed Microsoft would have to work hard to rebuild its credibility. The Bellevue *Journal American* wrote that Microsoft had committed its first strategic mistake. The Christmas edition of *Personal Computer* questioned the very usefulness of a windows environment and predicted its demise, asserting that it created nothing but extra problems for users. In the December issue of *PC Products,* an analyst with International Data Corporation argued that windows programs were a solution to a problem that never existed. *Forbes* magazine emphasized that the windows environment had not made VisiCorp and Quarterdeck successful. Sales of VisiOn and DESQ had been so weak that the two companies were on the verge of collapse—only Quarterdeck survived. And *InfoWorld* coined the term "vaporware" to describe long-awaited, highly publicized software programs still not on the market.

The Windows delay affected the plans of a dozen other publishers, who had to postpone release of their Windows applications. The first applications written with the tools furnished by Microsoft were so slow that they would probably not have sold anyway. Was Gates losing his Midas touch?

Bill Gates defended his pet project. He believed that the advantages of a graphical user interface compensated for the relative slowness of the program. He argued that although some operations were very slow on the Macintosh, the benefits of its graphical user interface were unquestionable.

Manufacturers of IBM-compatibles patiently waited out the delay. Meanwhile, IBM announced TopView with great fanfare. In his column in the September 18, 1984, issue of *PC Week*, Peter Norton expressed how impressed he was with character-based open windowing systems such as TopView and DESQ: "While I agree that the future belongs to the graphics-oriented technology seen in the Lisa and Macintosh hardware and in Microsoft's Windows software, the present belongs to character-oriented machines. Two-thirds of all PCs use the character-only monochrome monitor and therefore can't run graphics-oriented systems such as Windows."

When TopView was released in January 1985, however, it was not a success. Among the criticisms of this product were that it consumed too much memory and did not include certain DOS commands.

WINDOWS PAINT AND WRITE

In early 1985, journalists' questions about the health of Windows embarrassed Microsoft representatives.

In January, the Microsoft marketing department decided to change direction for Windows. At first, it was to be a program shipped by manufacturers with their computers. The focus now shifted to a product for retail sale to end-users. Tandy Trower was named Windows product manager to implement this reorientation.

The programmers had initially begun developing two applications to demonstrate the capabilities of Windows. Write and Paint were designed in 1983 to resemble the two programs that were bundled with the Macintosh. Tandy Trower pushed for the completion of these two products, and also started development of desk tools such as the calendar, calculator, and card manager. He even dug up two programs originally written to help in the development of Windows: the clock and a Reversi game. These additional features meant additional development time, however.

One morning, Bill Gates called Steve Ballmer into his office. Gates had discovered a bug in Windows and was losing patience. He yelled that if Windows was not released by the end of the year, it would be the end of Ballmer's career.

During this time, Digital Research released its GEM graphical user interface, which received a warm welcome. Everyone agreed that the Digital Research environment was much closer to the Macintosh environment than Windows, and this made GEM popular almost immediately. Digital Research had forgotten one point, however. Apple also thought that the GEM interface was very similar to the Mac's and threatened to sue. It may seem surprising that Apple would attack a publisher over an interface that it hadn't invented itself, but the Cupertino firm was committed to protecting the "look and feel" of the Macintosh interface and therefore sued on that basis. It was a hard blow to GEM, which was selling extremely well: 150,000 copies had been sold almost immediately. Faced with the threat of this lawsuit, Digital Research decided to rewrite its graphical user interface.

WINDOWS BECOMES THE TOP PRIORITY

Windows was now Microsoft's most important project. More than 20 programmers were working on it, backed by a team writing the documentation, which changed weekly. Others tested the software. In all, over 30 people were assigned to

Windows. They worked day and night, with tough constraints: They had to make the program smaller, faster, and more stable. "The whole group was sweating blood trying to get this thing done," Neil Konzen recalls.

One morning, one of the testers, Gabe Newell, came to the office with his sleeping bag under his arm. He spent an entire month testing the desk tools without ever leaving the office, which earned him the nickname "Madman."

To relieve the pressure, the developers tried to have fun on a regular basis. Sometimes they invaded the kitchen to do a few chemistry experiments. Around two o'clock in the morning, while the Windows code was compiling, they made bombs and rockets using a mixture of sugar and saltpeter, and shot them off outside. These strange explosions attracted the attention of the Bellevue police, who soon arrived at Microsoft with dogs trained to sniff out explosives. The police asked a security guard about the blasts, but he feigned ignorance. In fact, the guard had participated in setting off the homemade rockets!

One night the programmers got the idea of making a stronger rocket fuel by melting the sugar before pouring it into the rocket. One of them decided to melt the sugar in the microwave oven, which caused the fuel to ignite. The explosion made a terrible mess of the kitchen, and smoke poured through the entire building. The culprits turned on the air conditioning and worked hard to clean up the mess before everyone else arrived in the morning.

At other times, music alleviated the tension. Mark Taylor persuaded a few colleagues to buy electric guitars, and they held late-night jam sessions in the hallways. One night several programmers took their amplifiers to the top of the building. After cranking up the volume, they played for the people on the street below, as the Beatles did in "Let It Be." Once again, the police came, but did not catch these disturbers of the peace. Doubled over with laughter, the programmers had already run back to their computer keyboards and were working on the Windows software. "We were kind of like college kids—we just had a good time," Neil Konzen says.

In May 1985, at the spring Comdex, Microsoft exhibited Windows and confirmed it would in fact be released in June. This time, however, the company took a low profile. The version they demonstrated could be used with a keyboard as well as a mouse. According to Microsoft, this request had come up through the distributor network because many users had expressed dislike for the mouse. Windows was also modified to support Program Information Files (PIF) from TopView. Some industry observers, such as Peter Norton, saw this as a sign that the IBM environment was gaining ground. Finally, Microsoft said Windows would sell for $95.

On June 28, 1985, the next date when Windows was supposed to be available for retail sale, Microsoft instead released a test version for software developers and computer manufacturers only. A few weeks later, it sent evaluation copies to the press. Microsoft's official goal was to get advice before putting the product on the retail market. In practice, Microsoft had to give concrete proof of what the final product would be like. Developers received a kit of software tools to help them write applications for Windows.

THE PARTY

Windows 1.03 finally came out in November 1985. Eighty-five percent of the software was written in the high-level language called C. The most critical parts were written in assembly language. It took 110,000 programming hours to create this first version of Windows.

On November 21, as if to set the problems of the past aside, Microsoft held a highly memorable conference to celebrate the end of the longest development cycle in its history. The major magazine editors were invited, as were the heads of the large PC distribution chains. The atmosphere was one of general hilarity. Stewart Alsop from *InfoWorld* opened fire in his own way by presenting Bill Gates with the Golden

Vaporware Award. John Dvorak from *PC Magazine* followed Alsop's lead. Before giving the floor to Steve Ballmer, Dvorak introduced him by saying that when Windows was first announced, Ballmer still had hair. Ballmer then launched into a witty description of the many ways his life had changed since Windows was first announced. When the Windows development began, he had been in charge of finances and had approved the proposed investment of 6 man-years for Windows, which would be distributed on a single diskette. Now, 80 man-years later, Microsoft was selling a product with five diskettes for $99. Now you understand, Ballmer told the audience, why they changed my position! He then became marketing director, and his first task was to make the Windows announcement to the press. Another transfer followed, and he became development director for Windows.

Over the laughter from the audience, Ballmer began reviewing some of the most interesting articles written about Windows in the space of two years. Then he described the trials and tribulations of 1985, which he called a very difficult year. Even Gates, whom he had known for a long time, had lost his patience. Ballmer recounted how Gates had called him into his office and chewed him out. He then went back and told his developers, "Kids, we must ship this product before the snow falls." They had made it, he concluded.

Before giving the floor to Gates, Ballmer sang a song and Gates, who seldom acted so unreserved in public, began to sing with him. Then the great visionary launched into an impassioned speech about the virtues of the graphical user interface. At the end of the show, a giant shopping cart rolled onto the stage. It contained the first 500 Windows packages, which were distributed to the euphoric crowd.

RECOGNITION

Jim Seymour, a writer for *PC Week*, came out in favor of Windows.

I am a Windows fan, not because of what it is today, but what it almost certainly will become. . . . I think developers who don't build Windows compatibility into new products and new releases of successful existing products are crazy.

Sure Windows is a slug on 8088 PCs, an impossibility on floppy-disk PCs. . . . But Windows is a product for the post-8088 world. . . . The secret of Windows in its present state is how much it offers program developers: They don't have to write screen drivers, . . . printer drivers; they can offer their customers a kind of two-bit concurrency and data exchange.

Seymour concluded by saying that high-end, Windows-only applications were on the way, beginning with a PC version of PageMaker, which was already a best-seller for the Macintosh.

The December 1985 issue of *PC World* said that "the future of integration [could] be perceived through Windows." Bill Machrone of *PC Magazine* called Write "a jewel in the crown of Windows."

. . . AND REJECTION

When Windows was released, however, very few machines could do justice to this environment. As several market analysts had emphasized, it required at least a PC AT for acceptable results. For decent color display, users needed an EGA screen like the one IBM had announced for its PC AT a year earlier.[1] Some manufacturers of compatibles, such as Compaq, still had not offered such a product, thinking the time for color had not yet come. In December 1985, not all IBM PC ATs included color monitors. And with a PC XT or a PC with two disk drives, Windows was unbearably slow.

Because of these factors, Microsoft's sales goal for Windows was a relatively modest 4,000 copies a month. The public, however, stayed away from Windows for two major

---

[1]EGA stands for Enhanced Graphics Adaptor: a standard for color monitors which was introduced by IBM at the same time as the AT (late 1984). The EGA monitor uses more dots per inch and therefore has greater resolution (gives a sharper image) than earlier color monitors.

reasons. It was very slow, and there were almost no programs to run under it. According to a survey by *InfoWorld* in December 1985, computer services directors preferred Windows to GEM and TopView, but they were still waiting for better integration capabilities. Everyone was waiting for IBM to release a graphical version of TopView before deciding on which environment to adopt. It was rumored that IBM might publish such a program by the second quarter of 1986.

In addition, an important defection occurred among the manufacturers. In November 1985, Tandy announced it would offer GEM for its microcomputers; its plans for Windows were canceled. Likewise, Apricot, Atari, Commodore, Epson, and Texas Instruments indicated that they preferred Digital Research's product over Microsoft's. In the case of the Atari, GEM became part of the ROM (permanent memory) of the new STs.

Nevertheless, some prestigious names remained on the list of manufacturers that planned to offer Windows as standard with their hardware: Zenith, AT&T, Data General, DEC, Grid, Honeywell, Intel, NCR, Olivetti, and Convergent Technologies. IBM, on the other hand, had decided to offer Top-View with its XT, after noting that sales of the stand-alone product were not taking off.

A more troublesome problem arose for Windows. Major publishers, tired of waiting for Windows, had lost interest in writing Windows applications.

In July 1984, Jon Shirley had told *Micro Software Today* that the publishers of the 15 best-selling programs were writing applications for the Windows environment. One year later, in July 1985, the four largest software publishers besides Microsoft announced that they had no immediate development project for Windows. Lotus, Ashton-Tate, Software Publishing, and MicroPro gave several reasons for this defection: Their primary clients had no particular interest in Windows versions of their programs. No one was certain whether this environment would last. The publishers stated that they would be interested in Windows when the time seemed more opportune. "Basically, our customers are not asking for it," explained a spokesperson for Software Publishing, whose pfs:Write and pfs:File programs were selling very well. The absence of the Windows versions of bestsellers Lotus 1-2-3 and dBASE III also noticeably slowed the sales of Microsoft's environment.

Furthermore, Windows was supposed to make application development easier because it handled the video and printer drivers. In practice, however, writing Windows applications was incredibly complex. Many programmers shied away from attempting development in an environment that had not yet proven itself.

Finally, the major publishers thought of Microsoft first and foremost as a competitor. If they released programs for Windows, they would help lend credibility to the environment and therefore make it all the easier for Microsoft to publish its own Windows applications.

Software publishers in the Macintosh world were politely interested in Windows. A spokesperson for Forethought said that Windows offered advantages over the Macintosh because it handled color and multitasking. T/Maker, a California software firm, said it planned on porting five programs for the Macintosh to Windows, but also to GEM.

Deep in the heart of Texas, however, was a programmer named Paul Grayson of Micrografx, who believed in Windows and proclaimed his convictions far and wide. Grayson never missed a chance to say that he considered Windows far superior to GEM and TopView. In July 1985, before Windows was even released to the public, Micrografx published its first Windows application: the draw program In-A-Vision. From the very beginning, Paul Grayson believed in Windows, and Micrografx paid dearly for this unswerving loyalty. Sometimes the company had to rewrite its program from scratch to keep up with the changes in Windows.

A RECORD SETTER

Windows will go down in the history of Microsoft as the product with the most records—the most cumulative delays and the greatest number of development hours. Windows monopolized more than 24 developers for over three years, not to mention the testing and documentation teams. And by the time it was released, Windows had had four product managers and three development directors.

A few years later, Windows set another record: Microsoft's best-selling software. It also got the company involved in a major lawsuit.

THE APPLE LAWSUIT

In July 1984 Jon Shirley described the philosophy behind Windows to the magazine *Micro Software Today*, saying that Microsoft had made it look very close to the Macintosh with the hope that many publishers would be able to write software for the Apple machine and then port it to Windows, and vice-versa. The documentation, he said, would be practically identical.

Apple, however, was beginning to look unfavorably upon PC graphical user interfaces such as GEM and Windows. When Apple threatened to sue, Digital Research decided to rewrite GEM and avoid the lawsuit. Apple tried the same tactic with Microsoft, which held its ground.

According to a story published in the *Wall Street Journal* (September 25, 1987), Microsoft did not hesitate to use "high-pressure tactics" to copy ideas from the Macintosh. Bill Gates threatened to stop work on Word and Excel (which eventually became Microsoft's most popular products for the Macintosh) "to extract a virtual blank check to borrow many Macintosh ideas for Microsoft's own products. These ideas included mouse-activated pull-down command menus and overlapping 'windows' of on-screen text."

On November 22, 1985, shortly after the release of Windows 1.01, Microsoft and Apple signed an agreement in which Apple permitted Microsoft to use certain visual characteristics of the Macintosh display in products such as Excel. At that time, relations between the two companies were good, and Apple hoped to benefit from Microsoft's collaboration as a software developer. Microsoft Excel, for example, significantly boosted Macintosh sales.

In late 1987, Microsoft released Windows 2.0, whose interface was much more similar to that of the Macintosh. Windows, meanwhile, had sold over a million copies and had begun to make a name for itself. When Microsoft released the PC version of Excel, Windows gained credibility overnight, and PC manufacturers began positioning their computers against the Macintosh.

These moves created mounting tension in Cupertino. Though Apple had previously viewed Windows as a clumsy PC product of little consequence, it now began to view it as a threat to the Mac. As many companies that had previously developed exclusively for the Macintosh began writing software for Windows, Apple executives realized that the Macintosh could soon lose the selling point of its unique user interface.

Tensions came to a head March 17, 1988, when Apple publicly announced it was suing Microsoft over Windows 2.03 and Hewlett-Packard over New Wave, its Windows-based environment. Bill Gates was especially shocked by the news because he had just seen John Sculley, yet Sculley had made no mention of a lawsuit. Microsoft was informed of the action only when a journalist called to ask for Gates's comment on it. "Lawsuit? What lawsuit?" was all he could reply. Apple had gone to the press before notifying Gates.

Apple's suit claimed that it had spent millions of dollars and several years developing the visual interface that had become the distinguishing characteristic of the Macintosh, and that Apple had refused to grant Hewlett-Packard's request for the license to these visual effects.

Hewlett-Packard therefore began developing New Wave based on Windows 2.03, which according to Apple "embodie[d] and generate[d] a copy of the Macintosh" graphical user interface. To support this claim, Apple said that during the New Wave introduction, the Hewlett-Packard product manager had touted the similarity between New Wave and the Macintosh.

Apple also accused Microsoft of violating a 1985 licensing agreement, saying that Windows 2.03, released in late 1987, was an illegal copy of the "look and feel" of the Macintosh interface. With the lawsuit, Apple sought to stop the sale and distribution of Windows, obtain all profits from the sale of Windows 2.03, and prevent Hewlett-Packard from releasing New Wave. Finally, Apple demanded that all copies of these programs be destroyed.

On March 18, 1988, William Newkom, Microsoft's vice president of legal affairs, responded to the suit, arguing that Microsoft had scrupulously respected the 1985 agreement.

Three days later, Microsoft's Steve Ballmer disclosed parts of the agreement, showing that Apple had granted Microsoft a license to use the visual display already incorporated into six Microsoft programs (Windows 1.0, and the Macintosh versions of Multiplan, Chart, File, Excel, and Word) in any present or future software application. Apple also gave Microsoft the right to sublicense these displays.

Microsoft asserted that the 1985 agreement implicitly covered Windows 2.03, so it had no intention of modifying Windows or applications written for it and would continue to produce and sell these products.

The primary difference between the first and second versions of Windows was overlapping windows, already a characteristic Macintosh feature. The Windows 2.03 desktop no longer looked like a well-organized desk, since the Microsoft engineers had all decided that executives' desks are never as neatly organized as the juxtaposed windows of Windows 1.03.

Apple chairman John Sculley explained his company's official stance during the Information Systems and Technology Conference in London on March 21, saying that the modifications to Windows between the first versions and version 2.03 did not fall under the licensing agreement. Hewlett-Packard's New Wave is based on Windows 2.03 and considerably reinforces the resemblance between the Macintosh and Windows interfaces, Sculley argued.

In April 1989, Judge William Schwarzer ruled that the 1985 agreement between Apple and Microsoft covered only version 1.0 of Windows. Microsoft held its ground and reiterated the initial argument that there was no difference between Windows 1.0 and 2.03.

On July 25, 1989, Judge Schwarzer handed down a decision that significantly reduced the scope of Apple's complaint. The judge had removed all but 10 of the 189 items that Apple said constituted copyright violations. The 10 remaining issues concerned the issue of overlapping windows and the appearance and manipulation of certain icons in Windows 2.03. Schwarzer ruled that the use of the visual display in Windows 2.03 could be traced back to Windows 1.0, which was covered by the 1985 agreement.

According to Apple's corporate public relations manager, Christopher Escher, in the July 1989 decision the judge also divided the case into two key issues: Microsoft's adherence to the terms of its 1985 license with Apple, and the validity of Apple's copyright on certain elements of audiovisual display.

In early 1990, Judge Vaughn Walker of the Federal District Court in San Francisco took over the case from Judge Schwarzer. Judge Walker had also handled the Xerox suit against Apple, in which Xerox tried to sue Apple over the same copyrights. That case was thrown out in early May 1990.

On March 6, 1991, Judge Walker denied Hewlett-Packard's request to declare Apple's copyrights invalid and rejected Microsoft's argument that portions of Windows were covered by its license from Apple. While Apple was pleased with this decision, viewing it as bringing the case one step closer to trial, the judge also granted Microsoft's request to consider the copyright issue on a function-by-function basis, rather than on the basis of the general look and feel. In mid-April 1991, Apple broadened its suit to include Windows 3.0.

The stakes are high for both sides in this lawsuit. If Apple wins, Microsoft could be required to take Windows 3.0 off the market or pay royalties to Apple. If Microsoft and Hewlett-

Packard are successful in their defense, Apple could lose its market advantage of originality, as the way would be cleared for any firm to copy the interface features that have made the Macintosh unique. In light of these weighty consequences for the companies involved and for the entire industry, this suit will not be quickly resolved.

16

Excel in Windows

The rules were changing in the PC kingdom. In September 1986, Compaq offered a compatible built around a new Intel microprocessor, the 80386. The difference was that this time, Compaq had not waited for IBM to take the first step. The Compaq Deskpro 386 was the most powerful PC on the market, and it took IBM more than eight months to produce a competitive product in this category.

Compaq was able to make this move because it knew IBM was losing its controlling grip on the PC standard. Compatible meant any PC that could run the popular programs at that time, such as 1-2-3, Word, WordPerfect, and dBASE III Plus. Such a machine needed to include an Intel microprocessor and the MS-DOS operating system, an architecture that Compaq called the industry standard architecture (ISA). IBM itself could not release a PC that veered from these standards because the public would not accept it.

In England, Alan Sugar raised another challenge to Big Blue. By offering PCs for less than $1,000, Amstrad gave the price reductions begun in Taiwan the official support of an entire distribution network. In the United States, Dell started selling PCs by mail at rock-bottom prices, while maintaining top quality after-sales service.

WINDOWS AND PRESENTATION MANAGER

At the same time, Windows was not taking off as hoped. It lacked a star application that could attract the market. Microsoft decided to develop such a product itself.

At the Mac Excel introduction in New York in 1985, Bill Gates had hinted that one day Excel would be ported to the PC. Steve Jobs's presence had made it difficult for Gates to take a stronger stance. Gates added another piece to the puzzle in the May 27, 1985, issue of *InfoWorld.* "In the future, you'll see us develop on Windows first and then move applications over to the Mac."

This message, in conjunction with other declarations by Gates, clearly indicated that Microsoft firmly intended to offer applications that would function similarly on the PC and on the Mac.

The summer of 1985 was marked by a joint-development agreement between Microsoft and IBM for the next operating system for IBM's next-generation PC. In November, Gates met with IBM representatives to convince them to adopt Windows as the official graphical interface for their computer, but IBM turned a deaf ear. It had not yet made a decision on the future of TopView, and rumor had it that IBM was considering a graphics solution developed by Digital Research. One spring morning in 1986, Bill Gates arrived at the IBM offices just outside New York City after a red-eye flight from Seattle. Bad news greeted him. For three years, he had advocated the idea of Windows, and Big Blue was the only large company that had resisted him to this point. Gates believed that sooner or later, even IBM would come around.

That morning, the IBM people, through Bill Lowe—the director of the entry-level systems division, who had initiated the PC project—said no to Windows. IBM had decided to develop a graphical user interface for the PC on its own.

True to form, Bill Gates did not accept this rejection, but defended his product. He emphasized that Windows had a two-year lead on IBM's product. Bill Lowe responded that IBM had expertise in areas such as networking, in which Microsoft was still a novice. Gates rebutted that Microsoft had a better understanding of what was happening in personal computers than IBM did. After two hours of arguing, Gates won a concession from Lowe. IBM engineers and

Microsoft engineers would work together to modify Windows according to Big Blue's desires. IBM would then decide whether it wanted to market the product, based on the results obtained. This joint development later gave birth to the graphical user interface Presentation Manager, which is to OS/2 what Windows is to DOS.

The year 1986 ended with an unusual distinction for Bill Gates: a special prize from *PC Magazine* in the "Technical Excellence" category. Usually these honors were bestowed on software products and not on individuals. *PC Magazine* had decided to make an exception this time and honor this visionary for his work as a whole.

Nineteen eighty-seven began on a note of excitement because it became obvious that IBM had something new in the works. Manufacturers of IBM compatibles were eating away at its market share. The toughest competitors were the manufacturers in Taiwan who offered PCs at extremely low prices.

On April 2, 1987, IBM announced its new personal computer, the PS/2, an attractive machine with a very sophisticated design. It was a far cry from the rough PC AT released in 1984: The design was sleek, and its screen inaugurated a new video standard for characters and graphics called VGA (video graphics array), further improving resolution and therefore making the screen much easier to read.

The PS/2 was a break with the standard PC that had developed over six years. It did not accept the expansion cards of the XTs and the ATs, because IBM had developed a promising new multitask bus called MCA (Micro Channel Architecture).[1]

---

[1]In September 1988, Compaq announced the formation of the EISA group, which offered an alternative to the MCA bus of the IBM PS/2. (EISA means extended industry standard architecture.) The EISA bus was a 32-bit bus like the MCA, but it could receive cards made for the AT. AST, Epson, Hewlett-Packard, NEC, Olivetti, Tandy, Wyse, and Zenith all endorsed EISA.

The day of the PS/2 announcement, IBM also revealed that it was writing a new operating system, OS/2, in conjunction with Microsoft. Microsoft was also collaborating with IBM to adapt Windows to OS/2, and the new product was called Presentation Manager.

ASSAULT ON THE SPREADSHEET MARKET

Lotus continued to dominate the American software market. According to InfoCorp, in 1986, Lotus 1-2-3 claimed 17.6 percent of all microcomputer software sales for all machines in the professional sector. Lotus had already sold 2 million copies of 1-2-3 and there was no sign of any real competition in the near future. The number two software product, dBASE III Plus by Ashton-Tate, represented barely half of 1-2-3's market share (8.1 percent). Microsoft's top software product, Word, was number five with 5 percent of the overall market. In contrast, in the Macintosh world, Excel enjoyed a popularity comparable to 1-2-3's in the PC realm with 75 percent of all spreadsheet sales.

A Datapro study published in July 1986 said that Microsoft was better positioned strategically than Lotus or Ashton-Tate. Of the three, Microsoft was by far the most diversified. Its two competitors made most of their revenue from one or two products. 1-2-3, for example, represented 60 percent of Lotus's revenue, whereas Excel represented only 8 percent of Microsoft's revenue.

In October 1986, the first signs of a shift in the ranking appeared. For the first fiscal quarter of 1986,[2] Microsoft's revenue reached $66.8 million compared to Lotus's $65.6 million. It was still too early for Microsoft to claim victory as number one, although it seemed within reach.

Toward the end of 1986, Lotus entered Microsoft's privileged market, Japan. Although it arrived several years after Multiplan, 1-2-3 made short work of Microsoft's product. The

---

[2]July to September 1986; the fiscal year goes from July to June.

release of the Japanese version of the spreadsheet was preceded by a shrewd marketing campaign accusing its competitor of obsolescence. One month after its release, the Lotus spreadsheet reached the top of the sales list and began selling about five copies for every copy of Multiplan. Microsoft executives at headquarters felt that Kazuhiko Nishi's carelessness was partly to blame for this.

Gates decided to attack Lotus on its own turf, spreadsheets. Microsoft could easily have directed its diversification toward the world of databases, but Gates preferred to focus his efforts on destabilizing his number one competitor. The specifications for the Windows version of Excel were designed with this goal in mind.

DEVELOPING EXCEL FOR THE PC

The development of Windows Excel began very soon after the completion of the Macintosh version; some of the programmers were transferred over to this new project. Microsoft worked closely with five companies (including Boeing and the accounting firm Arthur Andersen) that used Lotus 1-2-3 and had agreed to act as test sites for Microsoft's competitive product.

Jeff Harbers and 6 other developers began work on Windows Excel. At times, as many as 10 programmers devoted themselves to the project, while 40 people worked on the documentation and packaging. Bill Gates carefully monitored the development of Excel for the PC.

The PC world was committed to 1-2-3's functionality. Therefore, according to Jeff Harbers, Microsoft did an in-depth analysis of 1-2-3 to make sure the new product would be at the same functional level. Microsoft didn't want Lotus users to feel that they would have to give up a function that was useful for them.

In developing Excel for Windows, Microsoft used a technique similar to the one used for Multiplan in 1981: 80 percent of the functions of the program were converted into an intermediary code that could run on the Macintosh, in

Windows and in Presentation Manager. Only 20 percent of the product then had to be adapted to each environment. Microsoft was already preparing for the 1990s when it worked to make one software product available for all three of the most widely used environments.

The task of writing Excel for Windows turned out to be more difficult than expected. According to Jeff Harbers, Windows was a much more complex environment than Apple's.

So, at night, out came the electric guitars and the synthesizers, and jam sessions again rocked the office.

Bill Gates wanted Excel for Windows to be as fast as possible. This became the development team's top priority. They wrote a complex macro that put the spreadsheet through a rigorous nightly test which took five hours to run. Every time part of the program slowed down, the programmers put their all into tracking the source of the problem and fixing it.

In late 1986, Microsoft revealed a preliminary version of Windows Excel to certain privileged clients in the United States and Europe. They were very impressed by the emerging product, but they all raised one issue: It was not compatible enough with 1-2-3. In the beginning, the developers had planned to furnish an external utility that could convert Lotus files into Excel files. At the request of a large potential buyer, however, Microsoft agreed to change Excel so that it could read and write 1-2-3 files directly.

The Microsoft developers said that respecting the 1-2-3 standard forced them to do a certain number of things differently from what they had planned. Lotus 1-2-3 was a standard understood by many people who felt at ease with it, so they had to work with that standard. As a result, they didn't put all the features they wanted to into Excel. Writing the macro translator turned out to be particularly tricky because the languages used by 1-2-3 and by Excel are fundamentally different. "We had to write a program that was intelligent enough to understand the goal of a 1-2-3 macro and then convert it into a similar macro in Excel," Harbers explains.

In April, a few weeks after IBM announced the PS/2, the OS/2, and Presentation Manager, Lotus announced it was developing a new version of its spreadsheet called 1-2-3/3. Privately, the Boston firm was somewhat concerned about the possible repercussions of Excel on the PC, but publicly it came across as confident that Windows was an imperfect environment. Windows applications at that time stood out for their slowness.

During this same time, however, the Microsoft systems division was working on a new version of Windows destined to run twice as fast as the previous one.

MICROSOFT SURPASSES LOTUS

On August 16, 1987, Microsoft executives received encouraging news via electronic mail. The results for the fiscal year indicated that Microsoft had become the number one software company, beating Lotus for the first time since 1983.

When Bill Gates found out, he wrote a message to his top managers, who in turn distributed it to all members of the company. The message was titled "Microsoft is #1."

As conservative as we are about self-congratulation and celebrating our achievements, I have to say as today went on I got pretty excited about the fact that we are now the number 1 software company in every respect (sales, profits, units, leadership, people). In fact, when I think of Lotus's statement at the introduction of their annual report where they say, "There is increasing evidence that LOTUS is the preferred vendor, the preferred investment and the preferred employer," I think they are kidding themselves. We didn't just have somewhat higher sales than they did—we had $14M more in sales which puts us ahead for the 3, 6, 9 and 12 months (I think). Of course their sales may go past ours again and it's not really our goal to be #1, but I do get a real kick out of the fight [sic] that their big distinction of being the largest is being taken away BEFORE WE HAVE EVEN BEGUN TO REALLY COMPETE WITH THEM. Actually I found out these numbers about 5 p.m. so I've been enjoying it for only 6 hours and it will be a fact of no importance in a few days but I think it's really great.

When Gates said that the real competition had not yet begun, he was referring to the imminent release of Excel, a product designed to directly encroach on the turf of the publisher that was now number two.

In the meantime, Microsoft applied part of the strategy that had contributed to the success of 1-2-3. One reason that spreadsheet was so deeply entrenched in large businesses was the availability of a large number of useful programs called add-ins. With the goal of generating a similar market for Excel, Microsoft began approaching developers from the Lotus world such as Turner, Hall, and Funk.

RELEASE OF WINDOWS EXCEL

Windows Excel was launched October 6, 1987. Gates had decided to offer the spreadsheet solely for computers as powerful as the IBM AT and the Compaq 386, or better. Gates called Excel the future of spreadsheets, saying that Microsoft expected Excel to become as widespread on 80286 and 80386 machines as 1-2-3 was on the 8088 PCs.

Microsoft's marketing staff remained reserved about how much market share they could conquer with Windows Excel. At first, they made it clear that they didn't intend to compete in the low-end PC market. Although they did not officially indicate how much of the high-end market they hoped to capture, it was rumored that they would be pleased to get 15 percent of the sales of new spreadsheets for 80286 and 80386 PCs.

In an attempt to minimize the effect of the Windows Excel announcement, Lotus announced it was beginning development on a Macintosh version of 1-2-3. Apple chairman John Sculley himself broke this news to his sales force, apparently to counterbalance the impact of the release of the most popular Macintosh program for the PC. Sculley called the

Lotus announcement exciting news for Macintosh users in light of the importance of 1-2-3 and other Lotus products in the business market.

The failure of Jazz, however, did not bode well for Lotus's attempt to reconquer the Macintosh market. Furthermore, Lotus was still talking about releasing Modern Jazz, which was finally abandoned the following year.

In the past, other spreadsheets had tried to attack the 1-2-3 empire, but could not even make a dent. Microsoft was aware of this. "We don't expect to make a huge impact right away," Jeff Raikes explained to the *New York Times* (October 2, 1987). "But we are heading into a technology transition, and over the long term, we have a major opportunity." When reminded of the extent of Lotus's domination, Raikes remained optimistic. "We think this is a case where a competitor's strength is also its greatest weakness. In the case of Lotus, the strength is in an interface that users are very used to. But the world is moving toward a graphical interface. And Lotus is hoping that people won't want to switch."

Businessland was one of the official endorsers of Excel. Its chairman, Dave Norman, announced that his stores were standardizing around Excel. He had no doubt that a program like Excel was the best showcase for the capabilities of the new hardware. In other words, Windows Excel could encourage people to buy the PC AT or 80386 machines with sophisticated monitors. He also praised the open connectivity between the PC and the Macintosh and, beyond these microcomputers, toward minicomputers and mainframes. The 94 Businessland stores throughout the United States offered training on Excel.

Some large businesses were already beginning to defect from 1-2-3. Arthur Andersen had several thousand copies of 1-2-3 replaced by Excel, saying the latter was easier to use and performed better. The vice president of Manufacturers Hanover Trust said that Excel would be put on all of their 80386 machines.

Steve Ballmer responded bluntly to criticism that Excel required high-powered hardware, saying that if he had watered down the original idea of the product so that it could run on the entire installed base of PCs, it wouldn't even be worth talking about.

Excel officially arrived in stores October 30, 1987. The big surprise came when a new version of Windows was released simultaneously, which was far superior to the earlier version. The Windows 2.0/Excel duo was a big coup. Microsoft also released a version of Windows for 80386 machines such as the Compaq or the IBM PS/2 model 80. The new versions of Windows could support Excel elegantly, and Excel in turn demonstrated that Windows was a viable and exploitable environment.

RECEPTION

PC Excel was one of the landmark products of its time. Microsoft's spreadsheet was one of the best technical developments ever seen in the microcomputing world. This was undoubtedly Microsoft's best work, and it is easy to distinguish pre-Excel applications from post-Excel applications. For the first time, the company showed such a high degree of know-how that its product could almost be called a work of art, a masterpiece.

The November issue of *Business Software* began its benchmark tests of Excel with a series of photographs symbolizing the history of calculating tools. In the background was an IBM 604 electronic calculator, created in 1948. Just in front of that was an Apple II with VisiCalc, dated October 1979. In front of those was the IBM PC with Lotus 1-2-3, captioned January 1983. Finally, in the foreground, was an IBM PS/2 based on the 80386 and Microsoft Excel. Microsoft's own advertising group could not have done a better job of positioning the product.

In the December 22, 1987, issue of *PC Magazine*, Jared Taylor spoke in glowing terms of Excel. "Microsoft Excel. . . . could be one of those milestone programs that change the way we use computers. Not only does Excel have a real chance of giving 1-2-3 its most serious competition since Lotus Development Corp. introduced that program in 1982, it could finally give the graphics interface a respectable home in the starched-shirt world of DOS. Excel is unquestionably the most powerful spreadsheet you can buy." At the end of his article, the author picked up this theme again, claiming that "feature for feature, Excel is far better than 1-2-3" and "should put the fear of God into Lotus Development Corp."

The October 19, 1987, *Computer Letter* was harsh with Lotus for not remaining at the technological summit, saying that Lotus would be greatly affected by Excel, and that Lotus should have introduced the next generation of spreadsheets before Microsoft. The article insinuated that Lotus had failed to do so because it was incapable of such a move.

Jim Seymour, in his column in the October 6, 1987, issue of *PC Week*, tried to explain his view of the problem that Microsoft would face: corporate inertia. "As wonderful as Windows/386 is for the lucky 50,000 or so who've got 80386 PCs, and as good as Windows 2.0 may be for the rest of us with 286 machines, Windows and Windows applications make no sense on ordinary 8088 PC XTs and clones. Yet Corporate America remains a predominantly PC XT universe."

The October 12, 1987, *Software Industry Bulletin* said that the fastest-growing market for Lotus was small businesses of less than 100 employees. These companies could be encouraged to buy Excel or 1-2-3, but, according to the *Bulletin,* the biggest obstacle for Microsoft was that the distributors were shying away from selling anything besides 1-2-3.

Two months after its release, however, PC Excel was already reaping awards. In January 1988, *PC Magazine* gave it the prize for technical excellence.

INCENTIVES

Beginning in October 1987, Microsoft spent several million dollars promoting Excel: more than on any other product in the company's history, Bill Gates said.

First, the Kenwood Group of San Francisco made a 20-minute video telling the story of three spreadsheet users trying to persuade their boss that Excel produced the best-looking reports. The boss is typically skeptical about switching to a different product. The three employees secretly install Excel on a PC. Then, at night, they return to the office and try out Excel. One of the three argues in favor of their present spreadsheet. Gradually, he is won over by Excel's many great qualities. At the end of the video, the boss himself is convinced and even approves the purchase of an expensive high-end PC.

The first advertising campaign was called "The Soul of the New Machines." Although the campaign did not bring down the Lotus empire (which was too busy celebrating the sale of the 3 millionth copy of 1-2-3), a significant number of large companies decided to buy significant quantities of Excel. They included United Airlines, American Airlines, Boeing, Texas Instruments, Procter & Gamble, Coca-Cola Foods, and Pacific Northwest Bell.

In May 1988, Microsoft shifted gears with its "Win-Win" campaign. Appealing to users waiting for Lotus's 1-2-3/3, Microsoft proposed the following offer: Anyone who purchased Excel before January 31, 1990, could return it later for a 100 percent refund. This would allow users to try Excel and also evaluate 1-2-3/3 when it came out, and still return Excel if it didn't compare favorably.

One month later, Excel got a three-month respite when Lotus announced that 1-2-3/3 would be late. The Boston programmers were going to a lot of trouble to make their new program fit within the 640K of low-end PCs. In September 1988, Lotus announced a second delay, rescheduling the release of 1-2-3/3 for June 1989. It was a difficult year for the large publishers. Ashton-Tate ran into similar problems with dBASE IV. To a certain extent, they were going through what Microsoft had experienced three years earlier in developing Windows.

Some large companies took advantage of the Win-Win offer, notably Deloitte Haskins & Sells, a New York-based accounting firm that uses more than 6,000 microcomputers worldwide. Lotus held its own. In 1988, *Software Digest* ranked 1-2-3 tops in terms of overall capabilities. And when *PC World* readers were asked to vote for their favorite products, 1-2-3 took first place, just as in the past. Furthermore, to counteract the attractiveness of Microsoft's product, Lotus decided to offer an add-in with 1-2-3 that allowed page formatting like Excel's.

At the end of 1988, Microsoft claimed it had won 12 percent of the spreadsheet market with Windows Excel. This is particularly noteworthy considering that Excel was aimed at high-end machines. International Data Corporation published figures indicating that the supremacy of 1-2-3 was slightly reduced even though Excel's market share was still small (7.2 percent).

Some Microsoft executives felt that Excel wasn't catching on quickly enough. On January 25, 1989, Microsoft launched a second campaign to try to convert Lotus users who were still waiting to try 1-2-3/3 before switching to Excel, by offering free trial copies and nationwide seminars. The free trial copy had all the capabilities of the real product, except that the spreadsheets were limited to 16 lines and 64 columns. Better yet, Microsoft offered 1 2 3 users the chance to shift to Excel for the very modest sum of $75. To take advantage of this deal, they had to send in a Lotus 1-2-3 diskette. At the same time, Microsoft doubled the size of the Excel sales force. In all, Microsoft invested more than $5 million in this new promotion.

Here and there, Microsoft won important victories. In April 1989, two federal agencies selected Excel. The Reclamations Bureau of the Department of the Interior recommended the Microsoft spreadsheet for the next seven years and installed 1,250 copies. The Department of Labor decided to include Excel in its accounting system, which involved purchasing several thousand copies.

The two delays in releasing 1-2-3/3 clearly contributed to the weariness of some Lotus faithfuls. However, despite the growth of Excel, 1-2-3 continued to sell ten times more than

Excel (around 100,000 copies a month compared to 10,000). On the other hand, Microsoft's spreadsheet sales were progressing much more rapidly. According to one survey of microcomputer stores, sales of Excel grew 63 percent from one quarter to the next in late 1988, while sales of 1-2-3 declined by 13 percent.

To stop this downturn, Lotus began a campaign in which it encouraged people to buy version 2.01 of 1-2-3, by offering the next version for free.

In June 1989, Lotus finally released 1-2-3/3. The new product was acclaimed for its many capabilities. *Software Digest* judged it superior overall to Excel and all other advanced spreadsheets. Lotus made it through the darkest period in its history and came out on top, but it had paid dearly for the delays. Microsoft had now outdistanced Lotus in total sales by hundreds of millions of dollars.

Microsoft had managed to bring down an empire that the largest software publishers could not. It became clear that the 1990s would not be dominated by a single spreadsheet. Lotus 1-2-3 would have to coexist with Excel. A page of history was turned.

PART 7

FORGING INTO THE FUTURE

Microsoft's future is very, very bright.
Microsoft is in a key position in the industry—
in operating systems with Windows, DOS, and
OS/2, and in applications with Word and Excel.

–Paul Allen, co-founder of Microsoft,
president and founder of Asymetrix

17

The Youngest Billionaire in the World

In early 1986, Lotus, Microsoft, and Ashton-Tate unquestionably dominated the software industry. These three publishers combined held 30 percent of a pie estimated at $5 billion in 1985. Bill Gates summed up the state of the microcomputer industry in these words:

> In a sense, personal computers have become simpler: Now we have just the two architectures, the PC and the Mac. Back in the good old days we had 30 or 40 different machines that were totally incompatible, and there were a whole bunch of languages that people were messing around with. Because we've brought millions and millions of people in, we've had to make it more homogeneous, more standardized, so that they can get some sense of what's going on.

Manufacturers of IBM-compatible computers now rallied around a new standard imposed by IBM in the latter half of 1984 when it released its PC AT with the 80286 microprocessor and EGA monitor. Compaq was the first to fall in line, closely followed by ITT, Texas Instruments, Zenith, and Kaypro.

In September 1985, Steve Jobs resigned from his post as chairman of Apple Computer and announced that he was forming a new company, called NeXT, with five top employees from Apple. Apple responded by threatening to sue its founder for taking proprietary information.

For Microsoft, it was a time for noteworthy awards. *PC World* showcased the mouse and the Flight Simulator. *PC Magazine* bestowed awards upon Word 2.0 and Windows. A few months later, the Software Publishers Association handed out its Oscars: Excel triumphed in two categories, Best Management Product and Best Productivity Product. Windows did even better with three prizes: Best Technical Product, Best User Interface, and Best Software. In June, CompuServe named Windows Best Environment for 1985.

Computer magazines were not the only ones glorifying Microsoft. *Inc.* Magazine listed Microsoft as one of the fastest-growing companies. In 1986, an almost unprecedented stock market coup rocketed Bill Gates, at age 30, into the elite group of the world's richest men.

GOING PUBLIC

Ashton-Tate and Lotus had gone public in 1983, but Microsoft was cautious about making this move. Gates knew the moment would come sooner or later, but he tried to put it off as long as possible. His friend Mitch Kapor, chairman of Lotus, had painted a bleak picture of the formalities involved. Stockbrokers were rarely impressed with high-quality software, being more interested in how it translated into monetary gain.

Microsoft used generous stock options to attract talented people to the company. Except for one major outside investor (David Marquardt, who held 6.2 percent of the company), Microsoft was owned almost entirely by its employees. Bill Gates and Paul Allen held controlling majorities. Microsoft estimated that by 1987, more than 500 people would own Microsoft stock. When it grew to that size, it would have to register with the Securities and Exchange Commission

(SEC), which effectively would give the stock a very narrow public market. It is usually better for a company to make its initial public offering before it is required to register with the SEC so that it can ensure a strong liquid market for its shares based on the firm's growth rate and external market factors.

When David Marquardt and Jon Shirley broached the subject of going public in April 1985, Gates was hesitant. Microsoft was on the verge of three important events: launching Excel for the Macintosh, Windows for the PC, and possibly developing a new operating system for IBM. Gates thought Microsoft should ensure the success of those three events first. Otherwise, the company could easily be attacked by the financial press on any of those three fronts, which would undermine its public offering. On the other hand, if Mac Excel, Windows, and the future DOS were definite assets, Microsoft stock would look healthier and would attract more investors. That way, Gates and his associates would see a substantial increase in the value of their own holdings.

Another point bothered Gates. Unlike many software publishers, Microsoft had until now managed to avoid high employee turnover. If Microsoft went public, some executives could be tempted to sell their shares at the most opportune moment and then leave the company. Bill therefore decided to take a survey and base his final decision on what it revealed.

On October 28, 1985, Bill turned 30. In honor of the chairman's birthday, Microsoft held a roller-skating party in the warehouse area. In the back, a jazz band featured Paul Allen on guitar, though he was no longer with the company.

The following day, the board met to hear Gates's decision. He was now in favor of going public. Microsoft had just signed the contract with IBM to jointly develop the next PC operating system, and Excel had been well received by the press and the public. Development of Windows was almost completed, and it was finally due to be published. And Gates's survey of key people in the company revealed that he could count on their loyalty. Each one had agreed to not sell more than 10 percent of his or her personal shares. Microsoft was ready to become a publicly held company.

Frank Gaudette, the chief financial officer hired by Jon Shirley, was placed in charge of selecting the financial firms to act as managing underwriters. Streetwise and financially savvy, Gaudette was definitely the right man for the job. He suggested giving top priority to a first-rate Wall Street firm and backing that up with a firm specializing in technology in order to attract investors specifically interested in technology stocks.

Three firms made the candidate list for Wall Street leaders: Goldman, Sachs; Morgan Stanley; and Smith Barney. Four names made the list of technology investors: Alex. Brown & Sons; Hambrecht & Quist; Robertson Colman & Stephens; and L. F. Rothschild Unterberg Towbin. Microsoft also considered the Seattle firm of Cable Howse & Ragen.

Frank Gaudette met with representatives from all eight companies and asked them straightforward questions about how they would distribute the stock, to whom, and why, and why their names should be associated with Microsoft's.

On November 21, 1985, Gaudette submitted his conclusions to Gates and Shirley. He graded each firm on a scale of 1 to 5 in 19 different categories. Goldman, Sachs came out on top. Gaudette nevertheless felt that the determining factor should be the "chemistry" between Microsoft and the firm selected. He then left for a ten-day vacation to Hawaii to belatedly celebrate his 50th birthday. While he was gone, anxiety grew within the investment firms, who did not appreciate this delay. They besieged the Microsoft offices with calls for Gates and Shirley.

Upon his return, Gaudette phoned Eff Martin of Goldman, Sachs and invited him to meet with Microsoft executives on the evening of December 11.

The dinner meeting was held at the Rainier Club, an exclusive Seattle restaurant. Microsoft had reserved a private room for the occasion. Early in the evening the atmosphere was somewhat strained, partly because the two parties were not yet acquainted and partly due to the significance of the moment. According to *Fortune* magazine (July 21, 1986), "Gates . . . was tired and prepared to be bored. Shirley was caustic, wanting to know exactly what Goldman, Sachs imagined it could do for Microsoft." Martin and his three colleagues were used to this kind of test and tried to establish rapport by explaining how they went about finding and financing high-tech companies. Martin finally elicited Gates's interest by talking about pricing Microsoft's stock. At the end of the evening, Martin predicted that Microsoft could have "the most visible public offering of 1986—or ever."

Gates left favorably impressed with Martin's proposals. He voted for Goldman, Sachs as the leading firm. Now they had to find a "technology boutique," to complete the duo. Shirley leaned toward Alex. Brown, which for several years had been approaching Microsoft about handling its public offering when the time came.

On December 17, the principal parties met in the Bellevue offices. Gates, Shirley, and Gaudette invited their legal counsel to attend. Microsoft's legal affairs were handled by Shidler McBroom Gates and Lucas (the Gates is Bill's father), represented by William Neukom. The Goldman, Sachs and Alex. Brown representatives arrived several hours late due to thick fog over Seattle.

Bill Gates said he envisioned selling 2 million shares. Existing shareholders were likely to sell up to 10 percent of their holdings, putting approximately 600,000 shares on the market. The underwriters would have the option for some 300,000 additional shares. Overall, Microsoft would put about 12 percent of the company on the market.

After a long discussion with the Goldman, Sachs people, Gates advocated a price of $15 per share, slightly higher than the price-earnings multiple of microcomputer software firms such as Lotus and Ashton-Tate, since Microsoft had a more diversified product line, but slightly lower than the multiple of publishers of mainframe software, which are viewed as more stable firms. At $15 per share, the initial offering could bring in $40 million. The consultants felt Microsoft could go as high as $20 per share, since the market for good software stocks had been rising since September. Gates did not feel comfortable with that amount and stuck to the initial modest price.

After informing the SEC of its intention to go public, Microsoft had to prepare a prospectus. This is a delicate art, since investors are supposed to base their investment decisions on this document. Microsoft knew that its prospectus had to project a positive image of the company, focusing on recent successes. It had to explain how the company intended to ensure continued growth, without giving away any secrets to competitors about future directions. At the same time, the prospectus had to be realistic and could not exaggerate Microsoft's position, lest the SEC challenge the prospectus's validity. Above all, Microsoft was concerned that its prospectus be legally sound, to forestall stockholders trying to sue the company on the grounds that it had painted a false picture in order sell stock.

Before the company went public, it could not appear to promote its stock in any way. Neukom thus required Microsoft to temporarily keep a low profile in Gates's public appearances, press releases, and other outside contacts. At the same time, in order for the offering to be a success, Microsoft had to attract Wall Street institutional investors. Therefore, public meetings were set up so that Gates could explain to select groups Microsoft's reasons for going public. Gates was very annoyed when he was told he would have to play this role halfheartedly and restrain his enthusiasm about his "dream child." After being reminded of the lukewarm state of the stock market, Gates agreed to make the rounds of bankers and financiers, with Frank Gaudette at his side to cover the stock-related issues.

For three weeks, various participants in the December 17 meeting met with the Shidler McBroom lawyer regularly to give their input on writing the prospectus. William Neukom, who in the meantime had decided to join Microsoft, assisted in this task.

On January 8 and 9, as the lawyer checked the final commas in the prospectus, Goldman, Sachs and Alex. Brown brought their experts to Microsoft to examine the company's administrative, financial, and strategic affairs. They questioned Gates, Shirley, Ballmer, and Gaudette at length. Gates still thought an offering price of $20 was too high, but at the insistence of Goldman, Sachs, he finally agreed to consider a price in the $16-$19 range.

Microsoft filed its prospectus with the SEC in early February, and had to wait a month for a response. In the meantime, Goldman, Sachs and Alex. Brown sent out 38,000 prospectuses to all types of investors. Gates, growing tired of the whole process, had to prepare for the meetings with institutional investors, beginning February 7.

The young visionary who was always quick to launch into expressive speeches about the virtues of software and its civilizing effect on society was instructed to adopt a conservative tone, restrain his natural fervor, and limit his presentations to the information contained in the prospectus. Though this was a difficult task, Gates played his role so well that one member of the audience asked him why he didn't put more into his speech. "You mean I'm supposed to say boring things in an exciting way?" Gates snapped.

Frank Gaudette, on the other hand, took great pleasure in speaking to an audience full of bankers and finance people. He added a few clichés and corny jokes to his glowing report of Microsoft's lack of debt and its excellent performance throughout its short history. Gates too became more communicative as time went by and occasionally even dared to extol the merits of software, especially Microsoft's. Institutional investors turned out in droves to these informational meetings, and everything indicated they would strongly support the stock introduction.

On March 5, the SEC pronounced its verdict on the prospectus. It found a few areas of concern, but nothing that would challenge the essential information. A few days later, the lawyers managed to reach an agreement with the SEC about the necessary revisions.

Meanwhile, the stock market continued to rise, and Eff Martin asked Gaudette to persuade Gates to increase the number of shares offered and to raise the price to $20. Two major Microsoft shareholders consented to sell 295,000 shares.

Martin flew to Seattle to announce the good news. He showed Gates the impressive list of buy orders from institutional investors. Martin explained that the stock seemed off to a good start and would probably rise to $25 a share within the first few weeks of the initial offering.

The Bill Gates who then met with Shirley and Gaudette was nothing like the Bill Gates who had fought to obtain an offering price of $15. Suddenly, it didn't seem right to him that investors would instantly net $4 per share. "Why are we handing millions of the company's money to Goldman's favorite clients?" asked Gates, who now favored a substantial increase in the initial offering price. Gaudette explained that he needed to tone down his pretensions so as not to offend institutional investors. They finally agreed to raise the price to the $21-$22 range.

The three men then called Goldman, Sachs to inform them of their new decision. Eric Dobkin, in charge of common stock offerings, took the call and was upset by this about-face. He haggled with Frank Gaudette for over an hour, arguing that this new idea could cause certain symbolically important investors to avoid the stock, hurting its chances on the market. Gaudette responded brusquely that he had confidence in the public. He said that Goldman, Sachs was primarily serving the interests of institutional investors and that they had to choose sides. Dobkin persisted, but could not sway Gaudette. Completely dismayed, Dobkin consented to a readjustment around $21, plus or minus one point. The following Monday, six major investors announced they were no longer sure about supporting Microsoft's stock.

On March 12, Gaudette and Neukom met Dobkin and Martin in the New York offices of Goldman, Sachs. The news was fairly good. The stock market was doing exceptionally well, and half the investors who had been likely to drop out had announced they would stay in the game. The two parties agreed on a final price of $21. Now they had to determine the underwriting discount, or "spread," which includes commissions, underwriting expenses, and management fees. Normally, the underwriting discount was around 7 percent of the stock's selling price. Gates, however, had charged Gaudette to obtain a lower rate than Sun Microsystems, which had recently negotiated an unusually low spread of 6.13 percent when it had gone public. Gaudette therefore demanded 6.13 percent, about $1.28 per share.

Once again, Dobkin was shocked and fought for his company tooth and nail. He emphasized the effort Goldman, Sachs and Alex. Brown had expended to promote Microsoft stock to their clients and said they were partly responsible for the favorable way it was received. He concluded by saying he would not go below 6.5 percent, or $1.36 per share.

Gaudette faced a definite problem. He had very strict orders from Bill Gates but could not reach him to get further instructions because Gates was in Australia. The discussions began again, and each side agreed to modify its position. Dobkin went down to $1.33, and Gaudette moved to $1.30. Gaudette remained calm, and Martin and Dobkin finally left the room.

A few minutes later, Dobkin asked to speak to Gaudette alone. Gaudette softened his tone and revealed his dilemma: He could not go any higher without Gates's authorization. He nevertheless agreed to call Jon Shirley to get permission to raise the spread by one cent. Shirley gave his consent. The two parties finally agreed on a spread of $1.31 per share.

A BILLIONAIRE ON PAPER

Microsoft's stock began trading publicly the following day at $25.75, surprising many financial analysts who were expecting an opening price of around $16. The stock rose rapidly to $27.75 by the end of the opening day. Two and a half million shares had been traded. Microsoft's stock market value was estimated at $661 million, representing a clear success.

When Lotus had gone public two years earlier, its value had been estimated at $277 million.

Since he owned 43 percent of the company, 11 million shares, Gates's fortune was then worth $390 million. And with Microsoft's stock rising rapidly, Gates's holdings rose to $1.25 billion in less than a year. By March 1987, Microsoft stock had risen to $84.75. Bill Gates became a billionaire at the age of 31, entering the elite circle of the richest men in the world.

The October 1987 issue of *Forbes* listed William Henry Gates III as 29th on its list of the 400 richest people in America. That same month, a photograph of Gates appeared on the title page of *Fortune*. This magazine said that Gates "apparently made more money than anyone else his age, ever, in any business." His salary was estimated at $133,000. Paul Allen was number 87 on the *Forbes* list. His 22 percent holdings in Microsoft were worth "only" $640 million.

Such wealth couldn't help attracting marriage proposals. But for the eligible bachelor who was also the youngest billionaire in the world, it was impossible to discern whether his "suitors" were motivated by love or by money. Miriam Lubow teased Bill about this, but he just put off the subject to a later date. At age 31, he still had too many things to do before he could think about a family. "When I'm 35, I'll get married," he joked.

18

Microsoft Culture Today

After Microsoft's initial public offering, Bill Gates appeared on "Good Morning America." When asked about his new fortune, he played down the importance of his wealth and calmly responded that he was primarily concerned with his company and with developing software. He added that stock values fluctuated and that his wealth was relative to the price of Microsoft stock. Gates maintained this modest view of his wealth even in 1990, when it had grown substantially. Asked by Mark Stevens (*M. Inc.,* December 1990) what his money means to him, Gates replied, "I don't have any money; I have stock. I own about 35 percent of the shares of Microsoft, and I take a salary of $175,000 a year." Forced to admit that the $30 million worth of Microsoft stock he sold in 1989 was indeed money, Gates said that all it meant to him was not having to worry about what he orders in a restaurant and being able to have a nice house on Lake Washington.

Gates's primary concern has always been selling software. After the initial pubic offering, he devoted himself more than ever to Microsoft's business, working an average of 65 hours a week. Returning home from the office around 9 p.m., he often turned on his PC and continued working late into the night. Vacations were a luxury. In the first five years of Microsoft, Bill took only two three-day vacations. It wasn't until the mid-1980s that he began taking one week of vacation a year. In the spring of 1986, he even went to the extravagance of renting a 56-foot-long sailboat with a crew and spending four days cruising the Australian coast. He half apologized: "We'd just gone public, and I was sort of pampering myself."

Bill continued to be very prudent, considering the possibilities open to him with his new-found wealth. Tired of amassing speeding tickets with his Porsche, he bought a Mercedes diesel. His house on Lake Washington is only about half a mile from his parents' house, and he visits them about twice a month, usually on Sundays. To relax, Gates devours biographies as in his teenage years. He watches carefully for new biographies of great scientists, businessmen, or politicians. He says this helps him understand how such people think. "I've read more about Napoleon than anyone else, and I've read everything I can about da Vinci and Franklin Roosevelt." Bill particularly enjoys reading success stories about other companies. He says one of the best books of all time is *My Years at General Motors* by Albert Sloan because it explains how the company completely redefined the world of automobiles. Gates naturally tries to adapt the successful strategies of other great entrepreneurs to the realm of software.

THE REDMOND "CAMPUS"

In early 1985, Gates and Shirley decided to move Microsoft to Redmond, Washington, in order to make room for the tremendous growth of the company. Construction of a veritable campus began in April 1985. The buildings form an X with a large open space in the middle, and the surrounding landscape includes a pond with a fountain, and stretches of green lawn with meandering pathways. The complex is integrated into the wooded setting.

In March 1986, 700 employees went to work at the new campus. Each had his or her own office with windows looking out on the trees. The enormous pines seem to isolate Microsoft from the outside world.

Inside the buildings, technology is omnipresent, with all the company's computers linked for internal electronic mail. Bill Gates's office is exactly twice as big as the other offices. He has an IBM PC AT, a Macintosh, and a Compaq portable on his desk.

Today, a visitor strolling through the Redmond site feels more like he is on a college campus than in a corporate headquarters. Near Lake Gates, two programmers juggle, while just a short distance away, an Asian woman taps delicately with thin sticks on an Oriental harplike instrument that is lying flat on a polished stand. She is accompanied by a bearded guitarist straight out of the 1960s. Squirrels dart playfully to and fro, and ducks bask on the lawn, unfazed by occasional joggers, unicycle riders, and the other activities around them.

These rare moments of relaxation complement the intense activity that results from the employees' high level of devotion to the company.

The lifestyle of a programmer looks laid-back from the outside. Work hours are flexible; some programmers arrive at 9 p.m. and leave at 5 a.m. Their offices are decorated with stuffed animals, aquariums, bows and arrows, and other assorted collector's items. They dress however they want and often work barefoot. One member of the company says that whenever he goes to lunch in town, the friends he meets ask him why he isn't working. They can't believe he can go to work dressed as casually as he does.

"Writing software is a very intense activity, and we try to make it as pleasant as possible," Jon Shirley explains. One day, a visitor asked Charles Simonyi why the programmers were so casual. Simonyi simply replied, "Because it's good for business."

He is right. The external appearance of relaxation on the Redmond campus masks the unrelenting productivity.

Gates, himself a programmer, knows that programmers need a working environment with as few constraints as possible.

Many programmers try to compensate for the intensity of the intellectual work with physical activity. Every employee receives a free membership in the nearby health club. Some developers have built their own homes, others have taken up rock climbing or skiing. One does silversmithing as a hobby, while another competes regularly in marathons. Many are musicians, some trained, some self-taught. In addition to a concert pianist, Microsoft has many guitarists and synthesizer players in its ranks.

People in this privileged environment could easily develop a neutral attitude about the outside world, but in fact, many are concerned about human rights issues and civic affairs. When not discussing the best way to write an operating system function, developers can often be found near the snack machines arguing over the soundness of a government decision. Concerns about civil rights sometimes even reach top management. In March 1986, for example, Microsoft announced that it would stop shipping products to the Republic of South Africa in support of the antiapartheid movement.

The presence of many foreign employees gives the Microsoft campus an international flavor. Many of these individuals are translators. The French, German, Italian, and Japanese versions of Multiplan, Word, and MS-DOS, for example, are translated on site by nationals from those countries. While everyone tries to speak English, Spanish accents and German interjections add charm to the conversations overheard on the lawns.

THE BUSINESS PHILOSOPHY

Microsoft's current management philosophy has fallen into place over the years. The company believes in choosing the best, hardest-working people and turning them loose to prove themselves.

It is not uncommon for Microsoft to hire people with no professional programming experience or formal training. After all, neither of its two founders obtained college degrees.

Charles Simonyi has greatly contributed to honing Microsoft's recruitment efforts. The company spends large sums seeking out and then attracting the best people possible. Even when a candidate has impressive diplomas and recommendations, he has to answer a series of questions designed to test his knowledge and analytical skills. For a long time, Simonyi insisted on personally interviewing each potential employee in order to have the final say on hiring. He says: "There are a lot of formulas for making a good candidate into a good programmer. We hire talented people. I don't know how they got their talent and I don't care. But they are talented. From then on, there is a hell of a lot the environment can do.[1]

Each year, employees undergo a review. In 1985, Simonyi, Gates, Ballmer, Shirley, and a few others developed from scratch this system of rating and promoting employees. Microsoft uses three systems for rewarding employees who contribute significantly to the company's success: raises, stock options, and bonuses.

Everything flows down from Gates. He is very demanding of those around him. "Sometimes it takes a little bit to get used to working with Bill, because the level of excellence expected is very high. If you don't meet that level of excellence, he'll be sure and let you know," says Jeff Raikes, director of development of applications software.

"If you don't like to work hard and be intense and do your best, this is not the place to work," Gates says.

Gates is also known for occasionally losing his temper and being disagreeable. Developer Jeff Harbers explained that working with Gates toughened him up. At first, he felt bad after being reprimanded by Gates. Then he learned to

---

[1]Susan Lammers, *Programmers at Work*, p.18.

counterattack. "You have to be able to take this abuse and fight back. If you back down, he loses respect. It's part of the game."[2] Mike Slade said that "for a guy who is right so often, he's always willing to admit he's wrong. Mind you, it's not easy to convince him he's wrong."

An atmosphere of open, honest relationships prevails. Employees are encouraged to send electronic mail messages to anyone else in the company, regardless of position. And it is not uncommon to see Bill Gates conversing with employees in the company cafeteria. He says he enjoys taking time with people to discuss their projects and push them to go beyond their limits.

Microsoft managers strive to stay on top of market trends and maintain good business relationships with other computer firms. According to Jeff Raikes, Microsoft tries to be sensitive to how hardware companies perceive the firm. "I remember that when IBM came to visit Microsoft, we ran and hid all our Macintoshes. We didn't want IBM to know that we had so many Macintoshes then. Then when Steve Jobs brought John Sculley, we went and hid all of our IBM PCs."

Despite the size of his company, Bill Gates keeps the creative juices flowing by having programmers working in small groups. "It takes a small team to do it right," he says. "When we started Excel, we had five people working on it, including myself. We have seven people working on it today, and at the maximum we had fifteen people working on the program. There's too much that needs to work together to have so many people spread out on a program." Paul Allen says this strategy has been part of Microsoft's approach from the outset. "When you increase the size [of the company], the important thing to do is when you see a new product opportunity, have a small team go after that opportunity. That's what we always did at Microsoft. We had small teams working on different areas."

---

[2] *Business Week,* April 13, 1987.

The Microsoft campus is an exciting place where being good-natured and driven to excellence are the norm. Despite pressure from executives and relatively modest salaries— which, nonetheless, are complemented by stock options— Microsoft's annual employee turnover is around 10 percent, lower than average for microcomputer companies. And the creative energy of its people is tremendous. Jeff Raikes offers his own interpretation of what makes the magic of Microsoft. "This all filters down from Bill. The company has a personality. If you compare Bill's personality with the company's personality, you can see they're almost identical." The entrepreneurial drive and creative genius of Bill Gates are woven into the very fabric of the company.

19

Works: A Product for Beginning Users

Seven people sat around a table. They represented the diversity of corporate America. From the secretary to the director of computer services, they all needed to use software to perform their jobs. Microsoft had gathered them together in San Francisco to get their opinions on a new product under development: Works.

Microsoft was holding another of its meetings with pilot users to help bring its high-tech, creative speculations into line with the needs of everyday people. Microsoft representatives set aside their theoretical debates about future features, technologies, and marketing strategies as they face real end-users who view software in terms of the practical problems it helps them solve, such as how to prepare a project status report for their boss, or create a graph of their monthly budget for a managers' meeting.

Three men and four women attended this late-afternoon meeting in December 1986. When the Microsoft representative asked them which programs were used in their companies, five of them said Lotus 1-2-3. Two mentioned Microsoft Word, and two mentioned Ashton-Tate's dBASE.

The Microsoft seminar leader asked the users how they had come to use those products. Three responded, "My company has a list of approved software." Only two people had chosen their software themselves, using primitive criteria. "Somebody else had Word so I chose it too." "Lotus 1-2-3 looked more modern than VisiCalc."

A Microsoft programmer demonstrated a prototype of Works on a color Compaq computer. This integrated software package—composed of a spreadsheet, word processor, a database, and a communications module—was designed to be easy to use. With its online tutorial, Works is primarily geared to neophytes who have never used a PC or a software application.

Questions began to fly. Will this be compatible with Windows? Does the spreadsheet work like 1-2-3? The programmer calmly responded, continually emphasizing the key points of Works.

After the demonstration, the seminar leader asked for feedback from the participants.

What did you like best about this program?

- I like the fact that you can combine different functions. Right now when I do a report, I use three different programs.
- I really like the Mac, and this program looks a lot like the Mac.
- I'm usually intimidated by computers, but this program looks like it's easy to understand.

What things didn't you like?

- I wish it had windows.
- Yeah, at least two windows. And you should be able to move from one to the other.
- Automatic recording of macros would be good.

What is missing to make it perfect?

- I would like it to be more compatible with Lotus macros.

A lot of people say that. But their macros in fact are not so sophisticated. Why is that so important?

- It took a lot of time to learn Lotus macros. It's difficult to invest time in something else.
- I have used Lotus, but the spreadsheet you showed us seemed OK.

Who do you think this product is for?

- Home use, to make Christmas card address lists.
- Yes. In the office you need something more powerful.
- It would be a useful product for someone just starting out with computers. But I don't see how this product could replace what we're already using.
- One thing I like is the tutorial. With the software we use at the office, you have to look things up in the manual.

Can you give it a grade between 0 and 10?

- I give it a 7 because it looks easy.
- As a product for home use, I also give it a 7.
- It's interesting. I say 5.
- Six.
- I'd say 5. It's a program for the home or school. Not for the office.
- I frankly don't see why you couldn't use it at the office. I give it a 6.
- It's an excellent program for the first-time user. I'd give it a 7 or 8.

The Microsoft representatives returned to Redmond concluding that they had aimed correctly. Works was a product designed above all to make computing accessible to the neophyte.

INTEGRATED SOFTWARE

In 1984, integrated programs that grouped several applications into one product had begun to enter the market. Lotus Symphony, an early integrated program, began selling well, but was not as enthusiastically received as 1-2-3. One of the reasons for Symphony's poor showing was that it was difficult to learn. Ashton-Tate's Framework had the advantages of a graphical user interface in text mode and was based on a concept of windows similar to Microsoft Windows. Its spreadsheet, however, was too slow, and Framework was only moderately successful.

In 1986, demand for integrated software was very low. Symphony and Framework had made this type of program seem too complex for the average user. Then Software Publishing Corporation (SPC) launched First Choice. This sinking company had the idea of grouping four previously popular programs into one package. First Choice was so simple that the public was immediately interested. It finished the year in ninth place for annual sales, according to InfoCorp.

First Choice clearly showed that there was a market for an easy-to-use integrated program. Microsoft took note.

DESIGNING WORKS

The Works project began at the end of 1985 as an integrated product designed to serve primarily the low-end PC market. This was to be a product that could be understood and used by the public at large.

Since Gates wanted to promote the graphical user interface and had decided that in the long run, all Microsoft products would be ported to Windows, Works was defined as a Windows program.

After four months, the project floundered. The developers announced that when they used Windows on an 8088 PC, performance was mediocre.

Gates called a meeting with Jeff Raikes, Jabe Blumenthal, and the lead developers to address this problem. They decided to develop Works in text mode like Multiplan and Word, so that it would perform well on low-end PCs. Works would, however, have a "Windows look," with a mouse, pull-down menus, dialogue boxes, and other Windows features.

Once this foundation was laid, designing Works was easy. Microsoft already had many lines of code that could be used in Works. Large sections were borrowed from Word for the Works word processing feature. The spreadsheet was modeled on 1-2-3, since that product was so popular. Works turned out to be one of the easiest products to develop in Microsoft's history. The specifications did not change midstream, nor did the programming team.

THE WORKS TUTORIAL

Microsoft had established the CBT (computer-based training) division in 1983 to write the learning tools for its programs. In 1986, the tutorial for Word 3.0 played a major role in selling the product.

Development on the Works tutorial began in June 1986. Three programmers were writing it. In September, Barry Linnett joined the group and began defining the format of the lessons. As team leader, he was charged with writing the most sophisticated computer tutorial ever.

When Linnett went to work for Microsoft, he had never touched a PC in his life. He was a biology major in college, and not particularly predisposed to computer science. After backpacking across the United States, he stopped in Seattle. He liked the area and decided to stay for a while. That's when he became friends with Betsy Davis, who worked in Microsoft's CBT department. Barry was looking for work, so Betsy asked him to come help out in her department for a few days. Barry was enthralled with what he discovered there, and five years later, he was still there. Much of the credit for the outstanding Works tutorial goes to him.

Again, Microsoft had identified a gifted individual, directed his efforts to an appropriate endeavor, and utilized his energies to the fullest.

Linnett defined a basic pattern that would apply throughout the Works tutorial:

1. Introduce a certain task, for example, cutting and pasting text using the word processing module.
2. Demonstrate how the product accomplishes the task.
3. Allow the user to practice that task.

The first part of each lesson focused on the desired output. "At the beginning of a lesson, you have to motivate the user. Why do I want to do this? What do I get out of it when I'm all done?" Linnett explains.

Linnett believed that tutorial users should enjoy using the program as much as they enjoy watching television. He loved visual images and bright colors. He drew each screen with extreme care like an animated cartoon. The programmers were also encouraged to let their imaginations run wild. Instead of presenting endless pages of information, the Works tutorial relies on drawings and animation to convey ideas. "The biggest part of learning anything is how enjoyable it is. If you're having a good time, you're going to learn it. That's a fundamental part of education. . . . People like visual stimulation. . . . You want the CBT to be fun and interesting, because it's really important that they learn how to use [the product]."

From the snail race to a night scene in New York, all of the tutorial's images incited curiosity. The "tour" of the word processing feature began with an iron tool chipping away at a solid gray block. The caption said, "2000 B.C. In the beginning, there was chisel and stone." The next screen showed a hand writing sentences on a piece of paper with a fountain pen and an ink bottle. "1776 A.D. Then came pen and paper. It was faster, but one mistake could spell disaster." When the user clicked the mouse to continue, the ink bottle spilled all over the paper. Then a typewriter appeared. "1929 A.D. Then the typewriter arrived. Little mistakes could be fixed, but big changes meant retyping it all!" Then a PC appeared on the screen. "Today, the word processor has taken the labor out of writing . . . so you can concentrate on generating ideas, not on avoiding mistakes." The advantages of word processing were presented with several examples such as spell checking, replacing a word, rearranging paragraphs, and so on.

Once the tutorial introduced a task, the user had only to watch the screen for a demonstration. "The best way to learn [a task]. . . is to ask a person who knows how to do it and [have him] come and work over your shoulder and take the mouse and say, 'Look, this is how you do it.' That's what we tried to do [in the demonstration portion of the tutorial]—have that person standing over their shoulder doing it."

Each tutorial lesson ended with an exercise for the user to practice what he had just learned, as if he were actually using Works.

The programming team finished the spreadsheet part of Works in three months. To finish the 49 tutorial lessons on time, however, the CBT group needed significant outside assistance. In January 1987, nine other programmers joined the CBT division. This group represented a particularly diverse set of backgrounds. Their past jobs ranged from kayak instructor to park service ranger. When it came time to find examples for how Works could be used, this diversity was a bonus. In all, this group meticulously created more than 5,000 tutorial screens.

Each tutorial screen was programmed to react to the various actions of the user. For example, besides successfully performing the task and giving an encouraging message if the user pressed the correct key, the tutorial responded with further directions if the user pressed the wrong key. Programming the tutorial for the large number of possible user responses was a major feat.

One of the lessons included a snail race, which became infamous. The programmer responsible for this example was a student at the University of Illinois who had come for a summer internship at Microsoft. For his going-away party, the CBT division organized a giant snail race, with programmers disguised as snails. At the word go, they began slowly crawling down the hall. Visiting executives, arriving for a meeting with Bill Gates and Jon Shirley, walked in just in time to see these giant Microsoft mollusks creeping toward them.

Once a lesson was written, the CBT team tested it on all the novice users they could find. Friends, parents, nieces, and distant cousins all became guinea pigs, provided that they had never used a computer before. "It was fantastic to watch how people would react to it," Betsy Davis recalls. She says the programmers discovered that many things which seemed obvious to them were not at all obvious to the beginners. For example, when the tutorial asked them to press TAB, they typed out the word T-A-B.

In the end, the Works tutorial became a model for tutorials. Barry Linnett believes his team developed a unique solution to the problem of training users. The most surprising thing was that he had never studied art or computers.

WORKS IS RELEASED

Works shipped in September 1987. Because it was released about the same time as Windows Excel, Excel stole its thunder. Gradually, the computer magazines realized that Microsoft had made another masterpiece. They remarked that the know-how that went into the Works tutorial was astounding.

In March 1988, Microsoft hired Griggs Anderson Research to conduct a survey of Works users. They phoned 150 people, none of whom worked for hardware or software companies. The results showed that Works users hardly ever used any other program. When asked about how they learned the product, they all praised the online tutorial. When asked "What part of the documentation did you like the best?" most responded with the tutorial. Ninety-four percent had used it, and 77 percent said they were very satisfied. This contrasted sharply with the printed documentation, which was judged "difficult to understand" by three-fourths of the respondents. Eighty-six percent had learned Works with the tutorial, and 73 percent indicated that they refreshed their memory by going through the on-screen lessons.

Barry Linnett found this survey quite gratifying. "It's really nice for me. The weirdest thing about working here is you put a year or a year and a half of your life into something, and when you're all done, you've got this little floppy disk. Then you never see it again."

Every magazine that compared Works to other low-end integrated programs placed it far ahead of its competitors. The most surprising reward came in August 1989 from *InfoWorld*. This time, Works was no longer compared to just the low-end integrated software, but to others in the professional market, including Symphony, Framework, and Informix's Smart. To everyone's surprise, Works came out on top, tied with Framework.

20

Vision for the Future

In June 1987, at the meeting of the Boston Computer Society, Bill Gates announced that 250,000 copies of Windows had been distributed. By early 1989, Windows had sold 2 million copies and had become Microsoft's best-selling product, with 50,000 copies sold per month.

What happened? Excel, PageMaker, Designer, Omnis, and other successful Windows applications had turned this once disfavored product into a best-seller. Windows itself had also substantially changed. Version 2.0, released in November 1987 at the same time as Excel, made up for the poor performance of the first version.

In 1989, Windows applications flooded onto the market. The AMI word processing program, the SuperBase database, and the draw program CorelDraw all proved the usability of Windows. Microsoft was also adapting its primary products to Windows. The Word conversion was under way, and the scope of the project was immense. Word 2.0 was composed of 35,000 lines of code and Word 4.0 had 78,000 lines, but the code for Word for Windows was more than 400,000 lines.

Bill Gates promoted his graphical user interface more energetically than ever. In Paris in January 1989, he claimed that more applications were being developed for Windows than for any other environment.

Lotus, WordPerfect, and Ashton-Tate ignored Windows for a long time, preferring to port their products to Presentation Manager, the graphical user interface supported by IBM for its new OS/2 multitasking microcomputer. By the summer of 1989, however, it was becoming clear that the business world was warming up to Windows and looking forward to the announced improvements of the next version.

THE BIG DAY

Industry excitement over the next version of Windows built to a near frenzy in the first few months of 1990, until finally, the big day of the introduction arrived. Almost five years after its initial release in November 1985, Windows was finally going to live up to its potential.

Microsoft spared no expense in turning the Windows 3.0 rollout into a historical event. On May 22, 1990, some 6,000 people were on hand as the City Center Theater in New York City became center stage for the multimedia extravaganza. Gala events took place in 7 other North American cities, which were linked via satellite to the New York stage for a live telecast, and in 12 major cities throughout the world, including London, Amsterdam, Stockholm, Paris, Madrid, Milan, Sydney, Singapore, and Mexico City. The production included videos, slides, laser lights, "surround sound," and a speech by Bill Gates, who proclaimed Windows 3 "a major milestone" in the history of software, saying that it "puts the 'personal' back into millions of MS-DOS-based computers." He called Windows 3.0 "a better DOS than DOS."

Microsoft poured $3 million into these opening-day festivities alone, and planned to spend another $7 million promoting Windows 3.0 by advertising, distributing 250,000 free demonstration diskettes, and offering demonstrations and seminars. It was, in Gates's words, "the most extravagant, extensive, and expensive software introduction ever."

LONG-AWAITED WINDOWS 3.0

The star of that show, Windows 3.0, is the result of two and a half years of development by a group of 25 people who called themselves the "Win 3 team." Each developer was responsible for a certain part of the product and had a great deal of freedom to be creative in designing it—within the general framework determined by Bill Gates, who kept in close contact with members of the team via electronic mail and bi-weekly meetings, and continually challenged them to excel.

The most significant new feature of Windows 3.0 is its expanded memory specification (EMS), which breaks the 640K limitation of DOS. This improves multitasking, as Windows users can run several large applications simultaneously without worrying about running out of memory. This capability makes it easier, for example, to transfer data from a spreadsheet and a drawing from a graphics program into a report written with a word processing program.

The new version also provides networking features lacking in earlier versions of Windows, although critics say these capabilities are still rudimentary. Microsoft made Windows 3.0 easier to install and configure, included more desktop accessories, and changed the appearance of the screen.

Microsoft came up with the new screen design after a survey of Windows 2.1 users uncovered many complaints that the interface looked like it was designed by a programmer, with little regard for esthetics. The bright blues and reds of earlier versions gave way to muted tones with a more professional look, and many icons were redrawn to make them more recognizable. According to Tandy Trower, Microsoft's director of user-interface architecture, "Windows is trying to expand the marketplace by making an environment that's easier for new users."

A BIG SELLER

The long anticipation of Windows 3.0 heightened expectations to unrealistic proportions. Jim Seymour, writing in *PC Week* (May 22, 1990), was able to keep things in perspective:

This is the moment when Windows gets real: real as in a real alternative to working in DOS. Until now, Windows has been a novelty, a tease, an alluring but disappointing and sometimes infuriating glimpse of what graphical interfaces could be.

Although still far from perfect, Windows 3.0 will nonetheless end that criticism. It's really that good.... It was worth the wait.

The response to this milestone product was quick in coming. In the first two months after Windows 3.0's release, according to *PC Week* (July 30, 1990), Microsoft shipped more than 800,000 copies throughout the world. By the end of 1990, it had sold 1 million copies. When leading trade publications announced their awards for 1990, Windows 3.0 frequently took the prize. *BYTE* magazine (January 1991) bestowed its Award of Excellence on Windows 3.0, calling it "the first usable graphical user interface for the IBM PC to meet with widespread, enthusiastic acceptance by the DOS-based computing public." *PC Magazine* (January 15, 1991) included Windows 3.0 in its "Best of 1990" cover story, saying that Microsoft's product was "arguably the most successful new product of 1990." The December 1990 edition of *PC Computing* called Windows 3.0 one of the most valuable products of the year and praised the new version highly:

When the annals of the PC age are written, May 22, 1990, will mark the first day of the second era of IBM-compatible PCs. On that day, Microsoft released Windows 3.0. And on that day, the IBM-compatible PC, a machine hobbled by an outmoded, character-based operating system and seventies style programs, was transformed into a computer that could soar in a decade of multitasking graphical operating environments and powerful new applications.

Windows 3.0 gets right what its predecessors—VisiOn, GEM, earlier versions of Windows, and OS/2 Presentation Manager—got wrong. It delivers adequate performance, it accommodates existing DOS applications, and it makes you believe that it belongs on a PC. . . . This $149 program is the most successful attempt yet to provide a multitasking, graphical environment for the PC.

The new version of Windows has also received its fair share of criticism, of course. One of the biggest complaints is that Windows 3.0 requires fairly advanced hardware capabilities to perform well. Microsoft claims that the minimum equipment needed to run Windows 3.0 is an 80286-based PC with 640K of RAM, a hard disk, and an EGA monitor. Many observers, however, point out that in order to obtain acceptable performance, a user needs an 80386-based PC with 2 megabytes of RAM and a VGA monitor. According to industry analyst Peter Lewis (*San Jose Mercury News,* December 16, 1990), the older 80286-based PCs comprise the largest part of the installed base of microcomputers. Among other factors keeping consumers from actually using Windows 3.0, Lewis notes the cost in time and money required to upgrade to applications written specifically for Windows 3.0 and the current unavailability of certain major products such as Lotus 1-2-3 and Word-Perfect for this environment. (Lotus Development Corporation and WordPerfect Corporation have announced, however, that they are porting their products to Windows 3.) Furthermore, Lewis states, "computers rarely come equipped with mice, but without them, Windows is pretty unwieldy."

In addition to Lotus and WordPerfect, seven other major software companies announced support for Windows 3.0: Ashton-Tate, Borland, Informix, Oracle, Software Publishing, Symantec, and Xerox. Windows 3.0 will likely gain wider use as these firms begin to release their popular products in Windows versions.

Meanwhile, Apple Computer has kept a close watch on the Windows 3 hoopla. The director of systems software, Jim Davis, met with analysts around the time of the Windows 3.0 release to tout the benefits of Apple's new

System 7 (later released in May 1991), and persuade them that it is a far better graphical interface than Windows. "We've been at this business for six years," he said. *SoftLetter* (May 23, 1990) concurred that "Apple really does understand user interfaces a whole lot better than anyone else in this business. Moreover, given the inherent limits of the Intel-based marketplace—especially the hodgepodge of conflicting hardware and system-level standards—we doubt that even Microsoft ever will be able to close the gap." The threat to Apple, the writers note, is if many software developers begin offering almost identical applications for both platforms "because the Mac then becomes an undifferentiated commodity machine (at a higher price point)." In the end, the market will prove whether users in search of a good graphical user interface can wade through the confusion of hardware standards in the PC world or whether they will increasingly turn to the simplicity of a single operating system available on all Apple Macintoshes.

WINDOWS VS. OS/2?

When IBM introduced the PS/2 in April 1987, it also announced that it had been collaborating with Microsoft in developing a new operating system called OS/2 and a graphical user interface for it called Presentation Manager. IBM finally released OS/2 version 1.2 for IBM computers in late 1989. Microsoft's version for IBM-compatibles, OS/2 1.21, did not arrive until over six months later.

Many believed OS/2 would eventually replace DOS, but Microsoft has continued to improve DOS. (Version 5.0 is due out in 1991; see Appendix A.) At the Windows 3.0 introduction, Gates said Windows and OS/2 belonged to the same family and that OS/2 was the growth path from Windows. That same month, Steve Ballmer unofficially nicknamed OS/2 "Windows Plus."

Throughout 1990, though, IBM and Microsoft repeatedly redefined the relationship between Windows and OS/2, generating confusion and suspicion in the press. Writing in

PC Magazine (January 15, 1991), Charles Petzold looked back on 1990 and described the situation as follows: "The key words in operating systems are confusion, uncertainty, anxiety, and doubt. Unfortunately, the two guiding lights of this industry—IBM and Microsoft—are part of the problem rather than part of the solution. It's enough to make you want to buy a Macintosh."

Many PC users waited in vain for OS/2 2.0, which was promised to arrive by the end of 1990 but did not. Meanwhile, Windows 3.0 continued to gain new users. The debate in the computer press continued, with many writers admitting that while OS/2 and Presentation Manager are technically superior to DOS and Windows 3.0, they have become victims of poor marketing and the continual repositioning by their joint creators. Petzold pointed out that "the technical superiority of OS/2 and Presentation Manager over DOS and Windows 3.0 is almost universally unquestioned. But standards are not born of technical excellence. Rather, standards result from market trends and political power." He called OS/2 the "idiot savant of operating systems. Deep down, it's brilliant—powerful and versatile..., yet on the surface it's a mess." He sees OS/2 as the victim of "major marketing blunders" by both Microsoft and IBM.

Comparing Windows 3.0 and OS/2, Jon Udell, senior editor at large for *BYTE* magazine (June 1990), asked whether Microsoft had committed "corporate fratricide" with Windows and OS/2. His answer:

> Yes and no. Windows 3.0 addresses, and satisfies, many pressing needs. Rarely does an operating-system upgrade render existing hardware so much more useful. Windows 3.0 will delight longtime Windows fans and win many new converts. Developers are flocking to the platform and in some cases shifting their focus from OS/2's PM to Windows. The Windows momentum that has been building is about to become a tidal wave. But scratch the elegantly polished surface and you'll still find creaky old DOS.

THE MICROSOFT-IBM RELATIONSHIP

All the repositioning of OS/2 by IBM and Microsoft led many industry observers to speculate on the health of their partnership. In September 1990, the two companies announced a new division of labor on OS/2, with IBM taking the bulk of the responsibility for its development, and the trade press immediately jumped to the conclusion that this represented the first steps toward a "divorce." Lotus chairman Jim Manzi was widely quoted as saying this was "the Balkanization of the desktop," and writers lamented the confusion that would inevitably result for users.

Nevertheless, the two major players tried to neutralize these speculations by explaining that the move was intended to make OS/2 development more efficient and consistent. Their statements seemed to convey a promise of further cooperation. Lee Reiswig, IBM's vice president of programming, stated: "Microsoft and IBM see Windows as a long-term opportunity, not short-term. I think Windows is a DOS extension, and DOS is going to go on for years. It's not going to be replaced by OS/2." Microsoft's Steve Ballmer told *PC Week* (September 24, 1990) that Microsoft's long-range goal was to offer Windows for DOS *and* OS/2. In summary, he told journalists, "You may not understand our marriage, but we're not getting divorced."

In May 1990, speaking about the ongoing struggle for operating system dominance—which also includes UNIX to some extent—Bill Gates confidently stated, "There's no negative. This is Microsoft vs. Microsoft vs. Microsoft." Which is what worries many in the industry.

INTO THE FUTURE: INFORMATION AT YOUR FINGERTIPS

In November 1990, Gates delivered the keynote address at Comdex Fall held in Las Vegas. Before introducing Gates, the chief operating officer of the Interface Group, Jason Chudnofsky, announced that in cooperation with Microsoft, his group would stage a new trade show called Windows

World Exposition Conference in May 1991, concurrently with the spring Comdex. This certainly confirmed that Windows was catching on!

Bill Gates began his speech by contrasting his last experience keynoting Comdex in 1983 with this time. In 1983, he said, he spent "about an hour" preparing his speech, arrived ten minutes before he was to go on stage, plugged in the slide projector himself, and had to ask his father to change the slides because there was no one else available. How things had changed.

At the 1983 Comdex, Gates kicked off Microsoft's graphical user interface crusade, which has since won enough converts to merit an entire trade show based on it. This time, he imparted his vision for the future of personal computers. For the personal computer industry to continue to be "the very innovative, high-growth industry that it was throughout the 1980s," Gates said, there must be a common vision, which he suggested should be "information at your fingertips."

To illustrate his vision, Gates used four videotaped scenarios, each time "conversing" with the characters on the screen about ways they wished computers could be more useful for them. All the solutions he presented were based on projects currently under way in many different companies. "Information at your fingertips" will include seamlessly integrated applications, allowing users to focus more on the data they need than on the process of retrieving it from different computer files. Computers no larger than notebooks, able to recognize handwriting input from a stylus, will increase productivity for people working in the field. This, Gates said, will open "a whole new market that wouldn't have used PCs in the past." When used with desktop computers, the stylus will complement the keyboard, making tasks such as editing much easier.

Gates's vision also includes multimedia, which Microsoft has been working on for some time. With "an integrated mix of sound, text, graphics, and live motion on the computer screen," multimedia machines will "blur the lines between education and entertainment, dramatically expanding the possibilities of both," Microsoft claims. For example, as Gates demonstrated, users will be able to move from a map of the world to a map of North America to a map of the state of Washington. Then, after listening to the song of the state bird, they can choose an area of interest, such as the economy, and view pie charts or graphs depicting the regional economy. To know more, they can click with the mouse on the software sector, for example, to see a list of software companies in the area, and then click on the one they're interested in to find out more. In Gates's demonstration, selecting Microsoft brought up a video of the Microsoft campus and then of a meeting where Microsoft employees were "hard at work" devouring several pizzas.

The platform for all this, of course, is Windows. In order to fulfill his vision, Gates outlined several necessary steps: The personal computer must become more "personal," i.e., simpler both in terms of hardware and software, and less intimidating; technology must provide for transparent application integration as well as integrated fax, voice and electronic mail; networks must become easier to manage; and users must be given "easy access to a broad range of information." Meeting this "formidable challenge," Gates said, will require a great deal of cooperation among hardware manufacturers, software developers, and distributors.

In the "Information at Your Fingertips" white paper, Microsoft spells out its role in fulfilling this vision, placing heavy emphasis on standards. Microsoft admits it cannot do this alone: "All these new technologies await us. Unless they are implemented in standard ways on standard platforms, any technical benefits will be wasted by the further splintering of the information base." The company clearly desires, however, to lead the software industry into the future: "Microsoft's role is to move the current generation of PC software users, which is quickly approaching 60 million, to an exciting new era of improved desktop applications and truly portable PCs in a way that keeps users' current applications, and their huge investment in them, intact." Because of its dominant position in PC operating systems, Microsoft believes it is "in a unique position to unify all those efforts."

Bill Gates has never tried to hide his intention for Microsoft to set the standards for the software industry. His often repeated vision of "a personal computer on every desk and in every home" is frequently followed by, "and software standards as a way to make that happen." The question now is, will the rest of the industry go along?

Afterword

As the brief but breathtaking history of Microsoft illustrates, in this information age, eras can be measured in years, months, and even weeks, rather than in decades and centuries.

The end of 1990 and early months of 1991 saw Bill Gates and Microsoft continue the frenetic pace of both achievement and experimentation that have become their trademarks:

- Windows 3.0 was selling at 30,000 copies a week, propelling the Microsoft stock to an all-time high.

- Gates is actively working to develop a more powerful version of the OS/2 operating system—the system that was introduced jointly with IBM in 1987 to generally disappointing reviews.

- Microsoft's spreadsheet, Excel, is continuing to gain on first-ranked Lotus 1-2-3, and its Word for Windows is within striking distance of rival WordPerfect.

- Gates has launched new, diverse business forays that are remarkable in scope: expanding Microsoft internationally in new languages; working on a joint venture with Radio Shack to create a low-cost CD-ROM information disk; and even buying shares in an English publisher of illustrated books.

Bill Gates's relentless pursuit of unchallenged dominance in the software industry—batting down even inconsequential competitors and always seemingly three steps ahead of principal rivals—has brought with it a quickening wave of resentment, criticism, and even legal and regulatory challenges:

- A federal judge refused to dismiss Apple Computer's suit against Microsoft for copyright infringement, which was filed three years ago.

- Rivals such as Hewlett-Packard and Lotus are joining forces with other companies in cooperative efforts to stave off the Microsoft juggernaut; in the meantime, Microsoft's ties to IBM continue to loosen.

- And, the Federal Trade Commission is now investigating Microsoft for so-called anti-competitive practices.

As the decade of the 1990s proceeds, Bill Gates is being repeatedly reminded that leadership entails much more than reaping profits and basking in applause; just as often, it means being on the receiving end of boos and catcalls.

This much is certain, however: Bill Gates did not succeed in fostering a global revolution in microcomputers by being a people pleaser and playing it safe. He has made a tremendous impact on the way we work, communicate, and do business because he is a brilliant entrepreneur who refuses to rest on his laurels. The future is what drives Bill Gates and Microsoft—a relentless search for the next bold idea, the next great adventure. Flexibility, experimentation, agressiveness, risk taking, and an utter disregard for orthodoxy characterize the making of Microsoft. Indeed, these same qualities characterize the making of America.

Versions of DOS

Versions of DOS have kept up with the evolution of the PC.

DOS 1.0

Extensively adapted from Tim Patterson's QDOS (Quick and Dirty Operating System), MS-DOS, released in August 1981, was the operating system for IBM's first microcomputer.

MS-DOS 1.1 AND 1.25

On May 17, 1982, Microsoft released version 1.1, developed primarily for the new PCs with two disk drives. These new drives wrote information on both sides of a diskette, thereby doubling disk capacity from 160K to 320K. Microsoft also published MS-DOS 1.25, a similar version for IBM-compatible computers.

MS-DOS 2.0

In late 1982, IBM informed Microsoft that its next microcomputer would be the PC XT with a 10-megabyte hard disk. This new PC shipped in March 1983 with 2.0, which comprised 20,000 lines of code. (1.0 had only 4,000 lines of code.)

Microsoft made many changes to 2.0, the most significant of which was how it handled a hard disk. Like UNIX, MS-DOS 2.0 allowed a user to set up a hierarchy of directories under the main (root) directory. The user could assign a name to each directory and store related files and subdirectories there. For example, a user could create a directory named TEXT and store his word processing program under that heading. He or she could then save correspondence in a subdirectory called TEXT\MAIL, contracts could be saved in a subdirectory named TEXT\CONTRACT, and so on. With this method, a user could clearly organize all files on a hard disk.

MS-DOS 2.0 also offered a limited form of multitasking just for printing; that is, users could work in one application while another was busy printing a document. During the microseconds that the active application was idle, MS-DOS's PRINT function continued printing the document from the other application. This same method was later used in other Microsoft programs to handle communication of data "in the background" while another part of the program was functioning.

Until 1983, DOS represented only a small part of Microsoft's earnings, and only three or four programmers were working on it. Things began to change quickly when Lotus released 1-2-3, which ran under only the MS-DOS operating system. Within its first three months, Lotus 1-2-3 became the number-one-selling microcomputer application and the new spreadsheet standard for 16-bit operating systems, just as VisiCalc had been for 8-bit systems. This simultaneously caused DOS's popularity to skyrocket. By the time Digital Research published a version of CP/M-86 for the PC XT in fall 1983, MS-DOS was already well established as the standard PC operating system.

In October 1983, MS-DOS received a major endorsement from DEC, the world's second largest computer manufacturer. DEC had chosen to use MS-DOS as the operating system for its PC-compatible Rainbow computer. DEC said it chose MS-DOS over other operating systems because MS-DOS offered more commands and superior performance in handling disks.

MS-DOS 2.11

Some Microsoft clients had expressed interest in a version of DOS that would be easier to internationalize. This required adding a function to automatically adapt the date, number, and monetary symbol formats to those used in a given country. For example, DOS represented dates in the American format—month-day-year—whereas many European countries such as France use the day-month-year format. Thus, DOS displayed the date June 2, 1989, as 6/2/89, which a French person would interpret as February 6, 1989. Furthermore, DOS represented decimal points as periods, whereas many European systems use a comma to indicate a decimal point. These small details were annoying to DOS users in Europe, who wanted a version that followed their conventions.

To meet this need, Microsoft released MS-DOS 2.11 in March 1984. It was sold worldwide and translated into more than 60 languages. Only IBM refused to use it.

By June 1984, 200 manufacturers had acquired the MS-DOS license.

MS-DOS 3.0

For the next version of DOS supported by IBM, Microsoft was interested in multi-task capabilities, but Big Blue—already in development on the PC network adapter card—was more concerned with networking. (With a network, several interconnected PCs can access the same files and use the same printers.)

In August 1984, IBM released the PC AT with the faster 80286 microprocessor and MS-DOS 3.0, which did not support networking, but did support the AT's 32-megabyte hard disk and the new high-density 1.2-megabyte diskettes. DOS 3.0 also included the options developed by Microsoft for internationalizing the operating system. This time, the code was 40,000 lines long, ten times longer than 1.0.

MS-DOS 3.1

In November 1984, Microsoft released this networking version of DOS, as well as MS-Net, a program to handle file sharing and user access to a shared hard disk.

Three principal suppliers of PC networks—Corvus, Ungermann-Bass, and 3Com—immediately announced their endorsements of 3.1. In April 1985, Novell, the biggest name in networks, announced it would adapt its software to the Microsoft standard.

In late 1985, Ashton-Tate released dBASE III Plus, the network version of dBASE. This popular database manager used 3.1 and MS-Net and helped establish them as networking standards.

MS-DOS 3.2

Released in March 1986, it supported 3½-inch disk drives such as those used in portable computers.

MS-DOS 3.3

When IBM introduced the PS/2 computer in April 1987, it officially announced its joint development (with Microsoft) of OS/2, a more advanced operating system, and the Presentation Manager graphical user interface. Before these two software products were actually released, however, version 3.3 appeared. One of its selling points was that it could support a 32-megabyte hard disk.

MS-DOS 4.0

In June 1988, Microsoft published 4.0, which had a graphical/mouse user interface like Windows. Much of this version was designed by IBM with the goal of making DOS easier to use.

In late 1990, MS-DOS still represented a healthy 19 percent of Microsoft's annual revenues.

MS-DOS 5.0

Yet another version of the operating system is scheduled to be released by mid-1991. 5.0 is said to provide more working space on PCs with at least 1 megabyte of system memory. Beta versions of Microsoft's 5.0 included task-switching abilities similar to multitasking in Windows, but not as powerful. It will allow several applications to be loaded, but only one to run at a time.

Key Dates in Microsoft's History

1975

January: *Popular Electronics* magazine announces the release of one of the first microcomputer kits, the Altair by MITS, based on the Intel 8080 chip.

February: Paul Allen meets with MITS and introduces Bill Gates's BASIC for the Altair.

March: The Homebrew Computer Club is founded in Menlo Park, California, by Steve Jobs and Steve Wozniak.

August: Bill Gates and Paul Allen form Microsoft.

October: MITS releases a version of Microsoft BASIC for 4K and 8K computers.

December: The Z80 microprocessor, an 8080 clone with superior capabilities, is released.

1976

January: Tired of seeing his BASIC openly copied in amateur computer clubs, Bill Gates publishes an

"Open Letter to Hobbyists" in a newsletter for Altair users.

March: Dave Bunnell organizes the first World Altair Computer Convention in Albuquerque, New Mexico.

July: An improved version of Microsoft BASIC is sold to well-known companies such as General Electric, NCR, and Citibank.

November: Computerland opens its first store in Hayward, California, and quickly becomes a national distribution chain for microcomputer products.

December: Shugart introduces an inexpensive 5¼-inch disk drive ($390).

The first word processing program for microcomputers is released—Electric Pencil by Michael Schrayer.

1977

February: The first Tandy Computer Shack franchise opens in Morristown, New Jersey.

April: The Apple II and the Commodore PET are introduced at the first West Coast Computer Faire in San Francisco.

May: MITS is sold to Pertec, which refuses Microsoft the right to license its BASIC to other developers. A lawsuit ensues.

July: Microsoft begins selling its second language, FORTRAN, for microcomputers with an 8080 microprocessor (such as the Altair).

August: Tandy begins selling its computers through Radio Shack stores.

Fall: Microsoft sells the BASIC license to Radio Shack and Apple.

Microsoft sells its first BASIC in Japan.

December: Microsoft wins the lawsuit against Pertec and officially obtains the right to license its BASIC to other developers.

Microsoft's yearly sales reach $500,000. Microsoft has five employees.

1978

April: Intel introduces the 8086 16-bit microprocessor, with increased speed and more memory.

June: Microsoft begins selling its third language, COBOL.

August: MicroPro introduces WordMaster, the predecessor to WordStar.

Fall: Microsoft creates a subsidiary for the Far East and begins sales in Japan.

December: Microsoft's yearly sales reach $1 million. Microsoft has 13 employees.

1979

January: Microsoft moves to Bellevue, Washington.

May: Dan Bricklin and Bob Frankston introduce the first version of VisiCalc at the West Coast Computer Faire.

June: Microsoft creates a retail sales division for end-user customers.

Microsoft announces its BASIC 8086 at the National Computer Conference.

MicroPro introduces the WordStar word processing program, which for the next several years is the most widely sold program of its type for the microcomputer.

August: Wayne Ratliff develops Vulcan, a database manager later renamed dBASE II.

Microsoft releases its Assembler language for the 8080/Z80 microprocessors (Microsoft Macro Assembler).

September: Convergent Technologies asks Microsoft to develop a FORTRAN for an 8086 machine.

December: Microsoft's yearly sales reach $2.5 million. Microsoft has 25 employees.

1980

February: Microsoft acquires the license to UNIX from Bell Labs and begins developing XENIX, a microcomputer version.

April: Tim Patterson begins developing an operating system for the 8086 chip.

Robert Leff and David Wagman found Softsel, one of the first software distribution chains.

June: Steve Ballmer, a college friend of Bill Gates, joins Microsoft as assistant to the president.

Seagate (formerly Shugart Technology) announces the first Winchester 5¼-inch disk drive.

August: IBM visits Microsoft, and Gates signs a contract to advise IBM regarding the development of a microcomputer.

Microsoft releases the SoftCard for the Apple II, enabling the Apple II to run CP/M software.

Hal Lashlee and George Tate form Software Plus, which later becomes Ashton-Tate and publishes dBASE.

September: IBM asks Microsoft to write BASIC, FORTRAN, COBOL, and Pascal for IBM's proposed microcomputer.

Tim Patterson shows Microsoft his 86-DOS, which he wrote for the 8086 chip.

Microsoft decides it wants to develop the operating system for the IBM microcomputer, based on Tim Patterson's 86-DOS.

Software Publishing delivers the first version of pfs:File, a very simple database manager. This package sells more than a million copies during the 1980s.

October: Microsoft buys the rights to 86-DOS.

Microsoft presents its offer to IBM to develop the four languages requested by IBM *and* the operating system.

November: Microsoft signs the contract with IBM and receives the first prototype of the IBM PC.

December: Microsoft's yearly sales reach $8 million. The company has 40 employees.

Apple goes public. Steve Jobs's shares are estimated at $165 million, and Steve Wozniak's at $88 million.

1981

January: dBASE II is released. This database manager became the best-seller in its category during the 1980s.

February: MS-DOS runs for the first time on an IBM PC prototype.

March: Microsoft establishes a nationwide retail sales network.

April: Tim Patterson joins Microsoft.

May: Xerox introduces the Star workstation, which has an innovative graphical user interface (with a mouse and pull-down menus). Later, the Star's influence is seen in Apple's Lisa and Macintosh computers and in Microsoft Windows.

July: Microsoft, formerly a partnership led by Gates and Allen, is reorganized as a privately held corporation and becomes Microsoft, Inc. Employees can now buy shares of stock. Outside capital is obtained by selling stock to Technology Ventures Investors of Palo Alto, California. Gates becomes executive vice president and chairman of the board, and Allen becomes executive vice president.

August: The IBM PC is announced.

Microsoft publishes version 1.0 of MS-DOS.

Don Estridge is named head of Microsoft's IBM PC division.

November: Microsoft moves to 10700 Northrup Way in Bellevue, Washington, and becomes Microsoft Corporation.

Microsoft begins collaborating with Apple to develop software for the new Macintosh computer.

December: Microsoft's sales for the year reach $16 million. Microsoft has 125 employees.

1982

March: Microsoft releases FORTRAN for MS-DOS.

For the first time, *InfoWorld* reviews MS-DOS products in its software section.

April: Microsoft establishes its first European subsidiary in England.

Mitch Kapor founds Lotus Development Corporation. Over the years, Lotus becomes Microsoft's prime rival.

Spring: Microsoft introduces GW-BASIC, which supports advanced graphics.

Microsoft releases COBOL for MS-DOS.

IBM releases Digital Research's CP/M-86 operating system for the IBM PC. CP/M-86 is the major competitor to MS-DOS.

June: PC DOS 1.1 is released, which handles double-sided diskettes on the IBM PC. Microsoft sells a similar product under the name of MS-DOS 1.25 for IBM-compatible computers.

Thirty developers have now published MS-DOS software.

The first IBM PC clone, the MPC by Columbia Data Products, is released.

July: James C. Towne becomes president of Microsoft Corporation. Bill Gates remains chairman of the board and CEO.

Intel introduces the 80286 microprocessor, which is later used by IBM in the IBM AT.

August: Microsoft introduces Multiplan, its first spreadsheet, for the Apple II, the Osborne 1, Intertec's SuperBrain, and several CP/M machines.

November: Compaq announces its first IBM PC–compatible computer, a "portable" that can run MS-DOS software. Compaq breaks all records in American economic history in its first year.

WordPerfect, a word processing program for the IBM PC, is introduced. It becomes number one in its category in the late 1980s.

Fifty microcomputer manufacturers have now acquired the license to MS-DOS.

December: Microsoft sales for the year 1982 reach $34 million. Microsoft now has 200 employees.

1983

January: *InfoWorld* chooses Microsoft's Multiplan as the software of the year and the IBM PC as the computer of the year.

Lotus releases the 1-2-3 spreadsheet. This program helps turn MS-DOS and the PC into industry standards.

Apple introduces the Lisa computer, with a mouse and a graphical user interface.

Time magazine features a microcomputer on the cover of its January issue and calls it "Machine of the Year."

February: Microsoft establishes a subsidiary in West Germany.

March: IBM announces the PC XT, which has a 10-megabyte hard disk; Microsoft publishes DOS 2.0 for the PC XT.

Microsoft creates a publishing division, Microsoft Press.

Lotus 1-2-3 rises to first place in sales on the Softsel list, where it remains for years.

Radio Shack introduces the TRS Model 100, one of the first portable microcomputers, which was developed by Bill Gates and Kazuhiko Nishi.

April: Microsoft introduces Microsoft Word and a mouse.

Microsoft releases new 16-bit languages for MS-DOS, including Pascal, C and BASIC Compiler.

Microsoft also introduces XENIX 3.0, a new version of the multiuser operating system.

May: John Sculley takes the helm of Apple Computer, replacing Mike Markkula.

June: Apple's 1 millionth microcomputer rolls off the assembly line.

July: Microsoft establishes its subsidiary in France.

August: Jon Shirley is named president and chief operating officer of Microsoft in place of

James Towne.

October: Microsoft signs a contract with Simon & Schuster to publish and distribute books from Microsoft Press.

Microsoft releases version 1.1 of Word, with many more features, including mail-merge capabilities.

Borland begins promoting Turbo Pascal through mail order for a very reasonable price. It becomes the most popular programming language for the PC.

Lotus makes its initial public offering.

VisiCorp releases VisiOn, a graphical user interface for DOS. It could run only a few programs and was poorly received.

November: Microsoft introduces Microsoft Windows, its graphical user interface for DOS. Twenty-three microcomputer hardware manufacturers support Windows. IBM is notably absent from this list.

Ashton-Tate makes its initial public offering.

December: DEC offers MS-DOS for its Rainbow microcomputer.

Compaq makes its initial public offering.

Microsoft sales for the year 1983 reach $69 million.

Microsoft has grown to 383 employees.

1984

January: Apple Computer introduces the Macintosh.

Microsoft offers Multiplan and BASIC for the Macintosh.

March: DOS 2.1 is released for the PC Junior, which is not well received.

Microsoft releases version 3.2 of its Pascal and FORTRAN languages.

Ashton-Tate announces Framework, a five-function integrated software package.

Microsoft publishes DOS 2.11 for the international market.

The French version of Multiplan becomes the number-one-selling software application in France.

April: *Time* magazine features Bill Gates on the cover.

May: Microsoft introduces Microsoft Project for managing and tracking projects.

Software publishers and computer manufacturers receive the first application development kits for Windows. Windows itself is overdue.

June: Microsoft becomes the first software publisher with more than $100 million in annual sales.

Ashton-Tate ships dBASE III.

July: Microsoft sales for fiscal 1984 reach $125 million. The number of employees has grown to 608.

Over 200 manufacturers have acquired the MS-DOS license.

August: IBM introduces the IBM PC AT with a 20-megabyte hard disk.

Microsoft publishes DOS 3.0 to support it.

Microsoft releases Microsoft Chart, a graphics program for the IBM PC and the Macintosh.

October: Digital Research introduces GEM, a text-based windowing environment for DOS. GEM is a competitor to Windows, which is still under development.

November: Microsoft releases MS-DOS 3.1, which can support PC networks.

The 2 millionth Apple II sells.

Microsoft releases Word and File for the Macintosh.

December: Apple has sold 250,000 Macintosh computers.

NEC asks Microsoft to write the Japanese version of MS-DOS for its PC-9801F computer. Twenty thousand PC-9801Fs sell in one year.

1985

January: IBM releases TopView, a text-based windowing environment.

Paul Allen, who left Microsoft in 1983 for health and personal reasons, founds Asymetrix. Steve Wood, another longtime Microsoft employee, joins him as vice president.

February: Microsoft releases version 2.0 of Word for the PC, which includes a spelling checker.

May: Microsoft announces Microsoft Excel, a new spreadsheet for the Macintosh.

June: Microsoft supports Lotus/Intel/Microsoft Extended Memory Specification providing for addressable memory space above 640K on MS-DOS machines.

Apple reorganizes. Steve Jobs retains his title of chairman but is stripped of his management responsibilities.

July: Microsoft numbers 910 employees and announces $140 million in sales in fiscal 1985.

August: IBM signs a contract with Microsoft to collaborate on the development of the operating system for its next-generation PC.

Construction begins on Microsoft's new headquarters in Redmond, Washington.

September: Steve Jobs resigns from Apple.

The millionth copy of Multiplan sells.

Microsoft officially releases Excel for the Macintosh,which is immediately successful.

November: Microsoft releases Windows 1.03, two years after the initial Windows announcement.

Lotus releases version 2.0 of 1-2-3, which can handle LIM-standard memory extension cards and spreadsheets of up to 4 million characters.

December: Ashton-Tate delivers dBASE III Plus, a network version of its database manager.

1986

January: Microsoft releases MS-DOS 3.25.

Richard Bressler and Portia Isaacson are elected as new members of the Microsoft board of directors. The rest of the board is composed of Bill Gates, Jon Shirley, and David Marquardt.

Apple introduces the MacPlus computer and the LaserWriter Plus printer.

February: Microsoft releases a French version of Windows 1.02. The largest French hardware manufacturers (Bull, Léanord, Groupil, Normerel) offer it as a standard with their PCs.

March: Microsoft becomes a publicly traded company. The stock is welcomed with frenzied buying. Gates becomes the world's youngest billionaire.

April: Microsoft has 1,200 employees and has done $197 million of business in fiscal 1986.

August: Microsoft announces Works for the Macintosh.

September: Compaq releases the Deskpro 386, based on the new, high-powered 80386 chip, for which IBM has not yet released a computer. It is the first time a major PC-compatible manufacturer beats IBM to the punch.

October: Microsoft announces Word 3.0 for the Macintosh.

Ashton-Tate ships the millionth copy of dBASE.

1987

April: IBM releases its new range of microcomputers, the PS/2. With the MCA (Micro Channel Architecture) bus, different from the bus used in the IBM PC and AT, the PS/2 distances itself somewhat from traditional compatibility.

Microsoft and IBM announce that they are jointly developing a multitasking operating system called the OS/2 for the PC and the PS/2.

May: Microsoft releases Mac Excel 1.04 adapted for the Macintosh II.

June: Microsoft and 3Com forge a strategic alliance to jointly develop and distribute the LAN Manager, a networking system for OS/2.

Microsoft sells its 500,000th mouse.

July: The end of fiscal 1987 shows Microsoft with $300 million in earnings and almost 2,000 employees.

Microsoft acquires Forethought, publisher of a presentation graphics program for the Macintosh called PowerPoint.

October: The government of Brazil wants to pass a law banning imports of software when an equivalent product already exists domestically. MS-DOS is one of the first products affected by this bill. Gates asks the U.S. government to enact reprisals.

November: Microsoft simultaneously releases Windows 2.0, Windows 386, and the PC version of Excel.

Microsoft releases Word 4.0 for the PC and Word 3.0 for the Macintosh.

December: Windows tops the 1 million mark in copies sold.

Microsoft releases the OS/2 operating system version 1.0 for the PS/2 and other 80286 and 80386 machines.

1988

January: A strategic alliance is announced between Microsoft, Ashton-Tate, and Sybase (a publisher of minicomputer software) with the goal of offering an OS/2 version of SQL Server, a program that manages networked databases.

Microsoft France announces that it controls 29 percent of the French market and has sold 300,000 products in 1987.

March: Apple files a lawsuit against Microsoft over Windows 2.03 and against Hewlett-Packard over New Wave.

Microsoft releases the PC version of Works with an outstanding tutorial.

May: Lotus announces that it has sold 4 million spreadsheet programs.

July: Fiscal 1988 results show that Microsoft has revenues of $590 million and profits of $123.9 million. The number of employees has risen to 2,800.

September: Compaq announces the EISA (extended industry standard architecture) group, which
proposes an alternative to the MCA bus used
in the IBM PS/2. Microsoft endorses EISA.

October: Microsoft releases the OS/2 LAN Manager,
developed in conjunction with 3Com to handle
networked PCs.

Presentation Manager, which covers the OS/2
with a graphical interface similar to Windows,
is now ready, so developers can now start writing applications for it.

November: U.S. sales account for 48 percent of Microsoft's
earnings.

1989

March: Microsoft releases Quick Pascal, designed to
compete with Borland's Turbo Pascal, the
most widely used PC language.

May: Bernard Vergnes is named vice president,
Europe, of Microsoft Corporation.

Michel Lacombe is named chairman of
Microsoft France.

April: Microsoft starts shipping SQL Server.

May: Microsoft releases Mac Excel 2.2, an improved
version no longer limited to 1 megabyte of
RAM. It can handle 8-megabyte spreadsheets.

June: Microsoft France has sold 50,000 copies of
Works in one year.

Two years after its announcement in the
press, Lotus releases 1-2-3/3.

July: Microsoft announces its results for fiscal 1989.
Revenues reach $803.5 million, with profits of
$170.5 million. Fifty five per cent of these earn-
ings come from outside the U.S. The number

of employees reaches 4,000 throughout the world.

Microsoft acquires Bauer, a California company specializing in development of printer-driver software.

October: Microsoft releases Excel for Presentation Manager. It is the first major application to appear for the graphics environment of the 1990s.

1990

May: Microsoft releases Windows 3.0, spending $3 million on the opening-day extravaganza, the beginning of a $10 million promotional campaign.

June: Microsoft President Jon Shirley resigns after six years at his post, and is replaced by Michael Hallman, a former Boeing executive.

July: Microsoft becomes the first software firm to achieve $1 billion in sales. Microsoft now has 5,200 employees.

November: Bill Gates delivers the keynote address at Comdex Fall in Las Vegas, presenting his vision of the future: "Information at Your Fingertips."

GLOSSARY

TECHNICAL TERMS

application: Also called application program. Software used to perform specific tasks, such as accounting, word processing, or drawing graphics.

ASCII: American Standard Code for Information Interchange. A standard code used to represent text inside a computer or transmit text between computers. It consists of 255 codes representing all text characters and several non-printing (control) characters.

assembly language: A *low-level* computer programming language. Assembly language interacts most directly with the computer hardware.

BASIC: Beginners' All-purpose Symbolic Instruction Code, a high-level programming language. In 1964, John Kemeney and Thomas Kurtz designed BASIC to be an easy-to-learn programming language. Because it is so simple, BASIC was quickly established as a common programming language for microcomputers.

benchmark test: A series of tests carried out on computer systems or software to measure performance relative to other similar systems or software.

binary system: A base-2 numbering system that uses only 1 and 0 as digits and is most commonly used in computer programming. See also *bit* and *byte*.

BIOS: Basic Input-Output System, part of certain operating systems, such as CP/M and DOS, consisting of drivers and other software designed to manage peripheral devices, such as monitors, disk drives, and printers.

bit: Contraction of "binary digit." The smallest unit of information that a computer can store. It can take a value of 1 or 0. Eight bits equal one *byte*.

bug: A programming error that can cause a program or system to malfunction or "crash" (become unusable).

bundle: The practice of selling an application and a computer together or two or more software applications together in a special promotion. For example, Microsoft Works was bundled with the Amstrad PC in 1989 and Microsoft Works for the Macintosh was bundled with the Quicken home accounting software in late 1990.

bus: The path along which information is transmitted in a computer. A bus is a set of electrical or electronic connections between the microprocessor and other hardware, such as the disk drives, logic boards, etc.

byte: A measurement used for computer memory or disk capacity. One byte equals eight *bits* and can store one ASCII character, i.e., a number, letter, or punctuation symbol.

CD-ROM: Compact disk read-only memory, an optical storage system in which information permanently recorded on compact disks (very similar to those used for music) can be displayed on a computer screen. The *Oxford English Dictionary*, the Bible, several encyclopedias, and commercial databases are just a few of the resources available on CD-ROM today.

CGA: Color Graphics Adapter, a standard for color display introduced by IBM in 1981. CGA circuit boards enabled monitors to display a 320-by-200-pixel four-color screen. In

1984, a higher resolution standard called *EGA* replaced the CGA standard.

chip: Informal name for integrated circuit. E.g., see *microprocessor.*

COBOL: COmmon Business-Oriented Language, a high-level programming language designed for business applications. It has been the most commonly used language for programming mainframes since the 1960s.

CP/M: Control Program/Microcomputer, one of the first microcomputer operating systems. In 1974, Gary Kildall developed CP/M and founded Digital Research one year later. By 1981, CP/M had become the standard operating system for microcomputer business applications. In the 1980s, after IBM selected MS-DOS as the operating system for its first PC, the CP/M market declined significantly.

disk: Also *diskette;* the most commonly used magnetic storage medium for microcomputers. "Floppy disks" measure either 5¼ or 3½ inches in diameter and are so called because the disk itself is made of pliable plastic, although 3½-inch disks are encased in hard plastic for protection. Application programs are sold in diskette form, and users store data on diskettes. See *hard disk.*

disk drive: A device used to retrieve information from or record information onto a disk. A computer may have one or more built-in disk drives, a disk drive may be attached as a peripheral device, or both.

DOS: Disk operating system, a general name usually referring to MS-DOS (by Microsoft) or PC-DOS (IBM's adaptation of MS-DOS). DOS remains the most common operating system for IBM and compatible computers.

EGA: Enhanced Graphics Adapter, a higher-resolution display standard than *CGA.* IBM introduced EGA in late 1984 in conjunction with its *PC AT.* EGA resolution is 640 by 350 in 16-color mode, representing a significant increase in display quality over CGA. In 1987, the EGA standard was replaced by *VGA.*

FORTRAN: FORmula TRANslation, a programming language developed in 1956 by John Backus at IBM, primarily used for handling scientific and mathematical formulas.

graphical user interface (GUI):   A method of displaying text and graphics on a computer screen using pictures and images formed by patterns of dots. A text interface, in contrast, displays information with only numbers, letters, and punctuation symbols. GUIs are thought to help make a computer easier and more pleasant to use. The Apple Macintosh computer has a built-in GUI. Microsoft Windows is software that puts a GUI on top of text-based DOS on IBM PCs and compatibles.

hard disk: A magnetic storage medium made of metal. A hard disk offers greater information storage capacity than floppy disks and may be built into a computer or attached as a peripheral device.

high-level language: A programming language—such as BASIC, FORTRAN, COBOL, Pascal, etc.—that allows a programmer to use instructions in a language similar to everyday English to control the computer. A program written in a high-level language must be compiled to translate the instructions into a form that the microprocessor can understand.

kilobyte (K):   A unit of measurement for computer memory. One K equals 1,024 (2^{10}) *bytes.*

low-level language: A programming language, such as *assembly language,* which is one step up from the machine instructions that the microprocessor can understand. It is very different from everyday English and requires advanced technical knowledge of the hardware.

mainframe: Any large computer system, typically with high processing speed and extensive storage capacity.

MCA: Micro Channel Architecture, a 32-bit multitasking bus introduced by IBM with its PS/2 computers in 1987. It doesn't support expansion cards made for previous PCs.

megabyte (MB):   A unit of measurement for computer memory. One megabyte equals 1,024 kilobytes.

microprosessor: The central processing unit (CPU) in a microcomputer. A microprocessor is an integrated circuit (or chip) on the computer's main circuit board. It uses electrical impulses to direct the operations of the computer, such as writing information into the computer's memory (saving the text of a letter or calculating spreadsheet totals, for example).

modem: A device for transmitting data from one computer to another over telecommunications lines.

mouse: A device that a user can move around on a flat surface in order to position a pointer on the computer screen at a desired location. A mouse includes a button a user can press to position the cursor at a desired point in a document, open or close a file, or select an item from a menu.

multitasking: A method that operating systems use to perform several operations simultaneously. With a multitasking system, a user can print a document, work on a spreadsheet, and receive data from a modem all at the same time.

operating system: A program essential to the functioning of a computer that establishes how data are handled when entered into or extracted from memory, and controls all the basic functions of the computer.

Pascal: A high-level programming language developed by Nicklas Wirth. Pascal is widely used in teaching computer science.

pixel: Contraction of picture element; each of the dots that make up a picture on a video display.

RAM: Random-access memory. RAM most commonly refers to computer memory that stores information temporarily while a user is working on it. When the computer is turned off, any information in the RAM that has not been saved onto a diskette or hard disk is lost. RAM can contain applications and information entered by a user.

ROM: Read-only memory. Permanently recorded information that a computer can read but users cannot change in any way.

S-100: The bus standard in the microcomputer industry before the IBM PC. The S-100 was also called the "Altair bus" because it was originally developed for that computer.

VGA: Video Graphics Array. A color graphics standard introduced by IBM with its PS/2 in 1987. VGA monitors offer a very high resolution of 640 by 480 in 16-color mode.

window: On the Macintosh computer or with Microsoft Windows, for example, a rectangular area of a computer screen in which a document or a running application is displayed. A window may also display the contents of a diskette or a hard disk. Users can open and close windows, change their size, and move them to different positions on the screen. It is possible to have several windows open at once, and they may overlap, depending on the system. The concept of windows was originally developed at Xerox and its first commercial use was on the Macintosh computer.

windowing environment: Software that enables several DOS programs on an IBM PC or compatible, for example, to be launched and run simultaneously in separate *windows*.

word processor: A machine or application program that enables a user to create, edit, reformat, and print documents with a high degree of flexibility. Word processing software often includes features such as a spelling checker, cut and paste capabilities within or between documents, a variety of layout options, and so on.

PEOPLE

ALLEN, PAUL: Cofounder of Microsoft, and a close friend of Bill Gates since their childhood. Today he heads his own software firm called Asymetrix.

ATKINSON, BILL: One of the programmers on the original Macintosh team at Apple, who also developed the popular MacPaint and HyperCard programs.

BALLMER, STEVE: A friend of Gates from Harvard, who joined Microsoft in 1980. In 1984, he was placed in charge of system software.

BLUMENTHAL, JABE: Hired by Microsoft in 1982 to assist Jeff Raikes in marketing Multiplan, he wrote the specifications for Excel and helped design Works.

BRAINERD, PAUL: President of Aldus. He invented the term *desktop publishing* by developing PageMaker, an application program that enables users to produce profess-ional-quality printed documents with a PC or a Macintosh and a laser printer.

BRICKLIN, DAN: Codeveloper (with Bob Frankston) of VisiCalc, the first electronic spreadsheet, which was also the first highly successful microcomputer application. In 1979, he and Frankston incorporated Software Arts. After Software Arts dissolved in 1985, he worked for a few months as a consultant to Lotus and then founded a new software publishing company called Software Garden.

BRODIE, RICHARD: Coprogrammer with Charles Simonyi of the first version of Microsoft Word.

BUNNELL, DAVID: Editor of a newsletter dedicated to the Altair computer. In 1983, he started *PC World* maga-zine.

CANION, ROD: Founded Compaq in 1982. Within three years of its founding, Compaq made the *Fortune* 500.

COLE, IDA: Former marketing director at Apple re-cruited by Microsoft in February 1985 to head the business applications division.

ESTRIDGE, PHILIP "DON": Head of the IBM PC project from its beginning in 1980 until his death in a plane crash in 1985.

FRANKSTON, BOB: Codeveloper (with Dan Bricklin) of VisiCalc and cofounder of Software Arts. When Software Arts dissolved, Frankston went to work for Lotus as chief scientist of the information sciences division.

FYLSTRA, DAN: Head of Personal Software, the firm that marketed VisiCalc beginning in 1979. Personal Software changed its name to VisiCorp in 1982.

GATES, BILL: Cofounder and chief executive officer of Microsoft.

GAUDETTE, FRANK: Head of finance at Microsoft. He was the primary Microsoft employee managing the company's initial public offering.

GRAYSON, PAUL: President of Micrografx, a firm that develops software for Windows.

HALLMAN, MICHAEL: President of Microsoft, who succeeded Jon Shirley in 1990.

HERTZFELD, ANDY: Principal developer of the Macintosh operating system and author of the Switcher program for the Macintosh. Switcher enabled users to launch several programs simultaneously.

JOBS, STEVE: Cofounder of Apple Computer, responsible for the Macintosh project. He resigned from Apple in 1985 after the board of directors removed him from management responsibilities. Jobs went on to found NeXT Inc., which released its first computer in October 1988.

KAPOR, MITCH: Founder of Lotus Development Corporation. In 1986, he left Lotus to study artificial intelligence and form a new company.

KEMPIN, JOACHIM: First director of Microsoft Germany.

KILDALL, GARY: Founder of Digital Research (in 1976) and developer of CP/M, the first microcomputer operating system.

KLUNDER, DOUG: Hired by Microsoft in March 1981 to work on Multiplan. Later, he was the lead programmer for Excel.

LACOMBE, MICHEL: Head of Microsoft France since May 1989. Prior to that time, he worked as marketing director.

LUBOW, MIRIAM: One of Microsoft's first employees. In 1977, she went to work at Microsoft as Bill Gates's secretary. She left Microsoft in 1990 to work for Paul Allen.

MANZI, JIM: President of Lotus Development Corporation since 1986.

MAPLES, MIKE: Vice president of applications development at Microsoft. He joined Microsoft in 1988, after leaving IBM.

MARKKULA, MIKE: The first investor in Apple Computer in 1976. He headed Apple from 1981 to 1983.

MILLARD, WILLIAM: Founder of Computerland stores.

NISIII, KAZUHIKO: Japanese computer hobbyist who took charge of Microsoft's business in Japan until 1986. He is head of ASCII Corporation.

OLSEN, KEN: Founder of Digital Equipment Corporation (DEC), and creator of the minicomputer. With growth in revenues of 30 percent for 19 consecutive years, DEC has become the number-two computer manufacturer in the world, behind IBM. He was voted Entrepreneur of the Year by *Forbes* in 1986.

O'REAR, BOB: Hired by Microsoft in 1977, he has been at Microsoft longer than any other employee. He is currently director of international subsidiary development.

OSBORNE, ADAM: Publisher of some of the first books about microcomputers in the 1970s and founder of Osborne Computer in 1980. The Osborne computer was a portable computer that sold well at first, but two years after its release, the company went bankrupt.

PATTERSON, TIM: Author of QDOS (Quick and Dirty Operating System), the precursor to Microsoft DOS. In 1980, he left Seattle Computer Products to work at Microsoft on adapting DOS to IBM's specifications.

RAIKES, JEFF: Director of marketing for Microsoft's applications division since 1984. He left Apple in 1981 to join Microsoft, where he began working on marketing Multiplan and Word.

RASKIN, JEF: Apple Computer's 31st employee and original leader of the Macintosh project.

RATLIFF, C. WAYNE: Developer of dBASE II, dBASE III, and dBASE III Plus, Ashton-Tate's best-selling database manager.

ROBERTS, ED: President of MITS, which in 1975 produced the Altair, one of the first microcomputers.

ROSEN, BEN: Venture capitalist who helped finance Lotus, Compaq, Quarterdeck, and Borland.

SACHS, JONATHAN: Codeveloper of 1-2-3, the electronic spreadsheet published by Lotus.

SAMS, JACK: Member of IBM's Chess Committee, which was responsible for developing the IBM PC.

SCULLEY, JOHN: CEO of Apple Computer since 1983.

SHIRLEY, JON: President of Microsoft from 1983 to 1990. Prior to joining Microsoft, he worked at Tandy for 25 years.

SIMONYI, CHARLES: Programmer hired by Microsoft in 1980. Former employee of Xerox PARC, he was the chief architect of the developers groups for Multiplan, Word, and Excel.

SINCLAIR, CLIVE: English lord, creator of the Z80, the first inexpensive microcomputer.

SLADE, MIKE: Microsoft's marketing director for Excel and other Macintosh software.

TOWNE, JAMES: President of Microsoft from July 1982 to June 1983.

VERGNES, BERNARD: Vice president (Europe) of Microsoft Corporation since May 1989. From 1983 to 1989, he was head of Microsoft France, where he helped make Multiplan and other Microsoft products extremely successful.

WARNOCK, JOHN: Author of PostScript and founder of Adobe.

WIGGINTON, RANDY: Author of MacWrite, the word processing software bundled with the Macintosh when it was first introduced. He also wrote the Full Impact spreadsheet, distributed by Ashton-Tate.

WOZNIAK, STEVE: Cofounder of Apple with Steve Jobs and designer of the first Apple computers.

PRODUCTS

Altair: One of the first microcomputers. MITS sold it in kit form through *Popular Electronics* magazine. Bill Gates and Paul Allen wrote the first BASIC for this microcomputer.

Compaq 386: An IBM-compatible computer released in September 1986. It was the first PC produced by a major manufacturer to use the Intel 80386 microprocessor, beating IBM to the punch by more than six months.

Compaq Portable: Computer released in 1982 that offered the capabilities of an IBM PC in a portable. It was immensely successful.

dBASE: A database manager published by Ashton-Tate. In the 1980s dBASE became the number one product in its category, with 2.5 million copies sold.

DESQview: A windowing environment, sold by Quarterdeck, which allows several DOS programs to run simultaneously.

Excel: Electronic spreadsheet published by Microsoft. First released in September 1985, it quickly became the best-selling software for the Macintosh. The Windows version released in November 1988 also met with immediate success.

Framework: An integrated software package designed by Robert Carr and published by Ashton-Tate in late 1984. It uses a type of windowing (terming the windows "frames") in which different types of documents can be manipulated.

GEM: A graphics-based windowing environment published by Digital Research. It uses overlapping windows but can run only one application at a time.

IBM PC (personal computer): The first personal computer released by IBM. It was built around the Intel 8088 microprocessor and sold with the MS-DOS operating system.

IBM PC AT: The successor to the IBM PC. Released in August 1984, the AT used the Intel 80286 microprocessor and a new graphics display standard called EGA.

Jazz: An integrated software package for the Macintosh released in mid-1985 by Lotus Development Corporation. It included a spreadsheet, database, word processor, graphics, and a communications module.

Lotus 1-2-3: A high-powered spreadsheet by Lotus Development Corporation which became the standard for electronic spreadsheets and the best-selling software in the history of microcomputers.

Multiplan: Microsoft's first spreadsheet product, designed to run on almost all microcomputer operating systems. It met with limited success in the United States, but was highly successful in France.

New Wave: A program developed by Hewlett-Packard designed to extend the capabilities of Microsoft Windows. In 1988, Apple Computer sued Hewlett-Packard over New Wave on the grounds that its "look and feel" were too similar to the look and feel of the Macintosh.

OS/2: An operating system developed jointly by Microsoft and IBM for the new generation of IBM personal computers. It has been the subject of some controversy between the two firms.

Presentation Manager: The graphical user interface developed jointly by Microsoft and IBM and designed to run on top of OS/2.

PS/2: A family of microcomputers introduced by IBM in April 1987. The exterior design was much more sophisticated than that of earlier PCs. It represented a break with the traditional IBM PC architecture as it introduced a new bus called MCA, which did not support expansion cards for earlier PCs.

SoftCard: A card developed by Microsoft for the Apple II computer. Released in 1980, it enabled the Apple II to run programs written for the CP/M operating system.

Symphony: An integrated software package for the PC developed by Lotus and released in late 1984.

TopView: A text-based user interface designed by IBM to run on top of DOS. It was released in April 1985, but withdrawn from the market in June 1987 after a poor showing.

Turbo Pascal: The most commonly used programming language for PCs. It is sold by Borland.

VisiCalc: The first electronic spreadsheet. Written by Dan Bricklin and Bob Frankston and marketed by VisiCorp (formerly Personal Software), it was so successful that many people rushed out to buy Apple II computers specifically to use this spreadsheet. It was later ported to the IBM PC and sold well until 1983, when Lotus 1-2-3 captured the market. VisiCalc sold 500,000 copies.

VisiOn: A program designed to enable programs to run in a multiwindow graphical environment. Released in November 1983, it was not very successful because it could not support standard DOS programs. Its failure in the market caused VisiCorp to go bankrupt.

Windows: A software product (developed by Microsoft) that runs on top of MS-DOS in graphics mode and enables users to run several programs simultaneously, each in a separate *window*. Windows makes a PC interface look similar to the Macintosh interface. In 1988, Apple Computer sued Microsoft over the "look and feel" of Windows, saying it too closely resembled the look and feel of the Macintosh.

WordPerfect: The best-selling word processing program, published by WordPerfect Corporation.

WordStar: A word processor released by MicroPro International (now WordStar International) in 1979, which rapidly became the star program for CP/M computers.

Works: An integrated software package published by Microsoft and geared toward novice users. It comes with a helpful online tutorial.

XENIX: A popular Microsoft-designed version of the UNIX multiuser operating system.

COMPANIES

Adobe: Publisher of the PostScript language used in desktop publishing. The Apple LaserWriter was the first laser printer to use PostScript.

Apple Computer: The leading microcomputer manufacturer competing with IBM. Apple makes the popular Apple II and Macintosh lines.

Ashton-Tate: Publisher of dBASE, the best-selling database manager.

Commodore: Major Canadian computer manufacturer, founded in 1958. In 1976, it bought out microprocessor manufacturer MOS Technology and began producing microcomputers. Commodore produced the PET 2001, C65, C218, and Amiga computers as well as several IBM PC compatibles.

Compaq: Computer manufacturer known for its portable computer and IBM-compatibles.

Computerland: The first nationwide distributor of microcomputer products in the United States. It was founded in September 1986 by William Millard.

DEC: Digital Equipment Corporation, founded in 1957. DEC manufactures mainframes and minicomputers, in particular, the PDP-10 and PDP-11 used by Bill Gates and Paul Allen in their high school days and in the early days of Microsoft.

Digital Research: Publisher of the CP/M operating system, founded by Gary Kildall in 1975.

IBM: International Business Machines Corporation. The leading computer manufacturer in the world.

Lotus Development Corporation: Founded by Mitch Kapor, and publisher of the highly successful 1-2-3 spreadsheet. From 1984 to 1986, Lotus was the number one software publisher in the world, before losing ground to Microsoft.

Micrografx: Software publisher founded in 1984, specializing in developing programs to run under Microsoft Windows. In July 1985, Micrografx published In-A-Vision, the first Windows application.

MicroPro International Corporation: Publisher of WordStar, the number one word processor in the early 1980s. In 1989, the company became WordStar International.

Microsoft: The world's leading microcomputer software company.

Softsel: Software wholesaler known for its weekly "hot list" of best-selling software.

Software Arts: Publisher of VisiCalc, the first electronic spreadsheet, founded by Dan Bricklin and Bob Frankston in 1979.

Software Publishing Corporation (SPC): Specializes in easy-to-use MS-DOS programs. Its best-sellers include pfs:Write and Harvard Graphics.

Tandy: Computer manufacturer whose Radio Shack subsidiary entered the microcomputer market in 1977.

Toshiba: Japanese computer manufacturer which in 1985 began specializing in portable IBM-compatible computers.

VisiCorp: Distributor of the VisiCalc spreadsheet. Originally called Personal Software and headed by Dan Fylstra.

WordPerfect Corporation: Utah-based software publisher known for its highly successful word processor, WordPerfect.

Zenith: Television manufacturer turned microcomputer manufacturer in the early 1980s. Zenith became a major supplier of portable PCs before being bought out by Bull in 1989.

Index